Life, Liberty & Resilience

A Man's War on Three Fronts

Steffan Tubbs

15 14 13 12   5 4 3 2 1

Life, Liberty & Resilience
A Man's War on Three Fronts

Copyright © 2012 by Steffan W. Tubbs
Highlands Ranch, Colorado
www.steffantubbs.com
ISBN 978-1-937250-06-5
E-book 978-1-937250-07-2

CONTENTS

ACKNOWLEDGMENTS

I'VE WRITTEN THIS BOOK DURING THE COURSE OF GETTING married, moving, two rainy springs, two hot summers, through the holidays, and during snowstorms. I've written in Hawaii, California, Mississippi, Louisiana, Tennessee, Guam, on airplanes, on vacation, on slow-moving computers, after work, half-asleep, and on multiple cups of coffee more times than I can count. Through the entire amazing process, I have never lost focus of my goal: to make sure you know about the amazing life of one incredible man. I quickly learned it is impossible to write a book without the love, guidance, and help of a strong circle of friends and supporters.

In alphabetical order, special thanks also go to: Key Blair, President of Columbus Marble Works; Peter Boyles; the Honorable Bruce Braley; Michael Brown; Mike Buchen of Colorado-based Skydex Technologies; Timothy Davis, founder of The Greatest Generations Foundation; Donnie Edwards; my documentary videographer, Andre Greller; John Horan of Horan & McConaty; my editor, Susan Janos; Nick LeMasters with the Taubman Centers, Inc.; the Honorable Ed Perlmutter; my mom, Linda Sleeter; my aunt and project guide, Jayne Sleeter; Key Bank of Colorado President, Tom Spillman; my attorney and often times counselor, Jon Tandler; and all of my other friends and even strangers who believed, like me, that Joe's story was worth telling.

No one supported me through the long days and nights of writing—or endured the time away from family—more than my wife, Lori. I love you so much. Thank you for being my backbone and cheerleader, proofreader, listener, and critic.

Our boys—Ryan, Nathan, and Jake—let Dad write when he should have been playing with them. Thank you, boys, for being so precious to me.

I lost both of my grandmothers during this project. My Gramma Zelma passed just before I began writing my first few chapters, and her dementia and onset of Alzheimer's prevented me from ever talking to her about Joe.

My Gramma Freda, even in her final month-and-a-half of life, read parts of Joe's story off my computer and was an amazing source of support and true love. She could not believe the way he overcame his obstacles and kept his focus on the inherent good in all of us.

This book is dedicated to her and to the generation of decent, hard-working people who changed the course of world history—through war and peace and through the black and white that threatened to permanently divide our country.

—STEFFAN TUBBS

FROM THE AUTHOR

Dear Reader,

Before you embark on Joseph LaNier's incredible journey, please note this is an unauthorized biography.

This book was written after more than 100 hours of my personal interviews with Mr. LaNier. The story that follows is based on those interviews and meetings, as well as information he delivered in speeches and public forums. Other information was gathered during trips with Mr. LaNier to various locations, both domestically and internationally.

As a journalist, I have a tremendous passion for WWII veterans and their lives before, during, and after their service. Based on government statistics, we are losing as many as 1,000 WWII-era veterans *every day*. Soon they will be gone.

As such, there is a public passion and interest level in our aging veterans and their incredible stories of service, dedication, and perseverance. Their memories and stories must be preserved for future generations.

I greatly respect Mr. LaNier and the men like him, who—despite incredible odds—served valiantly and changed the course of the 20th century.

I hope you enjoy his story.

Warm regards,

Steffan W. Tubbs

November 1, 2012

PREFACE

I FIRST MET JOE LANIER MONDAY, MARCH 7, 2011. HE CAME TO the Newsradio 850 KOA studios in Denver for an interview as he prepared to become the first documented African-American to return to Iwo Jima since the end of WWII. Joe came upon my radar after my good friend, Timothy Davis, President of The Greatest Generations Foundation, told me briefly about Joe's story. I was immediately intrigued and looked forward to our meeting.

I WAS BORN IN ESCONDIDO, CALIFORNIA—IN NORTHERN SAN Diego County—in February 1969. From the time I can remember, I wanted to write and become a journalist. I grew up on Electric Light Orchestra, The Eagles, and Van Halen; the Dan Fouts-era San Diego Chargers and the Tony Gwynn-era Padres; Ronald Reagan and the Iran hostage crisis; the Space Shuttle Challenger disaster; *The Day After* and George Orwell's *1984*; and the constant question and fear of whether we would soon go to war with the Soviet Union.

After graduating from San Diego High School in 1987, I attended San Diego Mesa College before moving away for the final years of my undergrad degree. My last two-and-a-half years of college (1990-1992) were spent along the beautiful Central Coast of California at Cal Poly, San Luis Obispo. I worked a lot in radio, both on campus and off-site, during my tenure there. Cal Poly's motto is *Learn by Doing* and I tried my best serving as news director at campus station KCPR-FM. I also hopped around that small market with stints at KDDB-FM in San Luis Obispo, KWWV-FM in Morro Bay, and KVEC-AM in San Luis Obispo, all in between and after classes. Each station was a stepping-stone in my career, and even then I knew more airtime meant more experience and thus a better chance of landing a job once I graduated. My lack of "real" experience was an issue.

After an unsuccessful attempt at getting a job at KTOK-AM in Oklahoma City, I headed up to Denver for the first time as an adult. But as I left Oklahoma, I remember I liked the place a lot. There were friendly people with an unspoken down-home spirit and Oklahoma City had much more culture than I expected. Little did I know I would be back in a much different capacity less than three years later.

In Denver a job interview awaited me at the legendary KOA-AM—a station with a stellar news reputation. It was a crapshoot but I got in to see news director Jerry Bell in the station's downtown high-rise. Denver was a big media market for a 22-year-old kid just out of college, but Jerry was gracious to meet and discuss my aspirations. He gave me a tour of the 13th floor news facility and hinted I was in the running for a reporter opening. There was hope.

When I returned back to San Luis Obispo, Denver was the only thing on my mind. Unfortunately, within a couple of weeks, Jerry informed me via telephone they had hired someone with more experience, but he left the door wide-open for me to keep in touch and get a couple years of experience under my belt. I was devastated, but continued a dogged pursuit of a job.

It was a godsend that right around that time word came that an all-news FM station was being put together in Fresno and I was later hired at KMPH-FM and KMPH-TV. It was the beginning of my first real, full-time job as a journalist. I covered the city council, arson, ribbon-cuttings, and murder—lots and lots of murders, including the infamous Carrillo's Club Massacre, May 16, 1993, when seven people were shot to death at a nightclub in southeast Fresno. Of the 87 murders that year within Fresno city limits, I figure I covered in some way, shape, or form at least 80 percent of them.

By early 1994, I was ready for a change. I decided to make another inquiry into Denver and called Jerry Bell. My timing was perfect. They were looking for a morning editor and he remembered me. I was offered $19,000.00 per year with a shift that began at

1:00 a.m., plus they also kicked in $1,000.00 for moving expenses. I headed to the Rockies in a U-Haul truck and started in April 1994. I will forever be grateful to Jerry for taking a chance on me. For more than a year I put together the newscasts and read headlines on-air twice an hour.

SHORTLY AFTER 8:00 A.M. THE MORNING OF APRIL 19, 1995— almost exactly a year into my job—I sat at my editor's position in the KOA newsroom preparing for my headline package at 8:15 a.m. Just moments before going on the air, our teletype machine to my right went into action and spit out an Associated Press bulletin:

OKLAHOMA CITY (AP) Explosion at courthouse in downtown Oklahoma City.

Of course it turned out to be incorrect. The explosion was at a place I had never heard of—the Alfred P. Murrah Federal Building. We followed the story for the next 45 minutes until our show ended for the day, and then the decision was made to send me there to cover the story. With nothing but a bag full of radio equipment and a cell phone the size of a small briefcase, I headed to the new Denver International Airport and was on the first flight out of Colorado to Oklahoma City (OKC). I knew it was serious when just before we landed, the flight attendant came over the intercom and asked if there were any doctors or nurses on board. My hair stood up on end. I arrived in OKC about six hours after the blast and I remember walking through a stunned Will Rogers World Airport. I hopped in a rental car and drove as fast as I could to downtown, where I stopped in a light rain to call in a live report to KOA. At that point, no one knew how many people were dead, who was responsible, or how something like this could happen. I walked among tens of thousands of pieces of broken glass, talked with stunned witnesses, and heard stories I had never thought possible. I spent five days in downtown Oklahoma City, many of the hours almost as if on autopilot.

I have often thought of the 168 people—19 of them children under the age of six—who died in the bombing, and my heart is still a part of the Oklahoma City community. I came back and KOA management urged me to undergo a post-traumatic stress disorder or PTSD counseling program, one I stayed in for more than three months.

Little did I know, but that was not the end of my involvement with the bombing; in fact, it was just the beginning. The subsequent trials of both Timothy McVeigh and Terry Nichols were moved to Denver, and naturally I was assigned to cover them both, gavel to gavel. I sat through as hundreds of items were entered as evidence and heard dozens of hours of witness testimony as the government presented its case. To me it was a no-doubt case. McVeigh did it. Through it all, I sat in the courtroom just feet from the mastermind. McVeigh and I would often make eye contact, but he would look right through me. At one point about three-fourths through his trial, one of his attorneys caught me at a court recess and asked me, "Are you Steffan Tubbs?"

"Yes."

"I'm Randall Coyne, one of McVeigh's attorneys. Tim wanted me to find you," he said as my heart skipped a beat. "He wanted you to know that he appreciated your fair reporting."

I didn't know what to say.

McVeigh only had access to a radio in his cell and he listened to KOA coverage both before and after his court appearances. To this day it remains a bizarre part of my career.

It was about this time that I started getting requests from ABC News Radio in New York to provide reports and conduct Q&As (or two-ways) with other radio stations around the country. McVeigh was eventually convicted and sentenced to death. His co-conspirator, Terry Nichols, was also found guilty by a Colorado jury but was spared the death penalty in 1997. At the end of his trial, I was offered a five-year contract with ABC News as their Los Angeles-based national correspondent, a position I began in February 1998. In what was a bit of closure for me both personally and professionally, I was on hand to report on—but not witness—McVeigh's execution at the federal prison in Terre Haute, Indiana, on June 11, 2001.

FOR NEARLY SEVEN YEARS I HAD THE TIME OF MY JOURNAL-istic life, traveling the world on assignment for the prestigious news organization. The late Peter Jennings became a brief mentor. I covered every type of natural disaster imaginable and had stints in Jerusalem, Mexico, and 30 of the 50 states. There were national political conventions, celebrity trials, the Oscars, Super Bowls, NBA Finals, World Series, the 2002 Winter Olympics, and countless light-hearted features and documentaries. There were also tragedies. I spent two weeks at Columbine High School in Littleton after the shooting rampage April 20, 1999. It was my first time back to Colorado since leaving KOA. I also spent a week at Ground Zero after the 9/11 attacks.

The three months of travel almost every year eventually grated on me. Because I was getting sick of being away from my newborn and three-year-old, I instructed my agent to start looking for a TV job, one where travel would be few and far between. In the spring of 2004, my agent called to tell me WNYW-TV in New York had seen my demo reel and wanted an interview. I flew to New York and three hours later was offered a job as an anchor/reporter. Several weeks later I packed up the family and moved to Connecticut. It was an adventure and I was willing to take the risk.

I MADE GREAT FRIENDS AT FOX 5 AND WAS RAPIDLY APPROACH-ing the end of my contract when I came in contact with my old program director at KOA. She offered me the morning co-host job on Colorado's Morning News (CMN) and after I declined twice, I finally agreed. New York was great but I was most certainly going to switch stations had I stayed. My final day on WNYW-TV came just a day after Hurricane Katrina ravaged the Gulf Coast. Instead of taking a week or two off between jobs, I flew from New York to Houston in early September 2005, and began my second stint at KOA from Texas as Katrina refugees flooded into the area.

One of the perks of co-hosting CMN came in late 2005, when I was informed I could travel with the Colorado Rockies to their annual Fantasy Camp program in Tucson in late January 2006. I would do the show from the KOA broadcast booth at Hi Corbett Field and then play baseball all day under the supervision of Rockies coaches and then-manager, Clint Hurdle. On our flight back to Denver, I received a voicemail from our producer. I finally picked up the message as I walked down Concourse B at Denver International Airport, Hurdle at my side. The message informed me the Pentagon had just called and they wanted to know if I would be interested in traveling to Iraq as an embedded reporter for two weeks later that spring. My mind raced. Of course I wanted to go! I listened to the rest of the voicemail and hung up the phone, then turned to Hurdle.

"I just got a call asking if I want to go to Iraq in March. I think I want to go. What do you think?" I asked the former big-league player as we walked.

"I wouldn't go! Think of the consequences!" he said, almost condescendingly.

"Yeah, true, but I'm going do it," I retorted, and Hurdle walked on ahead of me.

I ARRIVED IN KUWAIT AT THE BEGINNING OF THE SECOND WEEK in March. We had an overnight layover in Kuwait City before we boarded a heavily fortified C-130 into Baghdad. Packed in the back with returning troops, we wore flak jackets and Kevlar helmets as the plane did a defensive corkscrew landing into what had been Saddam International Airport. It was exhilarating.

I was embedded with members of the Army's 4th Infantry Division and flew to Camp Taji north of Baghdad via a Blackhawk helicopter. I soaked in as much as I could and when technology permitted, I fed stories back to Denver. Just weeks earlier, a former ABC News colleague, Bob Woodruff, had been severely injured in an IED explosion near Route Tampa, north of the Iraqi capital. I was embedded for two days with the team that saved his life. They told me I was the first journalist to be allowed back into the hostile area since Bob nearly lost his life. To this day my protectors, then Army Major—now Lieutenant Colonel—Mike Jason and First Sergeant John "Top" McFarlane remain dear friends.

For much of the remainder of my embed assignment, I was with the 4th ID troops out of Fort Carson, Colorado, and Fort Hood, Texas. I eventually hooked up with "Ghost Six" Commander, Army Captain Ian Weikel of A Troop of the 7-10 Cavalry, a West Point graduate and Fountain, Colorado, native. We instantly bonded and became fast friends as he welcomed me into their fraternity. I showed them respect and in turn, they did the same.

We went on one night patrol where I utilized night vision goggles for the first time ever in a combat zone. Weikel and his men shared their MREs with me and talked about home, thousands of miles away. He told me how the bad guys were going so far as to place IEDs in the carcasses of dead animals on the sides of the roads. As we rolled down on patrol, I sat in the back of the Humvee and listened to the young captain talk about his wife Wendy and their infant son J.T. back home in Texas. He also instructed me how to pop open ammunition canisters and feed the gunner should we become engaged in a firefight with insurgents and open fire. Being the only unarmed man in the area, I listened intently to every word.

Weikel and I reminisced about Colorado and planned to get our families together upon his return. I also promised him I would start a fundraiser on KOA and send as many soccer balls and dental supplies as I could back to them for distribution. He was elated. I interviewed him on my second-to-last day in Taji and broadcast it back to KOA via its 50,000 watts. Little did the two of us know, Ian's family and friends listened with pride back home in the Colorado Springs area.

It was the last time they would hear him.

IRETURNED HOME VIA KUWAIT AND A FEW WEEKS LATER, ON April 18, 2006, Ian Weikel was killed in an IED explosion north of Baghdad.

He was 31.

I found out the morning of April 19 at about 4:15 a.m. while I was seated at my desk in the KOA newsroom. It was, coincidentally, the eleventh anniversary of the OKC bombing. An email came in to me from a distant Weikel family member and the message, "Steffan, I thought you should know...."

It was just two days before our planned station fundraiser to send soccer balls overseas to Ian and his men. I wailed with emotion as I read the email over and over and over. I couldn't believe it. I had just communicated with him a few days earlier via email. My co-workers came to my side and comforted me as I told them what happened.

It took all the strength I had to go on the air less than an hour later, and my co-host, April Zesbaugh, and I openly cried on the air after our 5:00 a.m. newscast as I shared the story. I was devastated delivering the news to our audience, many of whom had been following "one of their own" in Iraq via our broadcasts.

Within two hours, it was confirmed by the Department of Defense. Ian was dead, killed instantly due to blunt-force trauma to the head after an IED, disguised as part of a guardrail, was intentionally detonated as he sat in the front passenger seat in a convoy of Humvees. It was quite possibly the same vehicle I had been in with him a few weeks earlier.

Our soccer ball and school supply fundraiser continued two days later in conjunction with my friends at KUSA-TV in downtown Denver. Thanks in part to my college friend, Trevor Slavick, who was touched by Ian's story, the *Little Feet* charity was born. As of this writing, more than 100,000 soccer balls have been donated to our troops overseas and to children in poverty in third world countries. The charity remains strong at www.littlefeet.com where one ball is purchased and the other is donated.

Later that week, the Weikel family asked me to deliver one of three eulogies at Woodmen Valley Chapel in Colorado Springs. On Wednesday, April 26, 2006, in front of more than 3,000 people, I barely held it together as I recapped my final days with Ian. I represented the last person in the room who saw him alive. Before the service, Dave and Beth Weikel welcomed me in as if I were their third son. Ian's widow embraced me and held me extra tight as she cried. Little Jonathan scooted around the waiting area, too young to walk.

I vowed to never forget.

I vowed that as long as I sat behind a microphone I would act as a beacon to make sure people—regardless of political affiliation or religious beliefs—would not forget the country is filled with families just like the Weikels. Their son's death would not be in vain. From that moment to present day, I end each of my broadcasts with a simple message, "Remember our troops."

IN EARLY MAY 2006, I HOSTED A POST-IRAQ-TRIP BRUNCH FOR members of our newsroom, sales staff, and select KOA clients. It was held in a local restaurant's banquet area and after food and drink, I went through a slide show of my pictures and stories from the gritty Iraqi landscape. I didn't know it, but a young Australian was in the audience and introduced himself after the program. His name was Tim Davis.

He explained to me he ran a non-profit designed to get WWII veterans back to the battlefields where they once fought, free of charge. Funding was based on contributions from private donors and many of the monetary gifts came in to honor a dad, grand-father, uncle, or brother who fought in WWII in either Europe or the Pacific. It was a fledgling charity but one that immediately piqued my interest. Tim explained how his uncles and grand-fathers fought as part of the Australian effort to aid the Allies in the South Pacific. Tim is more *American* than most Americans I know and is dedicated to getting these men the respect and the visit back to where they sacrificed before their generation fades away into memory. Since we met in 2006, I have had the honor of meeting the most incredible men and women in my life and have had the distinct pleasure of traveling across the globe with them as part of The Greatest Generations Foundation programs.

This is how I would come to meet Joe LaNier.

I LEARNED QUICKLY THAT WHENEVER JOE HAS AN APPOINT-ment, he always arrives early.

"It's good practice in case you get lost," he told me.

He arrived in the Clear Channel lobby at 9:20 a.m. for our 10:00 a.m. interview. Unfortunately I was tied up with a few things and didn't get down from our fourth floor newsroom until about 9:50 a.m. It was the first time I saw Joe in person. He was clean-shaven and wore slacks, a V-neck sweater, collared shirt and tie, shined shoes, and a blazer. A size 7-3/8" cream-colored, crisp felt Stetson cowboy hat completed his impeccable ensemble.

I came through double doors and introduced myself, and we sat for a few minutes around a small lobby table. My first impression was how incredible he looked for an 85-year-old man. He had great posture, a firm handshake, and a warm, inviting smile. His skin was dark cream, light for a black man. We did a little small talk before we walked to the bank of three elevators. Up on the fourth floor we turned the corner, entered a secure door, and walked down the hall to one of our production rooms. In preparing for the recorded interview, I figured we would be in and out in about 20 minutes.

We positioned ourselves in front of microphones and I gave him a couple of quick pointers to be sure he was in front of the microphone correctly. He made a passing reference to doing radio earlier in his life, which I thought was interesting. We then started our recorded conversation. In a matter of days, he was about to become by all accounts the first African-American to travel back to Iwo Jima.

His voice was warm and cozy with just a slight hint of southern dialect. I knew instantly he was an excellent speaker and would be a great interview to replay on our show the following day. I asked the questions and was mesmerized by his answers. We continued to talk and his stories fascinated me. I will never forget when something hit me during the latter part of one of his answers. I nearly blurted it out.

"You can't be that far removed from having slavery in your family, Joe."

He didn't miss a beat.

"My grandfather was a slave," he said.

I let it sink in as I shook my head and looked him in the eyes.

"Yes," he said, sensing my disbelief. "And I met him just one time, when he was 97-years-old."

I heard stories of boot camp, his time in Hawaii, on Iwo Jima, and in Okinawa. His story of how he came through Denver in 1946 blew me away. I heard about the injustice in Columbus, all the times he was called a nigger, and how he met his wife, a white woman. He shared his outlook on life. For an 85-year-old, his memory was impeccable and his delivery was pointed, smooth, and poignant. I was immersed in his story like few in my news career. He continued to speak and though I listened intently to every word, I couldn't help but think his story could be made into a movie or at the very least an incredible book.

No, he didn't receive the Medal of Honor like 27 Marines and 5 sailors on Iwo Jima. No, he didn't kill countless Japanese soldiers during a surprise attack. No, he didn't refuse to sit in the back of a bus in Alabama. But he was segregated in a U.S. Navy uniform and performed his duties without bitterness; he earned a Bachelor of Science degree in Pharmacy when the odds were stacked against him; and he went on to live a life of integrity, honor, and respect despite the world and conditions around him.

An hour later, we walked out of the production studio and I took Joe through our newsroom. I was honored to have the privilege to introduce him to our team and we said hello to several of my KOA colleagues that morning. We went back to the lobby and less than 90 minutes after we met, I felt I had reconnected with an old friend. We hugged and enjoyed a handshake goodbye, and I knew we would see each other soon.

We planned to meet again after his return to Iwo Jima as part of The Greatest Generations Foundation program. No one knew the devastating Japanese earthquake and subsequent catastrophic tsunami were just three days away.

Joe and Steffan at the Pacific War Memorial, Marine Corps Base Hawaii, Kaneohe Bay. December, 2011.
(John Riedy Photography)

For Freda

Occupy yourselves here with hope.
The joy of the day that's coming
buds in your eyes like a new light.
But that day that's coming isn't going to come: this is it.

—JAIME SABINES
b. March 25, 1926
(also Joe's birthday)

CHAPTER ONE

ANOTHER WORLD

We hold these truths to be self evident: that all men are created equal; that they are endowed by their Creator with certain inalienable rights; that among these are life, liberty, and the pursuit of happiness.

—THOMAS JEFFERSON

BY THE TIME HE CLIMBED DOWN THE STARCHY, TIGHTLY-wound rope ladder draped over the side of his ship and onto the landing craft that swayed below, most of the carnage had taken place. The dead Japanese far outnumbered the Americans, but the battle would continue for another month. For the past three days, the seas had been whipped by strong winds with swells of up to ten feet. It had been a rough journey for the teenager from rural Mississippi—from the tumultuous Pacific Ocean waters that made him seasick to the cramped quarters aboard his transport headed to "destination unknown" in early 1945.

As he made his way down that lifeline and into a world of death, he was about to become just another segregated "nigger" in a U.S. Navy uniform trying to survive on Iwo Jima.

Joseph Conklin LaNier II had never heard of Japan prior to the Pearl Harbor attack a little more than three years earlier and he knew nothing of the atrocities that had been carried out by the Empire across China and islands in the South Pacific. Save for a basic dogpaddle, the young Navy teenager really didn't know how to swim and he thought the earth was flat. He had no idea the shape of the United States or the geography of the planet.

★

JOE MADE THE DECISION TO JOIN THE NAVY IN 1943. HE WAS just 17 and had completed only his first semester of the ninth grade and was already academically two years behind his black peers in Columbus farm country. This happened as a result of entering school for the first time when he was seven. When the family decided to move closer to Columbus proper in 1935, when he was nine, he was forced to repeat the third grade.

The 1930s meant poverty and struggle and a fight to survive for most blacks in the South. It also meant a segregated society. The Depression hit rural farming communities especially hard, and Joe can still recall local soup lines in Columbus—depressed, desperate people in need of the most basic food and shelter to survive another day. It wasn't called welfare. Instead the blacks knew it simply as "relief."

His father was Joseph Lanier—or Papa as he called him—a man who, as a matter of pride, did just about anything to keep from asking for help or assistance. The family never went hungry, but they couldn't afford even the simplest of things. The children's clothing was either homemade or simple hand-me-downs.

Much to Papa's disappointment, Joe dropped out of school for a spell in the sixth grade, without so much as a discussion.

He was lost.

At 13, Joe decided to get a two-dollar-a-week job at a white-owned general store on Sixth Avenue on the outskirts of Columbus. His sole responsibility was to get food, clothing, and other goods to white customers across the area via the store-owned bicycle and its small basket wired to the front. All transactions were done on credit, so no money exchanged hands. They didn't trust blacks with cash.

When Joe delivered, he was forced to enter through the back door. Deliveries were made strictly to white families.

"I was called a nigger and that kind of thing, but that was normal. That was *normal*. It wasn't like I thought it was even mean. It was just so common. That's just what they called us," he said calmly during one of our first interview sessions at his dining room table. It was a place we would gather sometimes multiple times per week in the Denver suburb of Highlands Ranch.

"But when I have been called a nigger, it disrespects who I am."

B Y THE END OF 1940, THEIR LIVES TEETERED ON THE BRINK.

Papa was struggling to take care of the three children in the house—Joe and his two younger sisters. His mother was dead. Papa was out of work, save for odd jobs here and there that paid him less than three dollars a week. It was a struggle.

Across the country, young men—particularly those who lived in poverty—turned to the military to fulfill a sense of service, to find a way out of their socio-economic condition, or both. The collision of these two realities was about to dramatically change the LaNier family—and see a teenager enter war.

I N LATE 1943, JOE SAW AN ADVERTISEMENT IN THE TOWN newspaper, *The Commercial Dispatch.* It was an ad about the service. Uncle Sam looked directly into Joe's young face, finger pointed at him, right there in newsprint. There, in front of him, was a small black-and-white posting that changed the direction of his young life. Maybe this was the route he could take to escape the racism and poverty of northeastern Mississippi, but certainly not segregation.

He knew the Navy was segregated before he signed up—segregated like everything else. He didn't have to be told.

A small recruiting office kept normal business hours in Columbus, but it was there only to pique interest, answer questions, and funnel recruits to a larger office in Jackson. Without a lot of thought and without any family consult, Joe decided to go in, alone. At the Naval Recruiting Station, Columbus, a retired Navy-man-turned-recruiter named C.B. Roberts—now with the United States Naval Reserve—sat and talked with him. After their discussion, Joe was ready to enlist on the spot. However, he had no clue that in order to officially enlist he had to first convince Papa to sign the necessary paperwork. Joe had no idea he was too young to do it all on his own.

His sole motive for joining the Navy was poverty. He was primarily on his own, and the decision to enter the military changed the entire direction of his life.

Joe walked home with paperwork in tow and then explained to Papa how he could help with an U.S. Navy allotment every month. Papa agreed without hesitation. Of the multiple forms Joe brought home with him that evening, none was more important than NRB FORM 24A: Application for Enlistment. The filled-in blanks provided the Navy a snapshot of the boy's life:

> Last school grade completed: *Eighth*
> Reason for enlistment: *To Serve My Country*
> Address when registered: *RFD 5/Box 121, Columbus, Mississippi*
> Nationality: *U.S. Negro*
> Religion: *Methodist*
> Complexion: *Negro*
> Hair: *Negro*
> Eyes: *Negro*
> Blood pressure: *136/74*
> Do you wear or have ever worn glasses? *Yes*
> Remarks: *Measles, W. Cough, C. Pox. Two wisdom teeth erupt.*
> Are you well? *Yes*

At 17 years, 10 months, the examining Navy surgeon—Lieutenant Commander M.H. Jones—accepted Joe into the service. The teen was eager to leave the gravel roads and cotton fields of Columbus and take a chance. Papa and Joe both read the lines printed on *Form Eighteen*:

CONSENT, DECLARATION OF PARENT OR GUARDIAN
PARENTS OR GUARDIAN WILL READ
OR HAVE THE FOLLOWING EXPLAINED

An excerpt from his Navy contract below that line read: *"I am of the legal age to enlist...have never deserted...I have had this contract fully explained to me, I understand it...."*

Joe was listed as "ratings qualified" and ranked as V-6. In a non-binding Navy error, Papa's signature was actually next to the typed date of January 25, *1926*. It should have obviously read 1944, but no one ever caught the mistake. In a letter dated January 26, 1944, recruiter Branham Hume—another retired Navy-man-turned-recruiter—verified Joe's age and date of birth. Without the ability to locate his actual birth certificate, Joe's age had to be confirmed by Union Academy, his school at the time.

Both Joe and Papa signed their names under the line: *"I understand the foregoing."* There was no congratulatory hug, no handshake, or celebration in the LaNier home, but Joe was now a tremendous step closer to becoming part of the United States military in WWII. He signed a two-year contract, but every young man knew—whether they were drafted or they enlisted—their service was predicated on the duration of war.

When asked to list his skills, Joe wrote by hand in the space provided: *"Employed after school for past year and a half. Worked three months as presser machine, six months as porter, ten months as waiter, and bus boy, likes this type of work fairly well for the present would like to work in aviation machinist field."* The 17-year-old listed his main occupation as *service work*.

Most of the internal personnel records Joe would receive decades later showed how he was categorized: *NEGRO* was stamped at the top of nearly every page.

W ITH SIGNED PAPERS IN HAND, JOE HOPPED ON A BUS
in downtown Columbus and made the trek to Naval
Recruiting Station, Jackson—nearly 200 miles southeast of his
hometown. He arrived in Mississippi's biggest city on February 7
and had been instructed to report to the officer in charge at the U.S.
Navy Recruiting Station, 503 Post Office Building, for active duty
at 8:00 a.m. the following day. Joe was placed with a black family
he had never met and for unknown reasons he was put in charge of
two other recruits—Louis Jones and Oscar Ingram—both similar
in age and background. He was charged with making sure they
arrived in Illinois as scheduled.

The three Navy recruits left Jackson February 8 and headed
north by rail to Naval Training Station, Great Lakes and Camp
Robert Smalls. They arrived at the segregated base, inside the base,
the next day. Camp Smalls was named after a Civil War hero and
a former slave. It still stands today, relatively close to the windy
shores of Lake Michigan in North Chicago, Lake County, Illinois.
Black Marines were concurrently being trained—completely segregated—at Montford Point in Jacksonville, North Carolina.

President William Howard Taft dedicated Great Lakes on
October 28, 1911, but it was not until three decades later—with the
United States at war with both Germany and Japan—that the training site would open to blacks. Great Lakes was unique in that it was
the first U.S. Navy boot camp anywhere for African-Americans,
and as Joe walked on the grounds for the first time, he immediately noticed the large barracks, lined up in rows. The buildings
that stood in front of him—his new home for the spring—were
segregated. Blacks only.

Joe also filled out his application for National Service Life
Insurance, most certainly the first time he had ever thought about
his own mortality. He took out a $10,000.00 policy with a monthly
premium of $6.40 and named his sisters—Annie Ruth Lanier

and Gladys Lanier—as beneficiaries who would split the policy equally. The document was signed at Great Lakes February 23, 1944—exactly one year before the flag raising on top of Mount Suribachi, Iwo Jima.

IT WAS A STRANGE, NEW WORLD AT CAMP SMALLS. THERE WAS order, rank, and places to be. The schedule was regimented and everything was clean. It had to be. Joe received his dog tags almost immediately—serial number 722-26-24—after he arrived and was inoculated for the first time in his life.

Most of the white doctors in Columbus wouldn't see black children. As a little boy, Joe only saw the dentist after a tooth decayed and even at ten-years-old, he never had been given a toothbrush. The first doctor he saw was at Great Lakes—at 17. His first shots were given in intervals and were accompanied by lingering pain. They were administered in his left arm, which caused memorable swelling and soreness.

There was no way of knowing the young black men were such a small percentage of the Navy population. As other black men from across the country settled in at Great Lakes, they were put through the standard military routine. One morning, they were told to gather in a certain location and lined up for their physicals— their "small arms inspection." Everyone was naked in a huge room, lined up as they waited to hear the word "Next!" When it was time, they were checked for gonorrhea. The young men were bent over and sprayed with a bug-spray-like device as a precaution for crabs. Naval doctors also checked blood pressure, tonsils, eyes, and ears, as well as the lungs and heart. Joe had never been examined with a stethoscope. They told him he had an irregular heartbeat, but said he'd be fine.

I N FEBRUARY 1944, THE U.S. NAVY COMMISSIONED ITS FIRST black officers, known as the *Golden Thirteen*. While these 13 blacks were finishing their courses and training, Joe had just arrived at Great Lakes. Because of the lack of confidence in himself, he wondered exactly how he would make the necessary transition from poor Southern country boy to a proud member of the United States Navy. He knew his background could help him cope with the segregation within the military and as a result, it was easier for Joe than for blacks from the North who experienced true segregation for the first time in the Navy.

His rank was Apprentice Seaman through boot camp.

To this point in his life, he had never truly had a brand new wardrobe. There were no more denim overalls, ratty shoes, or homemade shirts; the Navy provided brand new clothing, in fact, some the newest items Joe had ever worn. Back home there was an occasional new shirt here and a new pair of pants there, but most of his personal items were used. As a young boy, he fantasized about clothes he saw in various catalogs. When he arrived at Camp Smalls, his civilian clothes were mailed back home to Columbus.

Each young man received two pairs of black shoes—one made of thick leather, the other a standard dress pair. In assembly line fashion, they were issued two pairs of Navy blues, two white uniforms, two pairs of underwear, two undershirts, socks, and two caps. Inside his "ditty bag" were the personal toiletries—shaving equipment, toothpaste, and toothbrush. He'd never possessed such personal hygiene items in all his life and everything fit into a Navy-issued green sea bag. Since Joe was the youngest in his outfit, he nicknamed himself "Sonny"—the name that was later stenciled in black on his lone large bag he would take to war.

Joe turned 18 just weeks after he arrived at Great Lakes, but there was no cake, fanfare, or celebration on March 25, 1944. Instead, it was business as usual, albeit in a brand new environment.

The days passed rather quickly.

Part of his Great Lakes training included ship recognition. One early spring day each man was placed in a dark room with silhouettes of ships on the walls, part of a drill to recreate what sailors may see on the horizon in a war zone. Each young black man entered a room and put on uncomfortable metal headphones and then had to describe the latitude and longitude of the ships on the fictitious horizon. They each spoke into a microphone attached around their necks as a superior in another room listened to their live descriptions. After the drill, Joe received his first kudos as a member of the Navy. He was told how clear his voice had come through over the intercom, and though he didn't know it at the time, his voice would pay dividends later in life. He also took a number of different courses and learned Morse code and flag communication as part of his training.

LIKE MOST MEN IN THE MILITARY DURING THE 1940S, JOE smoked. He began when he was 12 and had seen tobacco usage in his family since before he could remember. His grandmother dipped snuff and had teeth about as dark as her skin. His mother, Savilla (or Mama), chewed tobacco and Papa bought a cigar about four times a year to smoke only on Sundays when friends would stop by for conversation. Packs of cigarettes at Great Lakes were about the only thing Joe had to purchase during his boot camp days.

Laundry was done during free time, and being his meticulous self, Joe did his almost every day. While on duty, part of their boot camp routine included cleaning the wooden floors that covered a hangar used for ceremonies, gatherings, and drills. Retractable bleachers were on each side of the hangar and with all the foot traffic, the floor was constantly scuffed and dirty. A black group assigned to floor duty decided instead of spending hours on their hands and knees, there had to be an easier way to tackle the problem. They eventually placed steel wool on their shoes—tied with string or rubber bands—and they got the job done. They dubbed it the Great Lakes Shuffle.

The mish-mash group of black men from across the South and parts of the Midwest and North began to gel as a unit. They marched with rhythm and sing-songed through outdoor marching. The camaraderie made the days easier to take and while some of the men were homesick, Joe looked forward to every day as something new. He viewed this time in his life as an escape, much like a wealthy white teenager of the same age might look at going away to summer camp. They received gas mask instruction and went through the training chambers together. They bonded.

JOE CAME FROM A STRICT AND TOUGH SEGREGATED LIFE, YET he quickly learned what was meant by *Navy* discipline.

He was in about a month when he was placed on guard duty, which required a midnight wake-up. Earlier in the day, they had marched for miles and Joe was simply worn out. That night, he was caught—asleep while on duty. It never dawned on him that doing so in a combat zone could end with disastrous, deadly results.

Joe was immediately reprimanded for his inability to stay awake and as part of his punishment he had to make a visit to the company commander's office. There, he was berated and instructed to do his superior's laundry and as an added example, he was also told to clean the man's apartment on base. The extra duty was in addition to other responsibilities already laid out for the teenager.

Joe and his comrades dubbed their chief petty officer, E.M. Hanson, "Extra Duty Shorty" due to his small stature. The Texas native drilled them, yelled, inspected bedding and lockers, and at times would jump onto specific cots not up to his Navy standards.

"He didn't call us niggers. He would come around and talk to us and we didn't have to salute every time we went into his office. He didn't require a lot of the starchiness that goes with an officer.

I had very little trust in any white male from the South because all of my life, I had just seen so much. I'd seen the beatings," he said.

He trusted no one.

A<small>T TIMES, BASIC TRAINING SENT</small> J<small>OE INTO COMPLETE</small> exhaustion. He had very little contact with family in Mississippi and though he made acquaintances, he remained a loner. He often felt out of sorts in his scrawny six-foot, 130-pound frame. There was also something else that grated on him, even though it was one of the most basic requirements one could strive to meet as a Navy recruit.

He couldn't swim.

He had learned to dog paddle as a child in muddy swim holes back home, but getting into a pool and using the overhead arm motion was something completely foreign to him.

Even had he had the skills or desire to learn, public swimming pools were off-limits to blacks in his home state. All the black kids had heard it in some way, shape, or form growing up: most whites didn't want them in common pool areas because the blacks carried diseases that could get into the water supply. At the segregated Columbus Country Club, small white children were told they would die, yes *die*, if they got into water *with* or *after* a black person. At one nearby club, blacks could swim one evening a week: Wednesdays after the pool had closed for the day. That's because the operators drained the pool for cleaning and filled it up with new water for Thursday's opening.

No one in the Navy asked if he could swim. They assumed he couldn't because the officers knew most of their recruits were from the South, where those types of facilities weren't available to blacks.

One morning early into his training period, Joe and his fellow recruits ate breakfast at the chow hall and then all made their way to the Great Lakes training pool. Instead of panicking, he took it in stride and calmly changed into his swimsuit, the first one he'd ever worn. He floated and somehow got by, knowing he didn't have to prove he was an Olympic swimmer.

Nonetheless, stamped on his transfer papers, were the words *non-swimmer* and *Negro*.

CLEANLINESS AND TIDINESS WERE KEYS TO SURVIVAL AT this stage, especially for the blacks at Great Lakes, because they all answered to white naval officers. Segregation was, without question, in full force within the U.S. military during WWII. During my own research, writing and as I talked with people about a segregated military, I was amazed at just how many people—intelligent people and friends of mine—had no clue that the military branches protecting the greatest country on Earth were segregated until 1948.

The teen never expected anything different, even as he put on his United States military uniform every day during basic training. Yet he knew the significance of being there. He was a part of a new wave breaking ground within the Navy. Prior to 1944, there were no black seamen, only black stewards or cooks who served white officers.

The strenuous training and occasional word of the ongoing war thousands of miles away in Europe and the Pacific made it easy for Joe to quickly forget about the company commander, a fellow black man in his late twenties with one brown and one black eye. He never addressed the unit or exuded his authority and instead let those underneath him handle daily operations.

The days dragged on and the monotony became routine. Joe and his assistant company commander, Fitzgerald, would often kill time playing checkers. He once bet Joe he couldn't be beaten in a two-minute game. Joe took the bet and Fitzgerald proceeded to sit and stare at him for the next two minutes, and when time expired, Fitzgerald took Joe's money. Joe cried foul and the company commander helped get his money back but it was a lesson in semantics. From the incident, Joe would long remember that not everything in the Navy—or in life—was as it seemed on the surface.

The young black Apprentice Seamen did what they were told, yet they were still out of place. Not only did their color determine their placement, the cold and snowy spring of 1944 proved to be an obstacle. The Navy didn't care about the recruits being cold and certainly didn't care that some of the young men had zero snow experience nor had gone through a cold winter. One of the men had actually never seen snow and went snow-blind for a time. Another recruit was so slow and uneducated he didn't know his last name. They were not the most intelligent group of young men and as such were treated that way—stereotyped from the beginning. It was a hodgepodge mix of personalities; one of the seamen had even played saxophone in Count Basie's band, while others were just average folk from Kansas City, New York, and rural Mississippi.

Weapons training consisted of learning the inner workings of a carbine rifle. A clean weapon, treated with special care, could be the difference between life and death. Joe had fired a shotgun just once with his father when he was eight-years-old, but other than that had no experience with rifles or guns. His experience with firing that one shotgun blast was memorable, as he shot the family cow from across a pasture so she wouldn't eat the family's corn crop. The cow was at most annoyed, but Joe can still recall the kick of the shotgun as he pulled the trigger. At Great Lakes, it was basic mechanics with the carbine but there were no live-fire drills or other training exercises—nothing to prepare them for the potential of facing enemy fire in the Pacific Theatre.

AFTER THREE MONTHS OF EXHAUSTIVE MARCHING, cleaning, classroom training, and fieldwork, Joe LaNier graduated from basic training at Great Lakes April 17, 1944. He made $51.37 a month and of that monthly allotment, Papa received

$37.00 and $6.40 went to his life insurance premium. Joe was the first member of his family to join the Navy and he proudly returned to Mississippi by train for nine days' liberty. He soaked in his hometown and actually missed the place. Joe visited old friends and teachers and returned a bit older, a bit wiser, more of a man, and proud of his decision to enter the service.

The trip back South offered proof that things were, however, no different in the segregated city. One April afternoon during his brief time back, Joe went to visit Sanitary Laundry to see old friends at his old place of employment. When he entered the laundry's press area, he encountered the new foreman, a white man. Joe was asked a question and responded with a simple "yes" but was scolded and told to answer with a "yes, sir" because he was white.

O N THEIR RETURN FROM LIBERTY TO GREAT LAKES NINE days later, much to the unit's surprise and elation, 11 commissioned officers among the *Golden Thirteen* greeted them. The moment on April 26, 1944, remains one of Joe's most special wartime memories. It gave the young men a sense of belonging. These 13 were the highest-ranking black men in the Navy, and meeting them served as a tremendous morale boost. Joe was able to look up to these officers and viewed their promotions as an opportunity.

As the company prepared for its next assignment, the young black men were told to gather at the Great Lakes gymnasium. In uniform, they marched into the gym and took their seats on the wooden bleachers that lined the hardwood of a basketball court. They were about to meet their executive officer.

The gym went silent. The man who entered commanded instant attention. He was a LTJG, a lieutenant junior grade. It was an introduction that has stayed with Joe his entire life.

"I'm from Georgia," the LTJG began.

The "Golden Thirteen," Camp Robert Smalls, March 1944.
(National Archives)

"I'm telling you right now, we are gonna go and kick asses. We're gonna kick those Japs' asses, and we're gonna do our part to win this war. And I want you to know up front," he continued. His voice echoed through the rafters as at least 75 newly promoted black Navy Seamen Second Class sat and watched their superior officer deliver a stern warning.

"There's two kinds of niggers. There's a dead nigger and a good nigger. And we don't want no dead ones."

Joe and the blacks sitting with him were not impressed with the bold talk. He didn't like it but was so used to the word, it was just another typical insult. He ignored it the best he could.

It was too much for two enlisted blacks who decided they had heard enough and took a risk. They went to the commanding officer to report the incident. It paid off. Members of Joe's company would never see the LTJG from Georgia again. Rumor made its way around the company that he was demoted, but no one was ever able to confirm.

It isn't clear if word of the incident ever reached the desk of Captain Robert R.M. Emmet, commandant of Great Lakes operations. The WWI veteran had a superb career and received the Navy Cross for his duty as executive officer on the USS Canonicus (ID-1696). The converted passenger ship was a part of the mine barrage operation that laid some 100,000 mines in the North Sea in 1918, all in an effort to prevent U-boats from intercepting and destroying military and commercial vessels. Emmet's career continued as Captain of the USS Texas (BB-35) in Battleship Division Five from June 1, 1938, to May 31, 1940. An interesting anecdote: the Texas went on to provide weapons support for both the Normandy invasion and Iwo Jima. And it was aboard the Texas off the coast of North Africa a young reporter named Walter Cronkite began his career as a war correspondent.

Joe never met Captain Emmet at Great Lakes, but Emmet's initials are stamped on his entry papers.

AFTER THE RACIAL INCIDENT WITH THE LTJG FROM Georgia, Extra Duty Shorty was promoted and was charged with the unit until it was transferred to Pearl Harbor, Hawaii.

In addition to the racial slurs at the gym, the men found out they were headed out on a troop train the following day. It would be the last night Joe would spend in Chicago until the war was over.

He never regretted any time at Great Lakes. He had fun, established solid-if-not-friendly relationships, and the service started a new phase in his life. Prior to the Navy, he had no direction. Now, it was laid out in front of him.

The company spent that last night in the familiar surroundings of their segregated Great Lakes barracks and then it was off to the Chicago train depot the next morning, April 27, 1944. They were headed to "destination unknown."

Well before dawn, the company boarded a bus for the short commute to the train platform in downtown Chicago. Joe was about to leave the biggest city he'd ever seen and he didn't look back.

With fitted blue overcoats—pea coats—keeping them warm, the men boarded the troop train, a government-chartered passenger rail service. Each coach car had normal seating arrangements and for many of the blacks, it was their first train ride. For Joe, it was the fourth train trip of his life, and already the novelty had slightly worn off. It was a segregated train that pulled out of Chicago that morning and eventually headed west.

J OE HAD NO CONCEPT OF GEOGRAPHY. HE HAD NO IDEA WHERE he was in relation to the rest of the country, he couldn't point out a state on a map, and he had no clue where land ended and oceans began. Getting on the troop train that morning, Joe was unaware that if they stayed west on the tracks long enough, they would eventually stop in a city bordering the Pacific Ocean. The very tracks he would roll across—through prairie lands, corn, and wheat fields, through cities and towns, mountains and high plains— were laid by blacks and the Chinese two generations before him. During the trip, thick black smoke poured into skies above as the train rolled west. Inside one of the train cars, Joe talked at ease with Shorty about goals and his ambitions. It always came back to getting an education.

The first stop for the 75 people on the troop train headed west from Chicago was in Omaha, Nebraska. The troop train slowed and came to a stop in a place none of them had ever seen. Joe told me he vividly remembers it like it was yesterday.

Smiling female Red Cross volunteers dressed in crisp white uniforms were on hand to offer assistance and comfort for the young black men headed for more wartime training. These women had heard the reports from both Europe and the Pacific, and they surely knew many of the young men they came in contact with that cool Nebraska evening would not make the same train trip back home.

Troops were greeted as they disembarked from the hissing train for a meal inside an upstairs dining area at the Omaha train depot. Unbeknownst to the guests, upstairs was a lavish spread, at least based on Great Lakes' standards. There were tablecloths, plates, and silverware; flowers were on every table and friendly Midwest conversation available for anyone who wished to talk. For these civilians, this was their contribution to the war effort. The home fires and patriotic spirit would continue to burn so long as these men were away from home, protecting freedom.

As Joe got off the train, the tall, lanky teen was paired with a smiling volunteer—a white woman—who escorted him off the platform and into the depot. She gently took him by the arm and escorted him upstairs. It was the first time in his life he had been touched by a white female in a social situation. He never got her name but still remembers how she looked. To that point in his young life, it proved to be one of the most enlightening moments he had ever experienced. In Mississippi, for example, white women wouldn't put money in the hands of a black person in a retail setting. Instead, they would set it on the counter to avoid any human contact.

Waiters took their orders and served fresh, hot food to the troops as they sat at their seats at these fancy Nebraska tables. It was a far cry from the chow line they had already grown accustomed to during basic training in Illinois. Only blacks served blacks in service chow lines during World War II. This two-hour whistle stop in Omaha also became the first time Joe LaNier was served food, in a social situation, by a white person.

The Omaha oasis quickly came to an end. After the meal, Joe thanked everyone around him and walked downstairs and climbed back on the troop train. As the locomotive slowly pulled out of the depot, the Red Cross volunteers stood with smiles and waved as each illuminated window from every car crept by. From the inside, black faces could be seen looking back at these white women, dressed like anomalies on top of the depot's wooden planks. The young sailors inside nodded, smiled—some waved as the platform went out of sight.

He would never forget the face of the Red Cross volunteer.

JOE AND THE OTHER YOUNG MEN DIDN'T KNOW IT AT THE time but their next stop would be Salt Lake City, not exactly a bastion of activity for African-Americans in 1944. The troop train chugged along, crossed the Rockies, and made its way into the Utah basin. When the 75 blacks got off the train and into formation, it was apparently a sight to see. They were placed in parade formation and marched in rhythm as people stood and watched, as if they were some kind of show.

The train took on necessary provisions in Salt Lake and then headed out again, repeating the slow platform pull away the young black men had seen in Chicago and Omaha. But this trip out of a city was different, because within minutes, the train was headed out and seemingly into the middle of the Great Salt Lake. Joe had never seen so much water.

Because the training at Great Lakes was so intense and regimented, the company of black men primarily from the South had never ventured anywhere close to Lake Michigan while stationed outside Chicago. As the troop train rolled across Utah, water stared at them on both sides, with just a narrow strip of land holding the tracks.

The train rolled on through Utah, over the vast openness and deserts of Nevada, crossed the Sierra Nevada into California, and finally came to its destination at Camp Shoemaker in Alameda County, some 40 miles east of Oakland.

T HE BLACK MEN FROM THE NORTHEAST, MIDWEST, AND the South got off the train and headed to their segregated barracks. It was their home for three weeks beginning May 1, 1944. The 4,000-acre Navy base was a new, bustling place—commissioned January 19, 1943—with Camps Shoemaker and Parks (designated for Seabees) alongside U.S. Naval Hospital Shoemaker. Together, the three facilities were known as "Fleet City." The barracks and parade grounds held 20,000 men and hundreds of officers at the height of the war.

Boredom quickly set in. They passed the time playing horse-shoes and poker, waiting to find out what was ahead. It wasn't the wartime experience Joe had anticipated. Camp Shoemaker was basically a staging area for them while plans were underway to engage in major battles in the Pacific, an invasion of Guam, and the battle of Iwo Jima.

Joe and the young seamen soon received liberty and headed to Oakland and San Francisco, places Joe had never heard of other than the rumblings and the gossip that had circulated through the modest barracks. He fell in love with the Bay Area and all its newness.

San Francisco was the first big city Joe would remember, because in Chicago there was always night travel and the distance was just too great to see any of the skyscrapers. The Golden Gate Bridge left him in a state of awe as he tried to imagine how they built such a marvelous, monstrous crossing.

San Francisco would also be Joe's first foray into an integrated nightclub. It was the first time he danced with white women without fear of a lynching or other form of retribution. As sounds of the big band music played out onto the streets and teens danced the Jitterbug on the dance floor, the boy from Mississippi was nervous. He didn't know how to approach a white woman, let alone in a social setting. The tension was cut a bit because sailors were accus-tomed to buying dance tickets at fifteen cents apiece in order to get someone to dance with them. The dances with total strangers didn't last all that long before a bell would ring and another ticket was needed. The ladies worked for the nightclub and would consistently entertain members of the Army, Air Corps, Navy, and Marines.

The sailors were on liberty but had little money. Joe remembers sleeping on waiting room benches several nights at the train station in San Francisco. People in California seemed different to the young man and no one told him to enter through back doors or sit in certain places.

For Joe, a barrier had been crossed. He was 2,000 miles from home, in a U.S. military uniform, and for the first time saw that the entire country didn't operate the way it did in the South. While other servicemen drank alcohol, Joe refrained. He had tried "White Lightning"—homemade Moonshine—back in Columbus, just days before he entered Great Lakes. Since Papa didn't allow alcohol in his home, Joe actually got drunk at his sister-in-law Josephine's house next door. He was so inebriated he couldn't walk, and Papa came over, helped him back, and put him in bed. It was the last night Joe was home before he left for the Navy, and his father tucked him into bed.

In Oakland, Joe went alone and saw a movie at an integrated theater for the first time. Back in downtown Columbus, eleven cents bought a ticket but blacks had to go upstairs at the Princess Theater and sit in the crow's nest.

"That had more than one connotation, believe me!" Joe laughed, referring to the Jim Crow laws of the time.

The Mississippi theater had a separate entrance and a ticket booth labeled "colored." (Joe recalled to me how one particular day several years earlier, he stood in line on Fifth Avenue outside his hometown theater when a white ticket-taker—unprovoked— punched a black kid standing in line right in the face. He then continued taking tickets from others waiting to get inside.) Only whites took money from blacks at the Mississippi movie theater but in Oakland Joe paid a young black woman in her late teens. It was a small but brief feeling of liberation.

O N JULY 17, 1944, TRAGEDY HIT THE UNITED STATES NAVY in the northern portion of San Francisco Bay, yet Joe and the Great Lakes boys—indeed most of the country—had no clue. It would later become known as the Port Chicago disaster, where 320 sailors and civilians died and nearly 400 others were injured after a munitions explosion. Most of the dead in the Contra Costa County accident were African-Americans and only 51 of the bodies could be identified. According to various reports, the Port Chicago disaster and deaths accounted for 15 percent of all black Navy deaths in WWII.

The Port Chicago Naval Magazine was an extremely important locale for the loading of munitions headed for the Pacific Theatre but an area rife with safety concerns. Many poorly trained sailors handled bombs, torpedoes, bullets, mines, and shells under the cloud of war and pressure to perform. In subsequent investigations, witnesses termed their superiors as "slave drivers" and "Uncle Toms" with little regard for safety.

The initial fire and explosion on the Port Chicago pier triggered subsequent explosions and led to the high death toll. Two of the blasts registered on seismographs at the nearby University of California, Berkeley. Many of the survivors were transferred to nearby Camp Shoemaker.

In the weeks to follow, sailors revolted. Less than a month after the disaster, many of the same men impacted by the fire, explosions, and death were asked to resume their munitions loading at Port Chicago; what ensued led to the largest mutiny trial in U.S. Naval history. Nearly 300 who refused to follow their orders were told, among other things, that their actions were impacting military operations in Saipan. A total of 258 sailors were taken to Shoemaker for questioning, and 50 were placed in the brig. They became known as the "Port Chicago 50" and by September 1944, all were formally charged. Each man entered pleas of not guilty.

The trial lasted nearly two months and during closing arguments the 50 men were described in different ways: prosecutors painted the men as mutinous insubordinates while the defense described the defendants as shocked, confused, and traumatized. After less than 90 minutes of deliberations, the military court found all 50 men guilty of mutiny. The sailors were demoted to Apprentice Seamen and sentenced to 15 years of hard labor, along with a dishonorable discharge. After an extensive appeals process—led by eventual U.S. Supreme Court Justice, Thurgood Marshall—some of the sentences were reduced while others were left in place.

The U.S. Navy requested each family of a deceased sailor receive a $5,000.00 payment but Congressman John E. Rankin of Mississippi requested the amount be dropped to $2,000.00 per sailor when he discovered most of those killed were black. After negotiation, the total was set at $3,000.00. Rankin, who ran on a pro-segregation platform, was elected to 16 consecutive terms representing Mississippi's First Congressional District, including Joe's hometown of Columbus.

ON THE EVENING OF MAY 16, 1944, EXTRA DUTY SHORTY called his men together in the barracks and informed them he had received their orders. They spent one more night at Shoemaker, awoke the next morning to pack what little they had, and got ready for another "destination unknown." They boarded busses bound for San Francisco Bay and as the sun lit the spring morning, the seamen crossed the Bay Bridge and proceeded down to the harbor and the base of a converted merchant ship. It was the first ship Joe had seen in person.

He walked up the plank and for the first time in his life, he was aboard a ship. It was a converted merchant vessel with cramped quarters, yet for Joe they were perfectly acceptable seafaring accommodations. That night, it is hard to imagine what must have been going through the minds of the teenagers. Their first night on ship was spent getting acclimated to their environment, learning where the latrine and chow hall were located. As Joe put his head down on his small pillow, he pulled up his Navy-issued wool blanket and closed his eyes. They all knew the orders were to move out of San Francisco at dawn.

The next morning, he was up at dawn and went up on deck to see his surroundings. Out in front of him, the amount of water topped what he had seen in Utah just weeks earlier. The water he knew from back home was always muddy; here, it shimmered a green hue he had never seen before.

Joe was never overwhelmed with the potentially daunting tasks ahead of him. Leaving his rural, agrarian community, these places offered new sights and sounds, new people—even new food—and a naïve sense of adventure, at a time of global war. Yet from the simplest way of looking at it, it made perfect sense. He was excited. Their destination was still officially "unknown."

IN MARCH 1945, WHILE JOE SAT IN HIS FOXHOLE ON THE SHORES of Iwo Jima, something remarkable happened thousands of miles to the east at Port Hueneme, California. One thousand black Seabees—an entire battalion of Navy brothers he didn't know—staged a two-day hunger strike the third and fourth of March to protest Jim Crow laws and the lack of promotions during wartime. The hunger strike avoided potential mutiny charges. It was a risky maneuver and didn't change policy, and it wasn't the first uprising by black sailors. Just a few months earlier—Christmas Eve 1944—blacks had armed themselves against racist white Marines on Guam. In what became known as the Agana race riot, two enlisted black men were killed but justice was suspect. Forty-three black men were court-martialed and arrested; no whites were arrested or faced punishment. Race relations within the Navy were perhaps at an all-time low.

In the wake of the Port Chicago disaster, the Navy issued a pamphlet to its officers in January 1945, encouraging them to promote blacks on the same basis as whites. It held little, if any, merit and made no difference whatsoever to people like Joe in places like Iwo Jima.

O N THE DECK OF THE MERCHANT SHIP, HANDS READIED to disembark out of San Francisco Bay, while crews on the ground untied the ship and its final connection between the mainland U.S. Out in front of the vessel, tugboats slowly increased their engines and the merchant ship began to move; it was headed out to sea and into the Pacific Theatre. As it moved away from the dock, it cut slowly through the cold waters past Alcatraz and toward the Golden Gate Bridge. Joe proudly stood on the top deck and held the railing as the morning sea breeze blew against his tall frame. That morning was a perfect one, without fog to obscure one of the greatest views of any city in the country.

He remained enamored by the different colors as they left the bay and headed out into the ocean. In one of the more poignant moments of his long life, he watched as San Francisco moved away. He had never been taught about the horizon or that the world was, in fact, round.

Suddenly, without warning, San Francisco was gone. It dropped off behind the horizon behind him and for the first time since putting on his Navy uniform, he was scared. To that point, the newness of everything had overwhelmed him. Now it was quickly sinking in.

The merchant ship cut through the western Pacific, following a zigzag route in an attempt to avoid possible Japanese submarines, which were reported occasionally off the west coast.

Soon after departure, Joe felt a strange, sickly, unfamiliar sensation. He began to feel queasy and was soon seasick for the first time in his life, just a few hours off the California coastline. Everywhere the Mississippi native gazed stood massive amounts of water, as far as his eyes could see. He wasn't alone in his illness as country boys, city dwellers, and high school dropouts all felt the impact of the swaying ocean currents. Joe decided to get below deck to see if he might feel better by lying down on his small cot but that didn't help. It was then time for food, though he didn't really want to eat. He did, and it stayed with him for only about 20 minutes before he ran to the latrine.

Being from Mississippi, Joe had no clue there was actually a correlation between traveling on the ocean and feeling the way he did, so his next stop was to sickbay. His illness seemed to last an eternity. The doctors explained what was happening and comforted him not with medicine but with the message, "You'll get over it." Two days later, Joe was able to finally eat and keep things down.

He chuckled as he told me that it was around this time he had his first thoughts of trying to get out of the Navy.

Joe had no clue what lay ahead.

CHAPTER TWO

DESTINATION UNKNOWN

THE MERCHANT SHIP TRANSPORT LASTED SEVEN DAYS, THREE of which Joe felt as bad as he had ever felt in his life. The blacks being sent to the Pacific Theatre continued as passengers during their maiden voyage at sea, which meant they didn't work and didn't worry about their destination. It didn't matter. War was underway and they were headed into it. The ocean whitecaps continued to crest, the wind continued to blow, and the ship continued to steam toward the middle of nowhere. On board, there was never an announcement as to how much time was left in the journey or where they would eventually stop. One morning about a week into their journey, that changed.

Over a loudspeaker, the men were informed to head below deck and pack their belongings. They would disembark later in the day on the island of Oahu. Because Joe had never heard of Hawaii, everything remained new and exciting. It was a way to get paid, serve his country, and see places about which he'd never even been able to dream. It was hard to imagine Hawaii when the very word had no meaning in his mind. However, once Joe learned their destination was Pearl Harbor, Hawaii, he did expect to see remnants of devastation from the Japanese attack. His vision was based on what he had heard via his radio and had seen via newsreels from the crow's nest at his hometown Princess Theater in Mississippi.

On May 24, 1944, the merchant ship made its way into the Hawaiian island chain and cut through water off the coast of Oahu. It wrapped up the longest amount of time any of the black men had been away from land, and the seamen all stood on deck with their sea bags, ready to get back on the ground. The ship's deck stirred and conversations built as the palm trees came into view.

The warm Pacific breeze welcomed all of them to the island chain. They also noticed the tropical heat and Diamondhead off in the distance, though the only diamonds the boys from the South knew of were on playing cards.

The ship continued on its path into Pearl Harbor, and into the heart of the Pacific Fleet with battleships, destroyers, carriers, and frigates—some of the very vessels that were damaged on December 7, 1941—right there tethered to Ford Island. Joe saw the remains and wreckage of the USS Arizona (BB-39) but at the time its significance didn't really register. It served as a reminder to the young sailors to constantly remain on guard.

Joe's ship came to a stop off Ford Island, and the young men on deck were told to disembark and immediately get into formation. They trudged down with their green sea bags and marched to a mess hall to eat their first meal on solid ground in more than a week. After their first meal in Hawaii, the all-black unit marched to parked busses that drove them to their segregated new address at the U.S. Naval barracks—with an FPO of Navy 919—a quarter-mile away.

As Joe settled into his new bunk, he had no idea how long his unit would remain in Hawaii or what he would do in the interim. On Waikiki, locals and soldiers on liberty surfed near the pink Royal Hawaiian Hotel. Just two weeks before the black sailors arrived in Hawaii, famed aviator Charles Lindbergh made his first flight over Oahu and later wrote how "the surf looked wonderfully inviting." Joe agreed.

BACK ON FORD ISLAND, ORIENTATION FOR THE NEWLY arrived unit from Camp Shoemaker informed them where facilities were located and delivered a reminder that they remained a segregated unit. The Navy gave the blacks about three days down time to settle in and regain their land legs.

Extra Duty Shorty was in charge and handed out the various assignments to different groups of sailors. Joe's group was assigned to the boathouse, which prompted a thought of home. The knowledge he could gain from fixing boat engines and similar projects could help him back in Mississippi. At this point, the now 18-year-old had no clue how long he would be at war and was clueless as to what he wanted to do once he got back home. He constantly reminded himself he was behind in his education and since he had yet to complete the ninth grade, he felt at a distinct disadvantage. Yet there was a more immediate problem in front of him. Joe was told to report for duty in his Navy whites, which signaled to him he wouldn't be around greasy gearshifts or troubled engines.

He changed into his proper uniform and made his way down to the boathouse, where he was informed his job would be assisting the small ferry boats that took passengers from Ford Island to the Honolulu side. Every trip across the harbor, Joe saw a reminder of why he was in Hawaii: the remains of the Arizona were on his port side and the bodies of 1,102 men entombed just below the surface.

Joe's canopied boat was fairly small, seated as many as 25, and transported officers, enlisted men, and civilians whenever they needed a ride. He worked the day shift along with another black sailor and the coxswain who drove the small vessel. The coxswain was always a white sailor, never black.

Joe and three other crewmembers took people back and forth across the bay all day. His shift was usually 8:00 a.m. to 4:00 p.m. with two days off per week. It was mundane work and barely anyone noticed him. However, Joe felt that during his tenure—taking folks back and forth the 15 to 20 minutes each way across the sometimes oil-slicked water—he was as vital to the war effort as an admiral.

"I really felt what we did was important, and I don't know how much of that you can contribute to reality and the kind of system you were raised in. My parents always taught us, whatever you do, do it as well as you can do it. That was my attitude. When I look back on my career and my service, I really did think that was an important thing that needed to be done. We all felt that whatever contribution you could make was in the interest of helping to win the war."

J UST THREE DAYS PRIOR TO JOE'S ARRIVAL AT PEARL, THE AREA witnessed the biggest disaster since the Japanese attack. It happened in the West Loch section of Pearl's Naval Base but was kept top secret for nearly two decades. On Sunday afternoon, May 21, 1944, a mortar round on board LST-353 ignited nearby ships loaded with munitions and fuel. The massive explosion and fire killed at least 162 men who were preparing to invade the Mariana Islands as part of Operation Forager. Nearly 400 were wounded. The various vessels were fully loaded with supplies, ready for the trip out to sea to support the scheduled Marine-led invasion.

An initial fireball filled the sky and thick black smoke and flames burned for more than a day. Fortunately for many of the crewmembers, it was a Sunday and a large number were on shore leave for the day and away from West Loch, but blasts were heard throughout the greater Honolulu area, for a time spreading fear of another Pearl Harbor attack. The fact the skies were not filled with enemy aircraft calmed fears soon after.

The powerful combination of fuel, munitions, and other matériel sent a blast wave inland and out into the bay; 20 buildings on shore were damaged or destroyed and at least 200 men were blown off ship decks and into the harbor. Oil burned on top of the water for hours; flames burned with such intense heat, first responders were forced to keep back in the initial minutes after the explosion. Many LSTs and support ships began to sink and in the end, six LSTs and four LCTs were lost.

Wreckage was eventually dumped three miles off Oahu and kept top secret until 1960, an amazing amount of time for such a deadly accident to be kept off the radar for so long. Joe has no recollection of any talk of the billows of smoke that filled the Hawaiian air. It isn't surprising considering a press blackout was immediately implemented and the West Loch disaster categorized as *Top Secret*. The media received a one-paragraph statement a full four days after the incident stating there was "some loss of life, a number of injuries, and resulted in the destruction of several small vessels."

Because West Loch was kept under wraps and did not capture national attention, many survivors never received the recognition they felt they deserved. Survivors were told not to mention the incident in letters back home. Some eyewitness accounts say it was a simple act of careless smoking that led to Pearl Harbor's second-worst military loss during WWII. During the investigation, remains of a Japanese midget sub were found, one of five that came in December 7, 1941.

T HE DISTANCE AWAY FROM THE MISSISSIPPI COUNTRYSIDE often played with Joe's mind. He saw the farmland of Mississippi but then suddenly realized he was halfway around the world.

He never really missed anyone other than Papa and his grandmother, Louisa, back home. Joe was able to write his father for the first time back at Camp Shoemaker but wartime correspondence was rare and full of hurdles—namely censors and the timing of delivery—since mail to the Pacific usually came via San Francisco. One such delayed communication from home devastated the young sailor.

While at Pearl Harbor in 1944, he received word from Papa that Grandmother Louisa had died. She was 77 and the two were extremely close. Joe applied to go home to her funeral but the Navy denied the request because she wasn't his guardian. To this day, Joe's wife, Eula, feels it was a decision based on race.

THE HAWAIIAN ISLANDS WERE A UNITED STATES territory and under a state of martial law during WWII as recovery from the Japanese attack continued and U.S. military presence increased. Both territorial governors declared martial law from 1941 to 1944, thus dissolving all forms of state government. General Walter Short was the first military governor on Oahu but was removed due to his failures leading up to Pearl Harbor. Two more men held the position before the war ended. Those assigned to Pearl Harbor Naval Station, Hickam Field, Schofield Barracks, Wheeler Army Airfield, and other smaller outposts were still on guard around the clock as Joe began his brief Hawaiian stay. Large guns built into the Hawaiian hillsides watched over U.S. interests and the tens of thousands of civilian residents. It wasn't until August 21, 1959, that Hawaii became the 50th state.

JOE APPLIED FOR LIBERTY AND RECEIVED A TIME-SENSITIVE pass, which was his ticket to Waikiki. It was the first time Joe had extended time—after months in Hawaii—in a truly integrated situation. He was uncomfortable. He went alone and found himself where all the servicemen seemed to frequent: Hotel Street. What he didn't realize was that Hotel Street was the brothel section of Honolulu and it teemed with sex. Hundreds of women a day worked the streets, looking for interested takers. Some places charged three dollars for three minutes, almost in assembly-line fashion. It was officially "closed" by the time Joe arrived but had he been there a year earlier, he would have seen Navy men, Marines, and soldiers lined up down streets, waiting for their turn. Joe quickly figured out Hotel Street, even in 1944, wasn't the place for him.

Instead, he went to a nearby bar. For a young man from the South, Joe had more money than at any other time in his life.

Servicemen were there, the air was warm and tropical, and to relax, the 18-year-old Mississippi boy decided to have a few. He sat at the bar, handsome but stick thin. He wore glasses, but really didn't need them. He had always worn glasses, even back in Mississippi, but an added bonus was that he thought they made him look much older and smarter. At the bar in downtown Honolulu, for the first time in his life, he ordered a rum and Coke.

He got drunk and still doesn't remember how he got back to the base. The next day he was as sick as he was back on the ship that left San Francisco. To this day, though he can laugh about it now, he still avoids rum and Coke because of those bad memories.

On one of his next trips into the city during the late spring of 1944, Joe decided to try something he'd never done before. For the first time in his life, without any companion or a group of friends to accompany him, he went to the beach at Waikiki, dressed in his Navy whites.

With no companions to spend time with, he decided to do something bold and unknown: he rented a swimsuit and a surfboard.

It was the first time he had ever touched the ocean and most certainly the first time he had ever touched a long, wooden surfboard. He was clueless, so he watched the other guys catch waves at first, then ventured out into about five feet of water. Standing up on the board wasn't ever an option, but he did paddle around awhile— the only black man out in the waters off Waikiki. Joe wasn't even aware he needed a towel. From the crashing surf to the surfboard to the palm trees, it was all new.

Honolulu's iconic Royal Hawaiian was just a quick walk away from Joe's beach spot but he never noticed it. A hotel was a place Joe had never stayed and to him they represented nothing more than where a black man could work as a cook or a bellboy to serve white guests. The Royal Hawaiian served as President Roosevelt's headquarters when he traveled to the Pacific.

While Joe was on his surfboard for the first time, halfway around the world in Europe, the United States and the Allied forces were in the final stages of preparing for D-Day and the invasion of Normandy. For sailors like Joe, there were no updates from the battlefronts in Belgium, Germany, or France. They all knew the European Theatre had been dangerous and deadly but they were only focused on what was ahead of them. In most cases, Joe and his unit looked ahead perhaps only a few hours. They knew what they needed to know, and if they needed to know any more, a superior officer would tell them.

Joe never surfed again.

USO TOURS WERE IN FULL SWING BY THE TIME THE BOYS from Great Lakes settled into the islands and despite the segregated military, blacks were allowed to take part in the entertainment. One of the performers who made a mark on Joe while in Hawaii was the actress Betty Hutton. It was the first time he had seen a live stage production in person because blacks where he came from were not exposed much in the way of theater or the arts. As an example, he'd never heard—or heard of —classical music. It wasn't until college that Joe watched his first opera. When the USO performance was over, it was back to the segregated barracks.

There was a bizarre incident while at Pearl Harbor, one that to this day puzzles Joe. He was always the youngest in his unit, and one day he fell victim to the unit bully. It was in the barracks while Joe was in conversation when the bully tried to interrupt. He ignored the guy but the bully stepped in and cold-cocked Joe on the left side of his face and nose. Joe didn't do anything to retaliate. He didn't want to risk a night in the brig.

Decades later, Joe was treated for sleep apnea in Denver and during the examination he was told there was a blockage due to a past broken nose. He didn't realize it, but in 1944, the bully broke his nose.

Joe was alone most of the time. A loner. Back home, he had a lot of acquaintances but no real close friends and that was certainly the case while he was in the Navy.

Several times he would hop on the bus that constantly circled Ford Island and take it to an outdoor bar behind the laundry building. No one who served alcohol on base cared how old the uniformed customers were. If they could serve in the military, the feeling was they were old enough to drink if they wanted. Late one morning, Joe showed up, took a stool at the bar, and ordered a beer. The place was already crowded just before noon, as servicemen killed time between assignments. Lattice walls surrounded the place with small, circular tables scattered around the room. Joe struck up a conversation with a white soldier seated next to him, an Army guy about his age.

They drank beer all afternoon and didn't leave until close to dark. It had to be strange for other customers to see a white soldier talking to a black sailor, and while they could drink together, when they left they went to completely segregated barracks on base. They said goodbye, shook hands, and never saw each other again. Joe stumbled out of the bar, found his way to the bus stop, and went to sleep back in the segregated barracks.

NEW ORDERS SOON CAME AND JOE REALIZED HE HAD completed his final ferry mission from Pearl Harbor to Honolulu. His orders: report for laundry duty. *So much for feeling like an admiral.* When he got to his new job, he was reunited with many of the men with him at Camp Shoemaker back in California.

The laundry work was familiar and made him feel like he was back home. They loaded and unloaded machines and folded clothes. It was hot work anywhere, but even more unbearable with the tropical heat. Joe became friends with Nancy and Sadie, two friendly Hawaiian civilians. Sadie was the boss and Nancy was fascinated by Joe's hair. She wanted to touch it all the time due to its wiry texture. The two women in their forties and fifties were kind to Joe and they viewed him as a young man from a far-off land. Nancy thought surely Joe spoke some sort of African tongue and that English was his second language.

At the laundry, Joe met Mary. She was also 18, and every now and then the two of them would walk across the alley in front of the laundry and have lunch at the theater there on Ford Island. He was enamored by this beautiful, young Hawaiian but later found out he had read the tea leaves wrong. Mary only dated white servicemen.

The Pearl Harbor laundry job took Joe back to several of his previous positions just a few years earlier: the steam hisses, the smell of liquefied starch, and the rumble and tumble of wash machines and dryers. It was routine work that lasted nearly six months.

For fun, Joe continued to take his liberty into Honolulu and explored as best he could. He took almost every trip alone, which was exactly the way he liked it. The time alone helped him clear his mind, appreciate where he was, and experience all the new and different tropical surroundings.

Thanksgiving dinner 1944 was served on base at Pearl Harbor. The Navy cooks prepared turkey and the usual trimmings, served mega-family style. That holiday meal did not conjure up memories of his past or a longing for home, because Joe's previous time at home during the holidays was in extreme poverty. His first traditional turkey meal came in the service and these holidays provided the most bountiful meals of his young life.

After his mother died in 1940, holidays were never the same. There was no turkey at Thanksgiving and a special Christmas present was perhaps an apple or an orange from Santa Claus. Because things were so frugal, he never longed for home during the holiday periods.

Joe and his father continued to correspond infrequently during the latter part of WWII. After censors reviewed personal letters— and the time it took for the mail to leave Hawaii and travel to rural

Mississippi—much of the information was outdated. But it was a piece of his papa, a piece that kept Joe knowing, at least subconsciously, that he had not been forgotten. Joe also wrote letters every now and then to a childhood friend's mother back home but he never received any care packages like his fellow sailors.

ON DECEMBER 7, 1944—THE THIRD ANNIVERSARY OF THE attack on Pearl Harbor—there were commemorations but Joe and his black unit were not invited. Meantime in Europe, the final Nazi push against the Allies, the Battle of the Bulge, was just two weeks from beginning in the frigid Ardennes forest.

Christmas 1944, in Hawaii, was spent in much the same manner as Thanksgiving. There was the *Mele Kalikimaka* spirit but it was obviously hampered by war. For Joe, New Year's Eve and the start of 1945 were non-events. During the fall and winter, he and his fellow black sailors were not concurrently involved in gearing up for some invasion but instead, as Joe is fond of saying, the Navy acted as if it really didn't know what to do with these black men. What the unit didn't know was that the Navy, Army, and Marines were all in the final planning stages for the largest amphibious landing in the Pacific—second only to the Normandy invasion—in the entire war. The Battle of Iwo Jima was just weeks away.

Just after New Year's 1945, word again came from Extra Duty Shorty. He called his men into formation at the northeast corner of the barracks on Ford Island, their feet hot on the asphalt as the sun beat down. Without explanation he began to bark out last names and had some of the men move over into another line, away from the formation. He called "LaNier!" and 20 other people, then informed the group they were being transferred to the United States Navy 23rd Special Seabees.

He had no idea what a Seabee was.

The rest of the company was dismissed and then the XO explained that they were being transferred. After the group left, Joe asked to speak with Shorty in private. He asked his superior to explain what Seabees meant and what sort of opportunities lay ahead. Shorty was polite and in his Texas drawl explained the men would be a part of something similar to the Army's Corps of Engineers. They would unload ships and build tents, roads, and airfields somewhere in-theatre.

Joe had no idea how difficult some of those tasks were and had set his sights on becoming an officer. But without even a completed ninth grade education, Joe knew his background was certainly the educational equivalent of conduct *unbecoming* of an officer. Shorty consistently emphasized in order to become an officer in the United States Navy, it would all depend on Joe's commitment to getting an education once the war was over.

It was the last time Joe saw Shorty and to this day he remains appreciative of the respect the man in his mid-thirties showed to the unit of blacks under his command.

"I've often thought about him. If I had to make an assessment of why he was the way he was, he was very aware of what that LTJG said to us back at Great Lakes. He was a decent person and treated all of us that way. It just never crossed my mind I would never see him again. On the basis of what was available at the time, I think he did as much as possible for a person in his position."

The 23rd Seabees was comprised of 34 officers, tasked with overseeing the newly formed battalion. On January 2, 1945, Joe and nearly two dozen of his fellow black Seabees reported to Naval Barracks, Manana, T.H.—also in the Pearl Harbor area of Oahu—ready to take their next step into WWII.

CHAPTER THREE

THE BEGINNING

J OSEPH CONKLIN LANIER II WAS BORN FRIDAY, MARCH 25, 1926, in farm country, inside the bedroom of a rented home six miles from the center of Columbus, Mississippi—population no more than 3,000. Outside two magnolia trees swayed in the wind, while inside Mrs. Mary Boles, a midwife, helped 34-year-old Savilla LaNier deliver her fifth son. There were the usual assistance items: clean towels, warm water, and home remedies near the side of the bed. A kerosene lamp stood nearby.

Savilla pushed, strained, and grimaced in pain one final time and Joe was born into his new world. The cute, healthy little boy with a slightly receding chin took his first gasping breaths in-between his first screams. With his umbilical cord cut, he was cleaned, wrapped in blankets, and tucked into the bosom of his mother. There was no doctor to announce the time of his arrival or his official length and weight. After the birth, Mrs. Boles walked across the wooden floors to the front door, past the nearby cow pen, and back to her house two miles away. One month later, the LaNiers filed Joe's birth certificate with the State of Mississippi and the State Board of Health, Bureau of Vital Statistics. He was officially recorded as *state file number 11011;* the certificate read he was from colored parents—a farmer and a farmer's wife.

P APA RENTED THAT SMALL HOME FROM MR. HICK McClanahan, a railroad engineer who traveled back and forth from Columbus to Birmingham, Alabama. The family lived there until Joe was nine, on the southern edge of 40 mostly-wooded acres. The surrounding fields were covered in fruit trees, rows of corn, cotton fields, and other crops. This was manual-labor land. Papa made much of their furniture by hand, including the chair where Joe sat and cried as they took his first picture in 1930. It was the earliest documentation of Joe's life, a picture unfortunately lost decades ago.

Two younger sisters, Ruth and Gladys, came in 1930, and 1932. Joe, his older brother, and his father usually slept in one room, while his mother slept with the girls a few feet away. The home had two small rooms. There was a living room and bedroom in one, while the other served as the kitchen area. Papa later built an actual kitchen, which expanded the living and sleeping space into two bedrooms. They were cramped.

Across the dirt road in front of the LaNier home, a German family worked the farmland. Mr. Reich was a hard worker and six-year-old Joe would watch from his yard as the man worked the fields even at night, under a full moon. He worked the plows with mules and horses, going up and down the rows. Eight families had farms within walking distance and during certain times of the year, the air smelled of fresh corn.

When young Joe was old enough, about once a month he would hop in his father's homemade wagon, pulled by two horses, and ride down the bumpy dirt roads into town. Whites drove the few cars that were on the road. Papa owned a four-door Model-T he bought in Birmingham before Joe was born but it didn't run. That didn't stop a little boy from climbing in and pretending to drive to far-off places, rolling past great buildings and neighborhoods that floated in his young mind. In Columbus cars were rare, even for the whites, and paved roads were few where Joe lived. As the dust would fly up in the distance, children would often run out to the dirt road simply to see a car pass.

Sundays were community days. Friends and acquaintances would come over to gossip, socialize, and share a supper or dinner. It was also the day of bartering, where people traded this for that, settled old debts, or made new ones. The men gathered at the LaNiers' for monthly haircuts and as they sat around, each would take monthly turns acting as the barber. There was no electricity, so someone was always responsible for making sure the scissors were sharp and ready to use.

BECAUSE THE LaNIERS LIVED IN POVERTY, THEY ATE WHAT the land and their surroundings allowed. The family ate pork from their hogs but cows were special and used only for milk production. Homegrown vegetables and fruits were staples. They also ate raccoon, opossum, rabbit, squirrel, duck, and other foul. Joe's older brother, Ira, did most of the hunting, while Papa worked the fields. Joe hated opossum and its fatty, greasy flavor and out of fear, he also avoided snakes, refusing to eat them. Mama cleaned the animals and did the cooking. They ate fish and eels on occasion, caught mostly in Luxapalila Creek near their home. The kids fished the old-fashioned way—with dried poles, a string with a hook tied to the end, and worms as bait.

Joe's maternal grandmother, Louisa, lived about a quarter-mile to the west and he loved spending time with her. She had coffee-colored skin, wore her hair in cornrows, and was always seen with a scarf tied around her head and a dress down to her ankles. Louisa Barnett-Green was born just two years after the Civil War ended; she dressed as if she were still in the 1800s and because she dipped snuff, her teeth were stained almost the color of her skin. She read paperback, dime-store romance books as often as she could. Joe loved Louisa and stayed with her as much as possible. She was a tremendous cook and baked delectable cornbread. On Sunday mornings she made mouth-watering butter rolls cooked in a special, sugary sauce that Joe can still taste.

Louisa was a religious woman, the daughter of a minister. As a part of her weekly ritual on the Seventh Day, she rose at 4:00 a.m. and whoever was in the house was awakened before dawn to Scripture readings and prayer. Whether winter, spring, summer, or fall, it didn't matter; until those two things happened, there were no rolls or signs of breakfast.

His older half-brother, Clarence Roberts, lived with his grandmother most of the time. The two often clashed with one another over Bible study and the "prayer meeting" at 4:00 a.m. On one particular Sunday morning, Clarence just wouldn't get up, so when the prayer was over, Louisa grabbed a stick and forced him up. She yelled at him to get out with an additional, "Don't come back here!" Clarence left. Joe recalled she was so angry she was shaking and asked him what he thought. He told her Clarence would be back. After all, they needed each other—him for the chores and her for the room and board. He eventually came back and all was forgiven. Unlike Clarence, Joe was usually able to wake naturally within minutes of a specific time, whether 4:00 a.m. or 7:30 a.m., and throughout his life he has found this to be the case. In those early years, however, roosters would often act as his secondary wake-up call.

During other parts of the week, Louisa would sit by her ash-covered fireplace and bake bread or "hoe-cakes" as she called them. A churn of milk was strategically placed near the warm fireplace so it could clabber, or form curds, until she could make homemade butter. Making hominy was also a specialty in the kitchen.

As for chores, Louisa did most of them herself. She worked a small cotton patch in her front yard, sometimes assisted by Old John, the mule, and Old Flossy, the cow. Joe spent as many days as he could with this woman, who showed him the love and attention as only a grandmother could.

THE LaNIERS EVENTUALLY MOVED ACROSS THE DIRT ROAD, which is now Mississippi Highway 50, and into a spare house owned by Boyd and Annie Banks Weathers. The rented place got extremely cramped because another family also moved in for a brief amount of time. Eleven people lived in just several hundred square feet, with the kids sleeping on the floor on homemade quilts.

In the small quarters, Joe couldn't escape his nickname, Gump, as in Andy Gump, the character with the receding chin from the funny papers. The name stuck with him well into his teenage years.

Family supper was a given. The LaNiers ate around a table in a new kitchen area Papa built; their food was served either in large serving bowls or the very pot in which the meal was cooked. Butter, biscuits, or cornbread and the entrée were always presented but during the week Papa would be out until well past sundown. Weekends proved to be the big mealtimes when Joe, Ira, Mama, Papa, and the girls would share a meal.

Their home was surrounded by peaceful farmland. In fact, it was so quiet all Mama had to do was walk outside and call Papa to dinner with a *"Joe-seeeeeph!"* It was the only thing he needed to come in from the fields. At their table, suppertime was quiet time. There wasn't a lot of talking but one of the family rituals was Papa's prayer before the meal. Then they went around the table. The children weren't allowed to simply state they were "thankful" for their food; they had to recite a Bible verse. Another rule was no hats at the table. For Joe, it was usually eat, get out of the house, and go play. Never in his life did he see his mother and father sit down and have a dinner alone—or have a single conversation, for that matter. He rarely ever heard his parents call each other by their first names.

The décor in the LaNier home was basic. There were no knick-knacks, mementos, or framed pictures adorning the walls.

Unbeknownst to the LaNier children, their father had somehow saved and was able to purchase two lots on North 14th Avenue in the Memphis Town area of Columbus, with gravel streets, no street-lights, and poverty-level homes. There was no electricity or indoor plumbing where they moved in 1935.

Joe never knew anything about his parents' childhoods but both Mama and Papa were born and raised in Columbus. There were no stories passed on from generation to generation and the only one he ever heard about his mother's childhood was when she talked about going to a function where they did the "Fall Off the Log" dance. He never knew how his parents met. They never talked about it, much to Joe's disappointment as he recapped with me his early years. What he knows about his parents today is from researching his family tree.

SAVILLA BARNETT WAS BORN JANUARY 3, 1892. JOSEPH Lanier was barely her senior, born June 15, 1891. Mama had been married before—from 1907 to 1913—to a man named Jake Roberts but he died after the couple had three boys of their own. She became a widow when she was just 21. She rebounded and fell in love with Joseph, and just three days before Valentine's Day 1914, they exchanged their vows at a Columbus church.

In the mixed family, Joe was the fifth of seven kids. Alexander Roberts had been born in 1909, Charlie Roberts in 1910, Clarence (Bud) Roberts in 1913, and Ira LaNier in 1915. Papa raised them all as his own children, though Alex and Charlie remembered their biological father. They called their stepfather "Mr. Joe," save for Bud, who called him Papa like Joe and the girls. Within the family, the children never felt like they were anything but full brothers and sisters. Despite the large, mixed family, Joe explained to me many times how he felt like an only child. He was eleven years younger than Ira, four years older than Ruth, and six years older than Gladys.

AS OUR INTERVIEW SESSIONS CONTINUED, I BEGAN TO understand Joe and his past. It was not a surprise how he viewed women and longed to be accepted by females. His own needs, combined with the societal mores of his generation and the loss of his mother, were easily explained as he recapped his life with me. A case in point is Annie Laura Erving.

Annie was 12 and Joe had never seen a girl so pretty. He was so insecure he never knew what to say, so he sent notes via her friends. He never got a note back but knew he loved her more than anything in the world. Joe would often go to a small grocery store across the street from his school and buy a penny sucker which then promptly went into his back pocket. Annie would sneak behind him and "steal" it. That would make his month—if she stole the sucker, it had to mean she loved him equally as much. Just a stroll past her house made him feel better. One day Joe and his best friend, Charles Lewis, walked a great distance over to Annie's house and saw she was outside watering flowers. Joe finally asked what she was doing and she said, "I'm watering the flowers." Joe fumbled and told her he only saw grass. When the boys left, Charles chided his friend because in his estimation, Joe should have told her they were the prettiest flowers he had ever seen. Needless to say, Joe and Annie never became a couple.

It is safe to say before he met his wife, Eula, Joe felt abandoned by women. His mother died early in his teenage years, he was never close to his two sisters, and girlfriends never seemed to fulfill the relationship for which he hoped. Joe placed stock and emotion into his associations with women, yet almost inevitably they would hurt or disappoint, or both.

In 1934, Mama went to visit Charlie, who was sick in a Birmingham, Alabama, hospital with appendicitis. It was the first night in his life Joe went to bed without his mother in the same room. He felt abandoned. He was sad until she came home and could not imagine his mother not being there for him. Joe remained insecure and lived with the fear of rejection and abandonment for much of his early life.

ALEX AND CHARLIE WERE LONG OUT OF THE HOME AND lived on their own before Joe was born. When Joe was six, Clarence, the brother to whom he was closest, moved to St. Louis. Charlie was "the prodigal son" who lived just 15 miles to the north in Hamilton but rarely came home due to his career as a railroad section hand. Charlie was long considered the family bootlegger in the dry county and rumor had it he would get a "tip"

from the local sheriff that a raid was imminent. When it came time for the raid, the liquor was hidden, save for one quart. That quart was always promptly delivered to the county sheriff, no questions asked. He would "arrest" Charlie but down at the jail, his cell was left unlocked. The next morning, Charlie got up and walked out before the sheriff arrived for the day.

Alex was 18 years older than Joe and lived in Demopolis, Alabama. Joe figures he didn't see him more than 20 times in his life and was ten before he saw him in person, but Alex was a caring soul. Every September he would send a box of clothes and pairs of shoes back home for Joe and his siblings. With his full brother Ira, it was a different story, despite the fact many that knew the family called Joe "Little Ira." There was a dark side to Ira, who inflicted severe beatings on Joe, 11 years his junior. There was a deep-seated reason behind his brother's anger but it was something Joe wouldn't learn about until he was 23-years-old.

It was a strict family. Joe remembers the "corporal punishment" they received as kids. Break the rules, get a whipping; it was that simple—considered *gospel* in the LaNier home. On one occasion young Joe found some matches and he and a friend started a grass fire. Another time Joe talked back to his mother in front of a group of adults. In both circumstances, they "worked on his building"—or whipped him—for upwards of 15 minutes. If there was a whipping in his future, he always preferred it come from Mama. One Wednesday afternoon Joe was playing with Ben, a black neighbor boy, down the dirt road from the rented Weathers' place. The field around them had just been turned and dirt clods in various shapes and sizes were all around. As they played, they saw the trail of dust off in the distance. The car got closer and closer and Joe, without thinking, did what eight-year-olds do and grabbed a small rock. As the car raced closer and passed them, Joe threw the rock and hit the car. It continued about 20 yards down the road, stopped, and backed up. The driver was a white man. Two black kids had just thrown a rock at his car and the result could have been disastrous. Joe started to run away but Ben grabbed him as the car's owner climbed out and began to yell. As it turned out, the driver knew the boys and they got off with just a scolding.

But Joe's troubles weren't over.

The following Sunday, Joe didn't attend church. When Mama came home, she took him into one of the small rooms in their modest home and whipped him for several minutes. As it continued, she yelled at Joe to never throw rocks again. The car's driver had seen Mama at church and told her about what had happened days earlier.

Joe knows that rock-throwing incident could have had dire consequences. The driver could have been a racist and beat him, or worse, and within the unspoken law of the land in Lowndes County, Mississippi, nothing would have been done about it. In his later years he understood why Mama was so upset. Had the man not known the LaNier family, his life could have been in grave danger.

Joe swears he never threw a rock again.

MAMA HAD AN UN-LADYLIKE BAD HABIT. SHE CHEWED Spark Plug tobacco and was very familiar with its *Fresher-Tastier* slogan. At the request of his mother, Joe would often walk down the dirt road outside his house and head east to Mr. Russell's store, about a quarter-mile away. (As with many people in Joe's young life, he knew them only by their last names.) There inside the general store, he would receive the tobacco wrapped in a large tobacco leaf. One day as he walked home with his mother's request, Joe decided to try a little of the funny-smelling brown stuff. He unwrapped the leaf, put a bit in his mouth, and started to chew. He kept swallowing the "juice" and became violently ill. He never touched chewing tobacco again but did begin smoking when he was 12 and smoked what he described as a "moderate" amount for 25 years before he quit.

Tobacco wasn't Joe's only foray into adventurous behavior. About a half-mile down the road from home, the country kids would gravitate toward Puckett's brickyard. The company dug clay on site to make bricks and with every fresh dig, a hole was created. They varied in size and one was so big the kids thought of it as a small lake, filled with Mississippi mud. These quickly became the swimming holes for a collection of four or five area black kids. Most of the time the muddy water wasn't more than a few feet deep but regardless there was never any adult supervision.

They swam in the buff and they'd splash around for hours until they were tired. Being eight-year-olds, when they reached the point of exhaustion they would simply stand up. That was possible with the exception of one deep swim hole, which was, of course, their favorite. Joe had never taken a swimming lesson or for that matter swam with an adult. He taught himself the dog paddle and thought it was sufficient enough to make it across the pool and impress his friends.

One hot Mississippi day, Joe swam out into about 15 feet of water and then realized it was a long way back to shore. He tried to stand but his kicking feet found no bottom. Scared to death, another kid pushed him to shore and just may have saved Joe's life.

He made it back to shore and his toes sank into the warm mud. He got dressed as his friends chirped at him. Even at his young age, he knew he dodged a bullet. When he came home, his mother was standing over a boiling pot washing clothes. It was usually Joe's job to fetch water for her on laundry day and when he got there she was well underway. With the near-drowning incident fresh on his mind and feeling guilty for being late, he didn't tell Mama what happened. Instead, he asked if she needed more water. She said no. Joe was pulling a classic case of child bait-and-switch. If he could do something nice and divert her attention, perhaps time would pass and she wouldn't find out. But deep down he knew it was just a matter of time before someone would tell her about the near-tragedy. He was so frightened, he went inside the house and went to sleep.

Call it a mother's intuition, Savilla knew something was up. He wasn't asleep that long when a commotion outside woke him. Joe looked out his front door and people were in their yard screaming. One of their neighbors, Mrs. Sarah Thompson, said in a demonstrative performance, "Lord, have mercy, Ms. LaNier! Your boy Gump almost drowned in that dumb swimming hole out close to the brickyard!"

Joe was certain his beating would come. But it never did.

It may have been scary but later that summer Joe went back to the same big swimming hole and as fate would have it, he almost drowned again. This time he was in a makeshift boat and actually floating when kids swam up to it. They climbed up and then used it to propel off into the water. The boat gradually took on water and flipped over. Joe hung on to its side, his feet hanging a few feet below. He couldn't feel the bottom as the water churned around him when he tried to kick. Terror set in once again and instead of simply holding on to the boat and letting his friends maneuver it on shore, fear and instinct told Joe to swim for it.

He finally got to shore but it was down from where they had entered. As a result, there was no easy way out. He was tired and reached for whatever he could grab. That turned out to be a handful of grass, which came up by the roots. Even at eight he thought his life was about to end. Luckily, a kid swimming in from the small, capsized boat came from behind and pushed Joe up onto the bank.

Mama and Papa never found out about the incident and he never went back for a third attempt.

Joe had a huge need to be accepted by his peers. He said as a result, he would sometimes do what his better judgment told him not to do. It was a glimpse into what would happen a decade later when Joe—who couldn't swim—decided to enlist in the U.S. Navy.

THE LaNiers belonged to the Colored Methodist Episcopal Church and attendance at Cross Road Church was mandatory within the family, never an option. However, there was just one circuit pastor, Reverend Blue, who would travel from location to location every week and deliver his fire-and-brimstone sermons. During "off" weeks when he was ministering elsewhere, various church leaders set the agenda. It primarily fell on the shoulders of Walter Hardy, an impressive, stern, devout man with a headful of white hair.

Hardy would often warn his congregation of the dangers of drinking whiskey or the "White Lightning" he knew was being produced in various backyards and kitchens around the area. He often proclaimed drinking whiskey was a sure "one-way ticket to hell." Members of the church understood this message, except one particular Sunday when Hardy became extremely upset. It turned out his own stash of whiskey was stolen from his hiding place out in the pasture nearby and he wanted to get to the bottom of the crime!

Church was the one place where the African-American community could have their own sanctuary, their own rules, and their own beliefs. Church lasted all day and on certain Sundays, they gathered for potlucks. It brought people together and built community spirit.

Even as a young boy, the church choir mesmerized Joe. They would sing their songs from the musical notes printed before them. Very few could read beyond a fifth or sixth-grade level and no one had attended college within the Cross Road congregation. They worshiped in a one-room building, a raised pulpit in the front, and the choir positioned to the pastor's right side as he preached. Rows of wooden pews sat on either side of the main aisle. Many times during the year, the inside of the church was so hot there was a constant—almost rhythmic—movement of hand fans held mainly by the women. Sweat was a constant on the brow of everyone inside.

Reverend Blue commanded respect as he read the Word. He would quote Scripture and then preach about it; all the while affirmations from the congregation would start to stir, until almost ready to burst. I specifically asked Joe to re-create the moment.

"It would build and build and build and after every few sentences Reverend Blue would insert a *'Haaahh!'* So it would go something like, 'And you know David did…*Haaahh!*' He had to have the ability to be a showman. It was like sing-song, like he was an actor, and the congregation would talk back to him. He would say something and they would reply back, *'Yessss!'* and *'Auuumen!'* and *'That's right!'* and *'Hallelujah!'* But my parents didn't do that; they were very reserved, so therefore I was too," Joe laughed.

Joe was enamored with what he saw on Sundays. People would dance in the aisles and fall to the floor. They would shake and gyrate, and their eyes would roll back when they felt the *Holy Ghost* within them. The preachers were Joe's role models. In his playtime, all by himself, he made his own tiny pulpit and a table and he preached outside to an invisible congregation. He would mimic what he saw from his seat in the pew.

Church was not just a weekly obligation; many times it was an event, especially when Reverend Blue came to dinner at the LaNier residence. On certain occasions he came with Elder Love, the man in charge of the circuit preachers in the area.

The family always knew when the preacher was coming to dinner because Mama would kill a chicken or the "gospel bird" as it was known. It was a pullet—a young, tender hen. Mama would pick it up outside and wring its young neck. "Old" birds were left for normal dinners and whenever the preacher was over, the kids could only eat after he was served. Mama would also impress everyone with coconut cakes, three-layer chocolate cakes, custards, and pies made primarily around Christmastime.

The LaNiers would go into the woods in early December to find their Christmas tree and then the freshly-cut cedar would be set up on a small wooden base in the one-room living area. The decorations included pieces of cotton that served as snow and tin foil for icicles. The holiday period was full of the spirit but nothing in terms of gifts. There were no store-bought toys and often an apple or an orange served as the only presents Santa Claus would bring to the LaNier children. One of the most memorable gifts young Joe received was a package of Zebra firecrackers, placed in one of his shoes before New Year's Eve.

As farmers, the LaNiers milked their own cow, made their own butter, and grew corn as much of the year as the ground would allow. A large garden outside their home provided vegetables for the table, from cabbage to turnips, mustard greens to peas and beans. At the end of each summer, Joe watched his mother can the various items to last through the fall and winter months. The peach tree gave them fruit and peelings from crabapples were used to make homemade jellies. True to the times, nothing was thrown away. Mama also made her own wine during the holidays, a drink young Joe sampled for the first time unbeknownst to his mother at the age of seven in their small kitchen. When she found out, he blamed it on his sister Ruth, who was punished for the infraction.

Outside, they had one cow and at least two hogs in the pen. Joe knew the cow was safe but fattening the hogs for slaughter always bothered him. They would fatten the hogs and then before slaughter, place them in a pen where they would go hungry. Joe can still remember the squeals of the pigs, night and day, and their last moments alive. Even at his young age, he felt it was cruel. His father and neighbors would use various methods to kill their livestock: a shot to the head, slice to the throat, or a sledgehammer to their skulls. The kills were always in the winter and then the meat was smoked and salted for the cold months.

As a boy, Joe never had his own cat or dog but he did catch a baby rabbit he was determined to keep as a pet. He decided to keep the animal under the house in a box. The next morning the stray, neighborhood cat left nothing but the bunny's fur near the base of the chimney. He learned yet another consequence.

Joe was a typical black kid in the poverty-stricken South. In the back of his mind, he longed for a different world where the two societies were one. But even at his age, he knew his "one society" dream would not come overnight. He respected his parents, was scared of the dark and the *boogeyman*, questioned white people and their motives, and as young as eight-years-old, feared God.

CHAPTER FOUR

SEGREGATED

Wᴀᴛᴇ ɴᴏʀᴛʜᴇᴀsᴛᴇʀɴ Mɪssɪssɪᴘᴘɪ ᴡᴀs ɢᴇᴛᴛɪɴɢ ɪᴛs normal dose of cold, January rains, and even an occasional snowfall, Joe was spending his final days in Hawaii. The group of young black men was now part of the Navy's 23rd Naval Construction Battalion, Special. The men from Great Lakes were part of a massive operation: they were about to become a small segment of the V Amphibious Corps (VAC) attached to the 5th Marine Division. VAC was comprised of the Marine's 3rd, 4th, and 5th Divisions during WWII and together they fought the Battles of Tarawa, Makin, Kwajalein, Eniwetok, Saipan, Tinian, and Iwo Jima. They fell under the 8th Naval Construction Regiment (second phase) led by Commander Rudolph Y. Taggart.

The new Seabees spent their next three weeks on the west side of Oahu at Barbers Point. To get there, they packed up their belongings and boarded small PT (Patrol Torpedo) boats for a relatively short ride west. Joe didn't know it but the Japanese called them "Devil boats."

The Hawaiian scenery was beautiful and he really didn't care about where they were headed on the Islands. This was an adventure and furthermore, the last thing he expected was a democracy in the service. Though Joe never found himself questioning orders, he found himself bored at the new location. There was nothing to do but kill time and once again, experience the military's famous "hurry up and wait" approach. There was no extensive training for them by any stretch. No drills, no firearms training, and no additional education on Japanese culture or how to beat the enemy. They did march and keep the grounds in and around the barracks clean and tidy but that was about it. In the meantime, an island away on Maui, the 4th Marine Division was in constant training as it prepared for battle with mock landings, drills day and night, and little rest. The 2nd and 5th Marines trained at Camp Tarawa on the Big Island of Hawaii under the same strict, tough training.

FROM 1941 TO 1945, THERE WERE APPROXIMATELY 2.5 million African-Americans in all branches of the U.S. military. Segregated units in WWII included the Air Corps' 332nd Fighter Group or Tuskegee Airmen, and the 51st and 52nd Defense Battalions comprised of the Montford Point Marines, members of the Army's 92nd and 93rd Infantry Divisions, the 4th and 5th Calvary Regiments, select infantry and cavalry regiments, tank battalions, field artillery regiments and battalions, tank destroyer battalions, and a parachute infantry battalion. At this juncture in the Navy, there were relatively few blacks in the Pacific Theatre and fewer than 1,000 on Iwo Jima.

Then-Secretary of the Navy Frank Knox had received outside pressure to promote more black officers, and knew firsthand and approved of the *Golden Thirteen* at Great Lakes. As Joe was getting acclimated at Camp Shoemaker, Knox suffered a fatal heart attack April 28, 1944, and was replaced by Navy Undersecretary James Forrestal. He was a man much more open to blacks being promoted in the "lily white" United States Navy.

From Robert Schneller's *Breaking the Color Barrier,* Knox was quoted as telling a naval admiral in the summer of 1944, he was "not satisfied with the situation" and didn't feel blacks in the Navy Negro were getting a fair break. The admiral told Forrestal he didn't think it could be done but would support a change. The new Secretary of the Navy was also keenly aware many white sailors resented blacks and vice versa.

From nearly 5,000 miles away, Joe and his fellow blacks were unaware of this new support from the highest naval rank in Washington.

They were the first black Seabees. Prior to joining this distinctive group, the only blacks in the Navy were stewards' mates who served officers and had to worry about things like where to correctly place a plate and fork. These black men were really nothing more than servants in the U.S. Navy.

Schneller stated blacks in the Navy peaked just weeks after atomic bombs were dropped on both Hiroshima and Nagasaki. On August 31, 1945, a total of 166,915 African-American enlisted men and women were among the ranks in the U.S. Navy but even at the end of WWII, 50.2 percent of them were either cooks or stewards. All of the Navy stewards remained black. There were still no black graduates from the Naval Academy in Annapolis, Maryland.[1]

O N THE REMOTE STRETCH OF BEACH NOT FAR FROM PEARL Harbor, Joe and the men had gotten used to the boredom of the new locale. It offered no liberty, no trips to Waikiki, and was devoid of the camaraderie at the laundry on Ford Island. After many long days, they finally received some direction.

"We gotta go," they were told.

The group left their secret location January 24, 1945, and headed back on the same small boat to just northwest of Pearl Harbor, at what was known officially as Iroquois Point, Area 7, Oahu, T.H. This would be their staging area for Iwo Jima. Yet instead of instant deployment, they sat around and waited. Finally, they received orders to move out and boarded their ship to the unknown.

The only information any of the Seabees knew of the action in the Pacific was from newsreels they may have seen on base. There was no gossip that made its way through the ranks or the barracks. There were no great tales of bravery or victory from far-off places of which they'd never heard. Joe said the lack of information they received was par for the course in how blacks were viewed. They didn't need to know.

"Most of us were treated as unequal all of our lives and we were not a part of the society. As we grew up, we had to go to the back of the bus; we had to go to the back of the white person's house. There was nothing public that we could go to, except where someone was selling us something—where somebody could make money. Your neighborhood was a specific place. You couldn't move into other areas; you had to be in these places. All of that, plus not having a feeling of belonging—you just accepted things. I didn't know anything different. To be any place out of the South was great because you were away from segregation."

Yet he was segregated as he wore a United States military uniform.

A GROUP OF FOUR SHIPS—THE SS Dashing Wave, SS Sea Runner, SS Cape Georgia and SS Cape Stephens—left Pearl Harbor on both the fourth and fifth of February, 1945, and sailed south toward the Marshall Islands. By the time Joe was settled into his new, cramped quarters below deck on this new merchant ship, he started to develop his sea legs. Thankfully, though he was seasick for a couple of days, it was nothing like the outbound trip from San Francisco. For nearly a month, the ship full of blacks sailed into harm's way, once again zigzagging its way through waters that could be infested with Japanese subs. The ship was not part of a large fleet and was protected by only a few smaller ships that sailed into the Pacific in tandem.

One of the most memorable aspects of the journey was the moment when the ship crossed the International Date Line in smooth-as-glass water. The crew made an announcement and then conducted a ceremony on ship but Joe didn't attend. He had never heard of the International Date Line and it fascinated him. It was an exhilarating moment for the young man from Mississippi, especially considering that his entire life he thought the earth was flat.

These passengers didn't know it but just ten days after their merchant ship left Hawaii, they headed into what had been a hornet's nest almost exactly a year earlier. The ship stopped off the coast of Eniwetok, a tiny, coral atoll deep in the Pacific. The Battle of Eniwetok began February 17, 1944, as American forces gained control in order to have a forward base in the region and thus a better striking capability on the Marshall Islands. Nearly 300 Americans and 2,700 Japanese were killed in the fighting.

Joe's ship left Eniwetok after a brief overnight respite—in complete darkness—and then moved on to its second refueling stop. With every mile, the men sailed closer to their official entry into WWII in the Pacific Theatre. They headed west through white-caps, swells, and occasional calm seas before the ship docked off Guam, site of a U.S.-led invasion less than seven months earlier. Joe looked from his vantage point in the harbor and saw land for the first time since the Hawaiian Islands dropped below the horizon. His ship took on fuel and supplies and after the overnight anchor off the largest island in the Marianas, moved once again the following morning. This time, according to multiple WWII Naval records, the ship joined an "immense convoy" ultimately headed for Iwo Jima.

Time was running out to take a proper shower on the ship and Joe was struck by how the Navy had special soap issued to them that would lather in salt water. He doesn't remember freshwater showers but does recall saltwater showers with water pumped in from the ocean. It wasn't until Great Lakes that Joe even took a shower, because as a boy, he took baths once a week on Saturday nights in the family's zinc tub.

The ship moved on to Saipan Harbor in the Northern Mariana Islands but once again the Seabees remained largely on board and were treated strictly as passengers. They did have time to take an occasional swim, and in their clothes, no less. They jumped off the ship's deck for relief from the intense heat. For Joe, it was the chance to prove he was one of the guys, despite the fact he couldn't swim very well.

THOUGH THE SHIP WAS PHYSICALLY INSIDE A HOT ZONE OF war activity, the black sailors were unarmed and hadn't touched a weapon in months. The Navy was sending them into battle but without recent—or proper—battle training. Joe remains convinced it was a racial thing in the sense that the Navy didn't know what to do with them.

They were never properly trained to fight. The military had a long history of keeping blacks in mess halls where they would clean and take out trash.

"I don't think they gave it a whole lot of thought. For some reason, there was a feeling we had that they thought blacks wouldn't fight. That's why they didn't put us up on the frontlines, because they didn't know how to do this," Joe said sternly.

He didn't know at the time but African-American soldiers had fought in every war since the Revolutionary War, yet were never treated better than second class. D-Day on Iwo Jima was just days away.

CHAPTER FIVE

INSPIRATIONS

IN THE FALL OF 1933, JOE ENTERED A SCHOOLHOUSE FOR THE first time. He was seven. Children didn't follow an academic calendar but instead started school after the last crop was harvested. There was no preschool, no kindergarten—they called it *primer*.

Joe learned how to read and write in a one-room schoolhouse, with kids of various ages all taught together. There was no blackboard or chalk and there were no desks; instead, the children sat on uncomfortable wooden benches. They had to buy their own pencils and books. They only wore shoes in the winter; during warmer months they walked to school in their bare feet. There was no homework but Joe did have simple books he could take home: *Nell, Jack & Jill,* and *My Dog Spot.* His parents never read to him at home.

Miss Annie May Feld was Joe's first teacher, though she herself probably never finished high school. She would walk around the room with a book open in front of her or she would stand in front of the children while she explained the day's lesson plan. Joe developed a schoolboy crush on Miss Feld during their two years together but it didn't last long.

Math wasn't one of Joe's strong suits but his real-life experience taught him a lesson in economics. As a young boy, he watched as a group of neighbors came together to make molasses—a staple in 1930s Mississippi. It was a barter system at its best. Mr. Willie Shirley owned the cooking contraption that cooked the juice of the sorghum cane but he didn't own any of the land that actually produced the cane. Joe watched huge metal pans, compartments, and rollers that squeezed the cane, collected the juice, and then cooked the contents. A nearby mule walked in circles, tethered to a tongue-like pole that turned the contraption's drums. It worked like a charm; as the juice cooked in individual pans, it got thicker and thicker. Gravity worked the material down from top to bottom. The final compartment contained the molasses, which drained into individual one-gallon containers. Mr. Willie owned the machine and got every third gallon. The farmers needed him and he needed them. It was simple cooperation and an economic benefit for all. It was how poor people in a rural area made do with what they had.

As a general rule, Mama and Papa were not affectionate with their children or one another. Joe never saw them embrace or hug. Never. No kissing or affectionate gestures. It was in part a sign of the time, an era where poverty and segregation trumped even the most basic human traits. It weighed on them. They didn't celebrate anniversaries or special moments. Joe saw little of that in his circle of family and friends but even so, he knew his parents loved each other and each of their children.

Joe is adamant his childhood was a happy one. They never went hungry and he was never burdened with the obstacles his parents surely faced. They made it work. Mama made nearly all the kids' clothes, save for the denim jeans they would pick up at the local general store. From his earliest memories, Joe and his family wore farm-work clothes except for one hand-me-down suit that was worn only on Sundays.

Papa continued working the fields while Savilla tended house and made sure her children kept up with their responsibilities. Joe was close with his mother but not in an emotional sense. He loved her and they were close, yet while she would hold and kiss the girls, she didn't show the same affection to her youngest son. He knew his parents loved him but he admitted to me on several occasions it would be difficult to prove.

Joe was an insecure child and up until the age of nine, spent large parts of his day either alone or babysitting. He began looking after his younger sisters when he was just six-years-old. He was a good kid but was overlooked in many ways by his family members and those in his neighborhood circles. It wasn't necessarily a bad thing, just a reality. With his older brothers out of the house, Joe filled the big-brother role for Ruth and Gladys, but they never played much together.

They were so poor the girls didn't have dolls to play with and many times, as a replacement, they used an empty medicine bottle for a doll's torso and a pine branch for her hair. Joe babysat them often, which is one of the reasons he feels his relationships with his younger sisters never flourished. Savilla tended house, worked the large garden, made their meals, and sometimes spent time in the fields with her husband. Doing laundry and cooking from scratch took time and effort.

Papa worked two cotton patches and sharecropped upwards of 20 acres of corn, sorghum cane, sweet potatoes, watermelon, and cantaloupe. Wild plum and crabapple trees and wild blackberry bushes dotted the property.

"He was always working, always gone somewhere doing something. He would get up 'before day' as we called it. That's how we lived. He was always up before daylight because whatever he was doing, he had to get to it. He had to walk wherever he was supposed to be. He was a remarkable man."

Joseph Lanier Sr., who never capitalized the "N" in his name, stood 5' 9" and weighed about 160 pounds. He had extremely dark skin and never knew his parents. Joe remains confident his father tried to live his life the way God meant him to live. There was no profanity in the home and Papa never spoke poorly about another person. He never taught them to hate.

"Living under a totally segregated system made it easy for us to hate white people but he chose to see the good in all of 'God's children.'"

Even so, Joe doesn't recall his father as a happy man. He consistently did things for others but never for himself —like the monthly Saturday treks into town, where he would get Joe a Baby Ruth for a penny.

THE LANIERS WERE LUCKY WHEN IT CAME TO MOTHER Nature. There were no severe droughts or floods, and though tornadoes were frequent in their section of Mississippi, they were spared any scares or damage.

Cotton was the cash crop of the land, dubbed "Sandyland" by the locals. In northeastern Mississippi, cotton would only grow a couple of feet high and only after it was fertilized. Compare that with the tales they would hear from migrant workers who came up from the Delta. There the soil was rich and black, and produced cotton plants so tall you could stand and pick most of the bush. In the Delta, the cotton could be picked in one motion out of its bowl; in the Delta, the fruit was sweeter and the vegetables heartier. At least those were the rumors floated around Columbus.

Picking cotton could break a person. It was always sunup to sundown or as Joe learned from an early age: *"can to can't."* They worked from the time they could physically see the cotton bushes to the time they couldn't. Work days were sometimes 15 hours a day and by the end of that time, the men and women could barely walk. They couldn't stand because they had crawled on their knees all day in the hot sun. To try to protect their knees, many workers cut pads out of old rubber tires.

In 1935, Papa's handmade home was ready. It was in Joe's third-grade year that the LaNier family moved six miles to Memphis Town, where he was required to take a standard reading, writing, and arithmetic test to enroll in a different school. Joe failed miserably. As a result, he was forced to repeat the third grade with his new classmates. Ms. Grace Harris was his new teacher, a woman who never married and was completely dedicated to her students.

In this new "city" school, everything moved at a much faster pace and during the first two years, Joe struggled. Ms. Grace took an interest in him and praised him for what he did right, and required him to fix the things he didn't do as well. Besides Papa, Joe's teacher had more impact than any other person in his life. Later in school, during the times where Joe would work in a nightclub until ten or eleven at night, Ms. Harris would let him sleep in class if she could tell he was exhausted. She would also spank them when need be and consistently emphasized the importance of an education. Joe continued his relationship with the Harris family over the decades, until Ms. Grace died at 100-years-old. The teacher never married but considered all of her students to be her own children.

Papa took care of his family and his own business the best way a man of his means could in the 1930s. He made monthly payments on about 20 wooded acres, four miles west of Memphis Town, where he cut down timber to sell to the Moss Tie Plant. The company used the wood—dipped into a creosote bath—for telephone poles and railroad cross ties. He would also make charcoal by slow-cooking it in a hole, or earthen kiln, with the timber and sell it to people in the neighborhood. There was always work to be done.

Papa never played with Joe. To this day there is a hint of longing for that but Joe told me repeatedly it wasn't for lack of love; instead, it was the norm of black society in the heart of The Depression. The time alone with his father usually came during their walks to the fields. Papa talked of military rank—how the silver maples they passed represented the silver bars of a first lieutenant. The second lieutenant wore bars of gold because gold was underground, below the tree. The colonel, with an eagle as a symbol, soared higher than the others. Finally, there was the general, whose star shined above them all.

The only thing that remotely resembled social fun was when the men came over every month or so to cut their hair. The women also gathered to make quilts and on occasion they made their own mattresses from cloth and excess cotton.

When Joe was about nine or ten, during certain times of the year he and his sister Ruth would often wake before the sun and "hire out" to go pick cotton for white farmers in the area. This would generate a little spending money but by today's standards it was hardly worth the work. He would walk down the road to a gathering spot and wait for the flatbed trucks to pull up. Black workers—mostly men—packed every square inch of the flatbeds.

When they arrived at the fields in darkness, the low glow of sunrise was usually just barely visible on the horizon. They were all dressed in overalls, with sacks slung over one shoulder. The sack dragged on the ground behind them as they moved down each row. Because of the delicate nature of cleaning out every cotton bowl, they couldn't wear gloves. It got to be rhythmic work and adult workers would often sing hymns and spirituals as they picked two rows at a time. The work earned them just 35 cents for every 100 pounds of cotton they picked. Joe's sister Ruth could pick 100 pounds in a day even though she was four years younger. Joe never earned 35 cents in one day but tried to get around it by tricking "the man." Some of the kids would weigh down their cotton bags with a little drinking water to make it heavier on the scales.

The rows of cotton looked endless to a child. There was also the work of clearing grass and weeds that would sometimes grow around the plant base. It was backbreaking work. Because of the Sandyland soil, the plants would grow their cotton so low to the ground the workers would have to scoot along on their knees—all day. Some people could pick 200 pounds of cotton a day—70 cents for a day of hard labor. It reminded Joe of what it must have been like being a slave. The only difference seemed to be that now they were paid at the end of every day's work.

At the end of each row, the pickers would hang their sacks to a metal hook on a scale and "the man" would note the weight on a piece of paper. From there, oftentimes sacks would be emptied into a large basket. Usually a water bucket and ladle waited for them at the end of each row.

For fun, after sundown and a full day's work, sometimes the older kids were allowed to ride on the front fenders of the trucks as they came back into town.

FROM THE TIME JOE CAN REMEMBER, HE WAS KEENLY AWARE there were two classes: white and black. The LaNier children were taught about it from their earliest memories. The stories remained alive in Lowndes County—stories of how Ku Klux Klan members would ride from 50 to 60 at a time on horseback nearly every night in the years following the abolishment of slavery. Kidnappings and murders were commonplace. The fear was passed down from generation to generation and well into the 1930s.

"If you didn't obey the law, it could be catastrophic for you. *Catastrophic.* Meaning you could be physically attacked—you could be killed, depending on the person. They didn't see you as another person. We were deathly afraid of the Ku Klux Klan because they would kill you! They would lynch you! We knew it was real and the stories were verbally passed down from family members. We were taught about the lines we just didn't cross because of the consequences. We saw pictures of lynchings, beatings, and other atrocities."

He collected his thoughts.

"You had to know. If you didn't, the consequences could be severe and so dangerous. We knew there was a difference between white people and us. You had to say, 'Yes, Sir' or 'No, Ma'am.' They never really had to sit us down and explain it all. We just watched them and learned. It didn't matter if my father was 50 and another white man was 20—it was, 'Yes, Sir' and 'No, Sir.' When you see that as a child, you know what you have to do. The white people controlled our existence."

Joe can recall as a little boy overhearing his parents talk about racial injustice in their community. He never said a word. It was another reminder how the young man should behave around whites. They were always careful. *Always.*

The only exceptions to injustice were those whites who developed relationships with blacks. Mr. Clarence (C.L.) and Mrs. Minnie Mabel McCaleb were from Tennessee and owned both the land the LaNiers lived on for a time and the mercantile down off Waterworks Road. Joe recalls them as good, decent, honest Christian people. To this day he still keeps in touch with their children, James and Joyce. Joe told me numerous times how Papa never did "owe his soul to the company store." The bills were settled up by the end of every growing season. Mr. McCaleb and Papa respected each other and remained friends throughout the rest of their lives.

T HE McCALEBS WERE IN BUSINESS WITH MR. ROY LAMAR, Mr. McCaleb's brother-in-law, and together they operated the Waring place, where Papa sharecropped. Mr. McCaleb owned the company store nearby—with dry goods and products from overalls to canned meats, vegetables, and fruit on display atop wooden floors. Outside, there was a busy blacksmith shop, with its hot irons, horseshoes, and the ever-present clinking and clanging of metal hammers on heavy anvils. Both white families treated the LaNiers with respect and fairness during the sharecropping years.

The McCalebs were the only white family Papa would allow the kids to work for because he knew they would not mistreat any of the children. Joe likened them to an oasis in the desert, almost an extended family.

I F ONE NEEDED PROOF OF THE TRUST AND THE BOND BETWEEN Papa and McCaleb, you had to look no further than what happened when Papa fell ill. He was hospitalized in 1954, while Joe was living in Chicago. Joe came to Columbus as quickly as he could.

"For blacks at a hospital in Mississippi, you pretty much received attention if the whites on the first floor didn't need any nursing care. Papa was put in the basement area with other blacks, with all the pipes exposed underneath the *real* hospital. When I saw him, he told me to call the McCalebs. There were no black nurses. A short time later, Mr. and Mrs. McCaleb came to the hospital and specifically told those nurses, 'You take care of him.' Papa was just overwhelmed. Some of the things McCaleb did were just contrary to the society at that time in terms of his relationships with African-Americans. He didn't seem to care. He did what he felt was the right thing to do. They didn't have to be decent! These weren't Northern sympathizers! He was from Tennessee!" Joe told me.

The McCalebs also ran the risk of being labeled "nigger lovers" in Lowndes County. The potential harm from the KKK was real for blacks and for whites who befriended them. But the deep friendship endured and survived; it lasted until Papa's death in 1966.

ONE CLOUDY EVENING, JOE WAS SENT OVER TO GET MILK from the Lamar family and after he grabbed the milk, it began to rain. Joe decided since there was a long walk ahead of him, he would wait it out on the Lamar porch. While he waited for the rain to cease, he fell asleep on the back stoop. Lamar's 13-year-old daughter, Eloise, came out a bit later and found Joe asleep. It startled her. Joe jolted awake, grabbed the milk, and left. Later, Papa found out about the incident and was not happy. Had the Lamars been different people, he could have been lynched. Nearly 65 years later, Joe reconnected with Eloise via the telephone. She remembered the incident and when he later returned to Columbus, they visited in person and talked about the old times.

TWO RAIL LINES RAN THOROUGH LOWNDES COUNTY: ONE train went to northeast Alabama and on to Birmingham, and the C&G ran from Columbus to Greenville, Mississippi. Black workers—section hands—maintained the railroads and were responsible for the upkeep and maintenance of the spikes, cross ties, and the tracks. As a little boy, Joe would walk down a mile or so to watch the hands move large sections of track one at a time.

The Memphis Town suburb was a close-knit community. White merchants like the McCalebs thrived because most blacks couldn't afford to raise the capital to quite literally raise a store. Caesar and Mamie Williams operated the only black-owned store in the area, just down the road from the LaNier residence. (Joe can recall Ms. Mamie due her size; she weighed 300 pounds and easily dwarfed her smaller-in-stature husband.) Mr. and Mrs. Cunningham lived across the street and so did Mr. Cobb. Across the street to the northeast, a mother and her seven daughters moved in and Miss Ida Neil and Ms. Mandy lived to the west. They did laundry for white families.

One of Joe's first jobs was delivering basketfuls of clean laundry for a nickel each. The ladies did laundry Mondays and Tuesdays, and Wednesdays through Fridays they used *smoothing* or cast irons to press the clothes. Papa was involved as well; he made charcoal from timber on sharecropped land and then would sell it to them as part of the cyclical process. The ladies would also use cedar branches to clear soot from the irons and several days a week, the earthy smell of fresh cedar would waft over part of Memphis Town.

During one delivery, Joe came to the front door of a white person's home and was immediately scolded by a woman inside. She yelled at him to "get his black ass" around to the back where he was supposed to go—which was the back entrance.

The ironic part of the delivery was that unbeknownst to Joe, he was delivering the laundry to the rented room of a lieutenant at the Columbus Flying School. Years later on Okinawa, Joe saw the lieutenant. They recognized each other and spoke briefly, happy to see each other so far from Mississippi. The odds had to be ten-million-to-one.

Joe always tried to make an extra dime here or there but is the first to admit he was a lazy child overall. I tend to disagree. He sold small bundles of kindling wood for a time and peddled them to local ladies who used the kindling to start their charcoal fires. At the end of the week, his work switched to shoeshines—Sundays only. He had black and brown polish and a little box that could be set up for people's feet. He shined shoes for a nickel and would take his nickels to the store to get pennies so they would rattle in his pocket; then the other kids would know he had money. That single memory elicited perhaps the biggest smile Joe gave during our interview sessions in regards to his childhood. He beamed.

The fine young man from Columbus, in a segregated society, made opportunity as best he could even when there was seemingly very little in front of him. Keeping occupied turned out to be a blessing for Joe because although he really didn't know it, his mother's health was declining day by day.

MAMA STARTED TO SIT AT THE TABLE MORE AND MORE with her eyes closed. She began to act differently in the early stages of 1937, when Joe was just 11-years-old. He can remember her sitting in pain but never questioned why and it was never addressed. At that time, children just didn't question things like that but she was listless and physically drained. Mama didn't slow down but cooking, cleaning, and chores became a struggle.

Joe recalled when he and Mama were outside on the front lawn one day in the late 1930s. He was sick and suffering from chills; usually the cure-all remedy was a teaspoon or two of castor oil, washed down with a bit of RC Cola, or Vicks VapoRub applied on his chest with a wad of yarn. (Another home remedy was Mama's "shuck tea," brewed with cornhusks; for headaches, his grandmother, Louisa, would put gypsum weed in a rag and tie it around his head.) But there was no home remedy that could make Mama any better.

During this particular afternoon, Savilla was in such pain she sat in her chair with her eyes closed; she didn't notice Joe leave to go inside to bed. When she opened her eyes, she was frightened and went into a panic looking for him.

It was shortly after that incident the family moved about three miles north to the McCalebs' Waring place property. Papa share-cropped for them, and built the cabin where the family lived. Papa had to continue to support the family but Mama continued to decline. Louisa often came over to cook because her daughter— whom she called "Sissy"—was simply too weak. The children were never told why.

For two years, Savilla became worse and worse. The drawn-out illness was never properly diagnosed and medical care was almost non-existent. It finally got to the point where the LaNier family had to move back into town, which forced Papa to end his working relationship as a sharecropper for the Lamars and McCalebs.

Despite her obvious health condition, Mama was never bedridden.

SAVILLA BARNETT LANIER DIED ON SUNDAY, OCTOBER 27, 1940.

Joe was on the front porch, shining his shoes and getting ready for church, with his grandmother, Louisa, and his brother. After a few minutes, Louisa left and went to the back of the house but Joe paid little attention as he worked on his shoes, dressed in his Sunday best. It was almost time for church. The day before had been a normal Saturday.

When the 14-year-old took the focus off his shoes, he realized both people had left and he was alone. Joe got up off the porch and walked around the dirt path to an open door of the addition Papa had built on the east side of the home. There, his grandmother and father were standing near the head of the bed positioned on the back wall. His mother was lying there under a blanket, with her head toward the bedroom wall. She was extremely sick. Joe remembers the moment as if it were frozen in time.

"I knew she was dying. I became very emotional," Joe told me as tears welled in his eyes.

His father had a look of sadness he'd never seen. There was no doctor present and his grandmother had her face buried in her hands.

Joe walked closer to the bed. No one in the room said a word as he slowly approached and clearly saw his mother's profile. Savilla's mouth was open and eyes set. It was a tragic image for the young boy. As she was taking her last breaths, he looked briefly at her and then quickly walked out of the room, overwhelmed with emotion. It was the last time he saw his mother alive, though she was minutes from death.

Savilla LaNier was 49.

THE NEXT FEW DAYS WERE FILLED WITH SADNESS AND VOID. Joe's memory of much of that week has been erased. The common diagnosis in 1940 was "heart attack." It was a common listing on death certificates and the chatter throughout families in poor neighborhoods. But Joe is convinced his young mother died of some sort of coronary artery disease. Their diets were full of fried foods, lard, fats, and oils. Savilla only saw a doctor on rare occasions and when she did, the family paid the lone black doctor in chickens and potatoes instead of cash. The doctor had just two years of medical school before he began to practice in Columbus.

It was years later before Joe started to piece together the final years of his mother's life. With his college courses, Joe surmised his mother died of congestive heart failure and not an "attack." Her brain wasn't getting enough oxygen, thus the listlessness. Her clogged arteries were not able to pass a healthy flow of fresh blood throughout her body and she undoubtedly had high cholesterol. Though she wasn't obese, she was extremely unhealthy. Savilla was a big woman, at 5' 9" and 200 pounds, and bigger in stature than her husband. She loved to eat meat and pig fat, used grease in almost every dish, and followed recipes that had been passed down through the generations.

Reverend George was one of the LaNier neighbors and presided over Savilla's funeral at Cross Road Church, about six-and-a-half miles east of Memphis Town. All seven of her children were there and most of the pews were full.

It was the first and only time Joe saw Papa cry.

The LaNier family sat in the front row, all with heavy hearts. Savilla's open casket was just feet from them. When it was time for family and friends to walk by the casket to pay their final respects, Joe stayed in his seat. He couldn't stand to see his beloved mother that way. Joe wanted to remember his mother in his own way and not by how she looked in a casket. He was in a state of shock and denial.

She was gone.

Joe was upset in the days leading up to the funeral. His family didn't seem to be acting sad enough.

"At the funeral, I was so emotional I could not contain myself. My mom was a beautiful lady; she was a great lady. I loved her very much. She took care of her family and she was a person I enjoyed being around. All my life I have wondered what kind of relationship I would have had with her and what kind of guidance I would have received. Her perspective would have been so much different than my father's ways. For the next year, I was a basket case."

The service concluded with readings from Scripture and then it was over. Savilla's coffin was taken away from the front of the church and Joe broke down. The funeral procession went down a dirt road a few miles away to a black cemetery on an old planta-tion. There was no money for a proper headstone at the time of her burial, something Joe vowed he would remedy before he died. Little did I know at the time of our interview session in mid-August 2011, that I would have a role in making his lifelong goal a reality and would soon see this cemetery with my own eyes.

CHAPTER SIX

IWO

Among the Americans who served on Iwo Island, uncommon valor was a common virtue.

— ADMIRAL CHESTER NIMITZ

O N SATURDAY MORNING, FEBRUARY 24, 1945, JOE'S SHIP swayed in the south Pacific.

Over the past few days, chow halls on other ships prepared steak-and-egg breakfasts for the men about to enter their own hell on earth. *Fattening them for the slaughter,* some recounted later. This was not the case for Joe and the blacks aboard the converted merchant ship; normal meals were served until they climbed down their rope ladders.

Defense Department aerial photo of Iwo Jima pre-invasion, February 17, 1945.
(National Archives)

It was already hot when the XO came down the hole and joined his Seabees below deck. They had been aboard nearly a month and had no official idea how much longer they would remain on the ocean. Yet deep within their young minds, they all knew their journey had to be nearing an end sometime soon. It had remained a "destination unknown" mission, until the executive officer made the memorable, spine-tingling announcement to his passenger-soldiers: "Get ready! We're about to land."

The 23rd Seabees would land on D+5 or five days after the initial invasion of Iwo Jima. The fighting and chaos was well underway as the blacks prepared to enter a living hell. Success was measured in feet and yards on the desolate island nearly 800 miles south-southeast of Tokyo. Enemy mines blanketed the island and pillboxes swarmed with Japanese soldiers. On this, the first Saturday of fighting, military logs reveal the 21st Marines tackled the airstrips while the 23rd Marines took heavy mortar, artillery, and rocket fire.

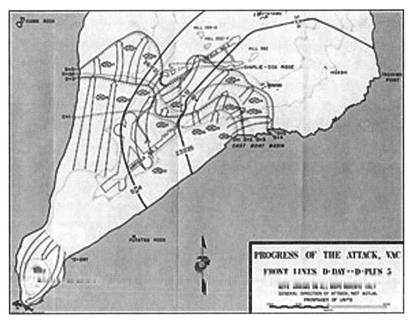

Previously classified Iwo Jima map, D-Day plus five February 24, 1945—the day Joe landed on Iwo Jima.
(U.S. Department of War)

The 24th Marines battled the frontlines as they continued to move north amid small-arms fire, grenades, and air strikes that filled the air. The morning was clear and relatively cool as the 25th and 26th Marines fought to advance and secure many of the enemy hills still controlled by the Japanese. The 26th lost 21 officers and 332 enlisted men on D+5 alone. The 27th Marines encountered 30 of the enemy at a sulfur hole and watched as many of the Japanese committed suicide. The remainder— in military parlance—were "mopped up." Just a day before, the 28th regiment had taken part in raising the American flag atop Suribachi, twice.

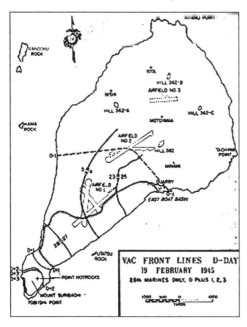

Previously classified 28th Marine Division Iwo Jima invasion map, February 19, 1945.
(U.S. Department of War)

Back on ship, Joe and his fellow black sailors listened in cramped quarters and heard their superior deliver a patriotic speech. They were told where they were headed. It was the first time Joe heard the words "Iwo Jima." He stood elbow-to-elbow in crowded conditions below deck as they were told of the island's importance to the overall war effort to defeat the Empire of Japan.

"We need this island because our planes have a range they can fly. If we are going to invade Japan, we have to do it from *this* island," the XO firmly stated. "The fighters who have to escort the bombers to their targets have a range and they have a range of their own. When you get on land, you'll be building roads, supplying ammunition to the frontlines, and unloading ships in order to get supplies on shore. Whatever you do, gentlemen, do *not* pick up anything on the island you think you'd like to take home with you! It could be a booby trap! You may see a rifle and it may look like someone left it there but that may not be the case."

For the first time since Joe officially enlisted and signed the additional Navy documents in Jackson, Mississippi, more than a year earlier, he received key information about what lay ahead of him and his fellow black sailors. What none of them knew was the invasion of Iwo had started at dawn the previous Monday and in the days that had passed, the U.S. and Japanese forces sustained incredible losses.

The XO finished his speech and went back above deck. Blood pressures rose. Anxiety set in for select individuals. The sailors didn't do much talking and went back to their cots to pack their belongings. All of their items had remained in their large duffle bags, save for the green camouflage pants, short-sleeve camouflage shirts, and standard-issue black leather shoes they wore.

Up on deck, Joe looked out and in the distance saw a speck of land in a vast amount of brilliant blue water.

There it was.

He stood and gazed at Iwo Jima and Mt. Suribachi for the first time as the ship slowly crept closer to shore. It had no real impact on him in terms of fear but he wrestled with the feeling of awe. Here was a boy from Mississippi, so far from home. He swears he wasn't nervous and wasn't concerned for his safety. In his mind, he was on a two-year cruise. Everything was new. He couldn't find his location on a map and it didn't matter. To this point in the service, he hadn't seen any violence and for the kid from Mississippi, war had no meaning. Yet.

WITH THE INFORMATION NOW OUT, THE SHIP'S CREW began talking and spreading what knowledge they had about the island's history and makeup. The fact Suribachi "was like a hotel inside" fascinated Joe, with its munitions, provisions, and soldiers who vowed to die before being taken prisoner. The black sailors all learned about the tunnels that ran throughout the island and how the Japanese had spent some 40 years preparing the small outcropping for battle. They heard about a track inside the fortified mountain that could transport large-millimeter weapons to various firing points at ships offshore. U.S. forces had secured about half the island by the time the 23rd arrived offshore D+5. For the new arrivals, they could never have imagined the chaos and carnage that had already taken place earlier in the week.

U.S. Marines up Red Beach on D-Day, February 19, 1945.
(National Archives)

Final preparations were made on board and the adrenaline level was as high as Joe had experienced since joining. With their bags, the black sailors all stood on deck as the sea breeze caught their faces and the tropical sun baked the top of their heads. Unlike the iconic images of Army combat soldiers in metal helmets embarking on the shores of Normandy, these black sailors were given steel helmets only *after* they arrived on land.

When the ship stopped, it rested off Iwo Jima's western shoreline, fairly close to the base of Suribachi and within artillery range of Japanese armaments. They encountered no resistance from the Japanese and though the island itself was still smoldering from constant naval bombardment and return fire, the merchant ship was never under any sort of attack. The true devastation on Iwo Jima was close in proximity but was located on the southeast side of Suribachi's base, where Green, Red, Yellow, and Blue Beaches had seen some of the most hostile action and death in the Pacific Theatre.

Small transport boats called LCVPs (Landing Craft, Vehicle, Personnel) waited next to Joe's merchant transport. Netting made of tightly-wound rope draped the sides of the ship and provided a moving ladder to crawl down.

It was time to land.

Joe carried his sea bag with all his possessions, which included a small Navy-issued Bible. When it was his turn, he carefully made his way down as he watched the LCVP move and sway below. The ocean current and swells consistently slammed the smaller boat into the larger one, only to soon be feet away with another swell. Salt spray covered the men and the smell of the ocean surrounded them. It was relatively quiet. Joe never looked back as he headed from the ship to the coastline.

They bumped their way across the small stretch of ocean separating them from the island. The *ping-ping-ping* of beach-based enemy fire ricocheting off the steel hull never came. Joe didn't know any different. Unlike the transports days earlier on the other side of the island—or the transports that landed on the beaches at Normandy the previous spring—it was quiet. They were not under attack and the transport was orderly and calm.

Just minutes later, the LCVP hit sand and pulled onto the shoreline. Its front opened and the men filed off and onto Japanese soil for the first time. Salt spray covered their faces and splotches of sea water darkened portions of their clothing. Joe quickly made his way up to the infamous black volcanic ash that makes up Iwo's beaches. Each man lined up and received a steel helmet, a spade, and a one-person tent pack. They were necessary pieces of equipment for the secured battle zone. Helmets came with straps but anyone with knowledge of combat knew to keep them undone. A landmine blast or concussion wave could snap a man's neck if the heavy steel helmet was attached under the chin.

Thirty yards from the surf's edge, Joe and his fellow Seabees scattered about and were told to immediately dig their own foxholes and set up their tents. They were just a few hundred yards from Suribachi—just 528-feet tall—and so close to its bottom they could not see the American flag, famously captured in the Joe Rosenthal photograph, raised less than 24 hours earlier. Joe's unit was in the harbor, off the southwest coast of Iwo Jima, when that historic event took place. They landed February 24, 1945, at the base of Mt. Suribachi and immediately went into foxholes.

The iconic Joe Rosenthal photo of the second flag raising atop Mt. Suribachi, February 23, 1945, which changed America's perception of WWII.
(National Archives)

It was only later in the campaign that Joe heard about the famous flag raising on the top of Iwo's only mountain.

T HE PROBLEMS BEGAN THAT SATURDAY AFTERNOON WHEN Joe realized he'd never been told how to properly dig a foxhole and this being the first tent he'd ever seen, he had no clue how to correctly put the poles through the canvas and set the thing up. There was no supervision and he had no idea how to put his tent together. While everyone around him dug foxholes, he did his best to pitch the tent.

"I figured I would just sleep on top of the ground. I looked at these other guys and figured, 'What the hell am I gonna dig a hole for?' That night, I was sleeping on top of the ground and it rained. I was flooded. So the next morning I dug a foxhole," Joe laughed.

African-American troops in foxholes on Iwo Jima.
(National Archives)

His first meal on Iwo Jima was a K-ration labeled "supper," with a canned meat product, biscuits, toilet paper, one four-pack of cigarettes, a can opener, matches, a bouillon soup cube, and a two-ounce, heat-resistant chocolate bar. Joe described the chocolate as "a brick you can't chew." Instead, you had to suck on it. The K-rations were served in boxes as breakfast, dinner, and supper and usually provided up to 3,000 calories per meal.

Each sailor received two quart-sized canteens of water per day. They used the water for everything, which explained the lack of bathing or shaving in battle. The Seabees lined up in the morning at a small water tank on wheels and the operator was strict to be sure each man received not a drop more than the allotment.

Joe LaNier fell asleep that night in the South Pacific, in a horrific war, at the base of Mt. Suribachi. At home in Mississippi, it was only Friday morning and Papa had already been up before the sun at work in the fields.

After a decent first night's sleep despite the rain, Joe woke the next morning to the sounds of his unit as they rustled around. His first full day was spent getting acclimated to his surroundings and soon after, the Seabees built a large tent to store the K-rations and protect them from the weather. Each man also checked out their mess kits, which included a tin cup, a small pan, and utensils. As the sun rose higher and the temperatures climbed, they used their knives and turned their pants into shorts. Their superiors never said a critical word. In fact, during Joe's time on Iwo, he and his men were never addressed by their commanding officer—similar to procedure at Great Lakes. They had heard he was a respectable man, a chicken farmer, but not once were they gathered for briefings or remarks that would typically come from the commander of an outfit.

The war on Iwo Jima and the effort to secure the island continued. The first few days they all watched the Japanese come out of Mt. Suribachi because they presumed—the enemy had run out of food. Some Japanese were captured, others were not so lucky. The U.S. forces knew they had been preparing for invasion for

Above the death and chaos on Mt. Suribachi. Note the activity on the beaches below.
(National Archives)

decades and because they had the high ground, they had the tactical positions: 75mm guns, mortars, and rocket launchers. According to countless men who survived Iwo, the enemy had howitzers, tank guns, and pillboxes that strategically covered nearly every square inch of the island.

The midday heat of the South Pacific was different from the sweltering Mississippi summers to which Joe was accustomed. They were closer to the equator and the increase in temperature, even compared to Hawaii, was immediately noticeable. Mornings were cool but conditions changed quickly. Many of the men went shirtless, even in the war zone. There was no sunscreen and the white officers would routinely blister and peel in the tropical sun. Joe turned red but because of the pigment in his skin, he never had any skin problems or concerns. Unlike in Hawaii and on the ship, no one ever went swimming off the Iwo coast.

Back on the beach, Joe looked out and could see a constant flow of ships coming in with needed supplies. There was never a time he didn't see at least some sort of vessel off the southwestern coastline. Smaller transport ships brought in trucks, ammunition, and food. To the north, he heard the fighting that would rage at times over the course of the next four weeks.

The consistent soundtrack on Iwo Jima was the tidal movement. Waves and the resulting white foam provided a stark contrast to the wet, black sand. In his downtime, Joe walked to the water's edge and was fascinated by the intricate designs the foam would leave in the sand.

His tent was within walking distance of Suribachi's base and nearby a dirt road curved around one side of the bare mountain. Bomb craters pockmarked the barren landscape. From his coastal vantage point, Joe could easily see tunnel entrances and could only imagine who was still alive inside and what they were planning. He knew they would kill him without a second thought.

In his early days on the island, Joe looked up from the beach and watched as engineers cut a road up the side of Suribachi. One soldier driving a bulldozer actually drove it off the side of the road and though it didn't tumble, Joe watched it hang there. The man was lucky to be rescued before the dozer rolled off the mountain.

Fast-paced activity was all around him. Numerous DUKWs (commonly known as *ducks*) could be seen not only on land but on

Two African-American duck [DUKW] drivers turn riflemen after their vehicle is destroyed, February 19, 1945.
(National Archives)

water as well. The ducks were six-wheel drive, amphibious trucks and were often operated by blacks, some of whom Joe knew. They were the workhorses and an enormous help in transporting matériel to proper destinations.

T HE CLOSE PROXIMITY TO THE OCEAN COULDN'T MASK THE smell of death on Iwo Jima. Joe noticed it immediately— a strong, strange, putrid odor his brain processed; he instantly knew the source. Within several hundred yards of Joe's beachside foxhole, American and Japanese corpses were rotting in that tropical heat and intense sunshine. There were also the acrid smells of cordite, gun smoke, diesel fuel, and exhaust.

Carnage on Iwo Jima's invasion beaches, February 19, 1945.
(National Archives)

"It was just a mess. Everything was topsy-turvy. You could see body parts as you went about your business. It was a common thing. I understood what was going on. I understood that I could die but it didn't bother me. I was never on the very frontline where people were shooting at me specifically. We came in behind people to help with what they needed to do."

Joe took stock of what he told me, and then continued.

"War is hell; I cannot imagine anyone taking exception to that. Once you are in the heat of battle, I can tell you, something takes ahold of you and it becomes almost routine at times."

Perhaps it was because these blacks were not in combat—perhaps it was racially motivated—but this group of Seabees handled weapons for the first time in nearly ten months *after* they landed on Iwo Jima. They hadn't possessed a weapon since Great Lakes. It had been almost a year since they had fired anything. Joe and members of his unit were each issued carbine rifles, a .44 sidearm, a leather holster, and a dagger-type, standard-issue military knife. Joe had never touched a knife and had no training whatsoever with the pistol.

"It made no sense," he said. "It makes no sense to give you a gun and then not train you how to use it. 'We don't need to train 'em. Give 'em a gun, point, and pull the trigger' was their mentality. They figured we wouldn't fight anyway."

When the sun set on the western horizon, night came quickly and Iwo Jima went into complete darkness. The moon helped but when the sky was void of its light, the island went pitch black. The stars were in the same sky but they looked so different from the skies Joe had seen as a boy growing up. The Big and Little Dippers were out of place. They were the same stars but positioned differently in the sky.

The Seabees were issued flashlights, which were lifesavers as they crawled back into their foxholes. Unlike soldiers and airmen on the frontlines in Europe, the Navy didn't issue Cricket Clickers—devices used at night to communicate and ensure someone approaching was a "friendly" and not an enemy. Joe frequently used passwords when he would enter secure areas and those passwords—passed down by senior officers—changed daily during combat operations.

Joe had learned by now that to keep the volcanic ash from collapsing inside his foxhole, he had to build up the inner walls with sandbags. At night, after exhausting days and extreme temperatures, he slept soundly, save for the frequent gunfire that would erupt nearby or the sirens that went off around the clock. The sirens usually indicated enemy aircraft were in the area, as the Japanese would fly planes overhead to pester and annoy the Americans. They were low enough to make god-awful noise but high enough to avoid shelling from batteries on the ground or from naval guns pointed into the sky. It became routine.

Joe lived in a beach foxhole in the Mt. Suribachi sector of Iwo Jima for two months. Two entire months.

A T FIRST HE HEARD COMMOTION AND THEN A SINGLE gunshot. Several people quickly moved toward the area 100 yards down the beach and Joe immediately followed. When he came upon the scene, he saw a Marine down on his haunches looking into the face of a dead Japanese soldier. His skull was gone, peeled back like a watermelon that had been cut open. Joe can still see the exact detail of the dead man and the Marine who hovered over the body.

"The dead Japanese was a young guy and his skull was gone. I remembered hearing that one of the tactics Japanese soldiers would use was to act as if they were surrendering but they would have hand grenades all around them with the pins out. When people gravitated toward them, they would blow up and you would go with it."

It was the first war death Joe witnessed.

"It was gruesome. I thought, 'How can you kill somebody?' And then I remembered there's no way to know if someone is really trying to surrender. With that individual, war sank in—but I still was not frightened of war. After that, we went back to business, as if nothing happened."

Joe had no interest in knowing any more about the dead Japanese soldier's body but it was likely disposed of in a mass grave.

In his foxhole, late in March 1945, Joe turned 19-years-old. In war, the days blended into one another and no one in the 23rd could, with certainty, know the date or even the day of the week. Time was, for the most part, unimportant and no one in the lower ranks wore a watch. His birthday came and went without so much as a thought. Once again, Joe mostly kept to himself but on occasion he would visit acquaintances in nearby foxholes. On Iwo, most everyone called him "Sonny," the name that was stenciled on his bag.

Two of his mates dug such an elaborate foxhole they actually shared it. That particular day, one of the young men thought it would be a good idea to clean his carbine rifle, which was common practice considering they could easily malfunction in the dusty, dirty environs. The men used oil and by this point could break down their weapons with relative ease and put them back together. Joe sat on sandbags piled up on the west side of the foxhole while his friend sat about eight feet away and cleaned his rifle. A canvas tent was pitched a few feet above their heads. When he was finished cleaning, the fellow Seabee forgot to clear the chamber and as a joke, he decided to pull the trigger. A bullet struck just beneath Joe and lodged into a sandbag. Had it been a foot higher, the bullet would have hit him.

WITH EVERY DAY THAT PASSED DURING THE BATTLE, THE front lines advanced north. After the western sector was deemed secure, the 23rd Seabees moved inland about 300 yards to a safer environment on a small terrace or *the plateau.*

The men put up rows of tent housing and plywood flooring, and finally after two months in foxholes, they were able to sleep on cots. The last time any of the men had put their heads down on anything resembling a bed was two months prior aboard ship, yet Joe had adapted well to his foxhole and was fairly comfortable several feet below Iwo's beach surface.

It was here on the plateau the Navy implemented a small makeshift chow hall with a Chinese cook. The man's hair was in long, straight strands and he looked like a Japanese to all the servicemen because that image was the type of Hollywood propaganda they received: the Japanese wore thick glasses and many had buckteeth. On one trip down to the beach to look at the surf, Marines on guard pointed their M3s at the cook before they realized he was one of the good guys.

Day work for the black men often consisted of unloading ships with supplies for the Army, Navy, and Marines. The equipment was transported to what they called "the dump"—a storage area that housed every kind of supply needed to operate a war on a remote island. Though the supplies came into one central location, Joe and the Seabees remained completely segregated. Their only contact with white men came in the form of their superior officers. It was rare to see a white soldier or Marine during downtime and if that happened, it would usually be from a great distance.

JOE LaNier remains a patriotic man, though on countless occasions in our interview sessions he specifically pointed out to me his patriotism and his appreciation for his country came *after* the war and in the decades that followed. But something deep within him gave him pause one evening early in his deployment on Iwo Jima.

From Mt. Suribachi, Lt. Ceil Dennis looks over the 21st Bomber Command. The tent city below is where Joe lived after he and the 23rd Seabees left their foxholes.
(National Archives)

After a long silence in one of our interviews, Joe reflected on an incident that is so clear to him it could have happened this morning. He recalled his fascination with the ocean. On a walk down to the shoreline, he watched the retreating surf and was mesmerized by the white ocean foam and the intricate lines in the black volcanic ash.

"I would just stand there and watch. I wore my sidearm on my holster. One evening as the sun set in the west, it was just beautiful. The sun was a dark, pinkish-red. Clouds—strips of them, white clouds—sat up in the atmosphere. The sun reflected off the ocean and sent light to the clouds above. The bottoms of the clouds looked reddish and up in the left-hand corner of my view, there was a space. I stood there and thought how that is where the stars to our flag could go. When I visualized that, the clouds—red on the bottom and white on top—separated and the same distance apart, blue sky still in the background, I saw a red, white, and blue flag, and for the first time ever, I felt very patriotic. And I didn't know why. Patriotism was not part of my vocabulary but at that moment it confused me. I was emotional about it. As I talk about it today, I think of President Obama and a speech where he proclaimed: 'In no other country could my story be possible.' That's why I'm emotional about it, even today. There's something about this country that gives me pride."

Joe became emotional.

"If you take it logically—where and how I lived as I was growing up—that would probably be the last thing I would be emotional about. But that sunset has stuck with me. I can see it exactly how it looked at the time I saw it."

Tears welled in Joe's eyes.

CHAPTER SEVEN

PEG LEG

In the name of the greatest people that have ever trod this earth, I draw the line in the dust and toss the gauntlet before the feet of tyranny, and I say segregation now, segregation tomorrow and segregation forever!

— ALABAMA GOVERNOR GEORGE WALLACE
INAUGURAL ADDRESS
JANUARY 14, 1963

AFTER HIS MOTHER'S DEATH, JOE BECAME MORE DISTANT from Papa, not surprising in that while Joe respected his father, the two never developed a close, personal, affectionate bond. It was just how it was in their era. Papa continued to work the fields and other odd jobs, as much as his sixth-grade education would allow. He still had to provide food, shelter, and clothing for his younger children but now without the support of his wife.

In reality, he didn't know what to do. Joe would often get up early and have a bit of breakfast—perhaps a leftover biscuit—and go to school until 3:00 p.m. After a long walk home from school he was hungry but Papa was out working odd jobs and there was never excess food available for snacking. As evening fell, Papa would typically make a fire in their small stove and quite often he would send Joe about a mile up Military Road to Miss Eubank's home, a kind white lady who owned a cow. Joe wasn't happy. The loss of his mother, his lack of interest in school, and his early teenage mood swings did nothing to solidify a house in emotional chaos.

Papa never dated another woman after Savilla's death.

Not surprisingly, Joe's relationship with his father spiraled downward. They got into spats, made all the more awkward because by now the younger Joe was taller and weighed more than his father. During one fight, Joe physically picked up Papa and moved him out of the way, which led to one of the worst incidents in Joe's teenage years. Papa called for Ira, who was in another part of the house. Ira, who himself often beat Joe, came into the room and held his brother down while Papa repeatedly beat Joe with a stick. The beating seemed to last an eternity. When it was over, Joe was severely bruised but knew it was irrational anger. He knew Papa was a good man.

Joe's best friend was Charles Lewis, a boy he met in 1936. They shared similar interests and sense of humor, and Charles' mother became a surrogate for the still languishing young teenager. For spending money in 1940, Joe delivered things on a bicycle for $2.00 per week and then the next year, he went back to school. Charles landed Joe a job working with him at Sanitary Laundry, where Joe pressed and folded clothes as hisses of steam spewed out from the laundry machines. The 15-year-old went to school during the day and then walked a few miles to work—a hot, steamy, noisy area in the back of the laundry. Joe worked from late afternoon until about 9:00 p.m. during the week.

He had no idea where his life was headed. His mother was gone and he was frustrated many times with his strict father. With the relationship strained, Joe decided to run away from home with 50 cents in his pocket. His first thought was to stay with his half-brother, Alexander, in Demopolis, Alabama, but there was one problem: Joe didn't know how to get there. Instead, he went over to a girl he had been seeing and told her he was leaving town. Joe also told the girl's mother but it was too late to leave that night. The girl's mother agreed to let Joe stay but he had to sleep in a swing chair out on the porch. He nearly froze overnight and went back home the following day. Papa put him right to work and they never talked about it.

On occasion, the beatings from Ira would come from out of the blue, unprovoked. They started to get serious when Joe was around

11-years-old. But there was a reason; a dark, family secret Joe wouldn't learn about until 1949. The secret was perhaps the reason why, in the late 1930s, Joe sustained a brutal beating at the hands of his brother. At the time, Ira worked at the Moss Tie Plant and one day Joe came to the yards to play on one of the train cars. Ira came out and without warning repeatedly punched his little brother with closed fists. Joe suffered a busted lip and bloody nose. The little boy immediately told his mother and that night, Savilla told Ira if it happened again, she would kick him out of their home.

FAST-FORWARD A DOZEN YEARS WHEN JOE WAS BACK IN Columbus on a college break. He decided to visit the Benton family, longtime LaNier friends. Miss Mary, her children, and Joe all knew each other well. During a conversation with one of the Benton girls, Mary came onto the porch as Joe talked about his father.

"Your father is dead," Mary said abruptly.

Joe didn't understand. In the conversation, completely out of context, Mary bluntly—and in explicit detail—told Joe that his father was actually her deceased husband. He was confused and devastated at the same time, and after trying briefly to understand, he left the Bentons' home in a daze. He walked home and immediately went next door to his father's home where Josephine, his sister-in-law, listened to what had happened earlier in the day. It was apparently a family and neighborhood secret.

She told Joe she had heard the rumor and at the end of their conversation, he told her not to tell Papa. But later, Josephine told Papa anyway. She told Joe she mentioned it because she was so angry at the fact someone could do that, even if it were true.

Joe finished his college break and went back to New Orleans.

After he settled in at school again, Joe received a letter from his normally detached father. In it, ne told his son he had heard the same thing and indicated the news was incorrect, *not* true.

Joe and Papa never had a face-to-face discussion about the allegations.

Joe tried to dismiss it. But then a childhood flashback came into his mind.

When Joe was no more that two- or three-years-old, he remembered seeing his mother having sex, at their home, with another man. Savilla had an affair with Mr. Benton and the two had sex in front of Joe while Joe Sr. was out working in the nearby fields. It was a dark, repressed secret.

The realization at 23, of what he had witnessed in 1929, had a devastating impact on him. A million thoughts began to circulate in his mind—first and foremost if, in fact, he was who he thought he was and if his siblings were really who he thought they were. There were no paternity tests available and few people ever suspected a woman like Savilla would be anything but faithful to her husband. To Joe, regardless, Papa was his father and that was that. He felt whatever happened was between his mother and God.

It then clicked with Joe, in 1949, why Ira went from being a loving—if not normal—brother to a young man filled with rage and deep-seated hate. Joe feels Ira learned about the affair in the late 1930s and resented him for being a bastard child. In order to deal with his own pain, Joe felt Ira took it out on him physically.

Ira was the only black person Joe knew who actually attended high school. He was married to Josephine Gardner, against her white father's wishes, and the newlyweds moved in with Mama and Papa. Sometimes they fought violently and mercilessly. Later, Papa built Ira and Josephine their own home on the vacant lot next door to the existing LaNier home in Memphis Town.

B ESIDES THE BIKE DELIVERIES AND THE LAUNDRY, JOE worked for a brief period of time at Ruth's, a white-owned clothing store in downtown Columbus. He walked three miles each way for little wage. Joe remembers one afternoon—in front of several white customers standing around—he bent down to pick up something. At that moment, from behind him, he felt the kick. The white manager of the store, totally unprovoked, kicked Joe hard and square in the butt. They all laughed about it. It was fun to see the black boy get kicked for no reason. The manager and his friends never said a word; they just stood there and laughed as Joe stood up. He stopped working there a short time later. Joe also cleaned the McCaleb house for a time where he was treated much better.

Oftentimes Joe walked three miles each way to work the fields with Papa. The young man would frequently fall behind his father as they made their way down gravel roads. They passed the poor black homes of Memphis Town as early morning smoke wafted out of poorly constructed chimneys. They made their way past a white neighborhood and a golf course, open only to whites. The country-side then opened up, with homes scattered sporadically across dozens of acres of farmland. The three-mile journey ended at "the big house," where Papa checked in to get any needed supplies for the day's work ahead. Joe helped at the barn by equipping the mule with its harness and then riding it to the "turn plow" in the middle of the field. It was the type of manual labor the young teenager despised. Inside, Joe was full of pent-up emotions as he tried to lead a life without his mother.

One afternoon a friend told Joe about a position that had come open at the 20th Century Nightclub, a local place on the outskirts of Columbus. It offered Joe a firsthand glimpse of the society in which he lived and the types of people he called his neighbors.

The nightclub near the Tombigbee River offered a place on the edge of town for whites to come and eat, drink, and socialize. Racist talk and behavior was rampant. It was not the place for a black teen but Joe needed the work and they needed the help.

I T WAS A SUMMER AFTERNOON, 1941. JOE WAS PLAYING POOL with some acquaintances at Billy Herndon's second-floor pool hall on Catfish Alley in downtown Columbus and what happened in the hours that followed could have ended his life.

The pool hall, in a typical pool-hall environment, was poorly lit. Several tables were scattered around the room, each with lights above that illuminated the darkened hall and gave the place atmosphere. The distinct cracking sound of balls crashing into one another filled the air. There were no whites inside; this was a place—along with other businesses along Catfish Alley—where the black community felt the most comfortable. They were among their own, the people who shared similar backgrounds and stories. They knew each other.

Joe arched over a table with pool cue in hand and squared up to take a shot at the white cue ball. Just then, a black boy, escorted by an off-duty deputy sheriff, came into the upstairs area.

"I was preparing for a shot and this guy walks in, I didn't see him, but I heard him. He said, 'Is that the nigger there?' I looked around and there is the sheriff and this young boy about my age. I was about 15. I didn't know he was talking to me because I didn't know this kid, so I ignored him. Best not to do anything. And the pool hall owner said, 'Joe, he's talking to you. You better go with him.'"

The deputy—in plain clothes during this encounter—was known among the blacks in the area as "The High Sheriff, Peg Leg Goosby." He had somehow lost his leg and in its place he wore a prosthetic stump. He limped when he walked. Peg Leg was in his fifties with a thin build and strong voice. To a kid, he was a mean, ominous man of the law. He was easily the face of segregation and racist behavior in their small southern town.

Peg Leg pointed across the room at Joe.

Joe swears he wasn't scared and because he had nothing to hide, he went with him.

Joe put down his pool cue and walked across the room where Peg Leg and the kid were standing. As people watched, the trio went out through the pool-hall doorway, down an inside flight of stairs, out another doorway, and stopped on the sidewalk below on Fourth Street. No one from the pool hall did anything. The men inside knew better than to say a word, though it could have easily been the last time they saw Joe alive. In the South in those days, this type of event was not unusual. Anytime a black was picked up by the police during that period, it could be the last time they were seen.

Joe paused.

"*Anytime* that happened. That's how that society was at the time."

A parked car waited in front of the doorway on Fourth Street. A man was seated behind the steering wheel, someone Joe did not know. (He later found out the man owned Etherton's Meat Market in Columbus. Joe assumed this man was Etherton himself and as he has told the story in subsequent years, the man is referred to as "Mr. Etherton," the owner.) In the back of the car sat another black teenager. He sat quietly with his head down. His name was James Peoples. Joe knew him only as "Peoples."

Peg Leg opened the door and pushed the stranger kid in the back seat first, then Joe. The door shut loudly behind them. It was a regular sedan, not a marked police car.

"You didn't have to get black folks in a cop's car. You just went to get them!" Joe told me.

Inside on the back seat, three pistols sat strategically in place, as if on display. Peg Leg and Etherton were also looking for something else—cash.

Before the car started, Peg Leg turned around from the front seat and over his left shoulder looked directly into Joe's eyes.

"How much of that money did *you* get?"

Joe had no idea what Peg Leg was talking about and had nothing to do with any crime.

"What money? I don't know anything about any money," Joe said softly.

Peg Leg turned around, and Etherton started the car and pulled away from the sidewalk.

Not a word was said as Joe and the other two boys sat in the back seat. They had no idea what was going to happen next but they knew they were not off to the sheriff's office to be booked into jail. They knew they were not going to face a judge. They all assumed they would be beaten. The only question was how and how severely.

The three handguns sat next to the boys the entire trip out of town. Were they loaded? Could they use the guns to get out of the potentially deadly situation that may have been in front of them?

It didn't matter. Joe never thought of touching one of them.

"They could have had a gun loaded but they knew I was not going to pick up that gun and use it, because that was a death sentence! Period. They were not worried about us. We were, in their minds, sub-human. We might as well have been three dogs in the back seat. Not only did they know that if I picked up one of the guns, it would be a death sentence for me, it also could be a death sentence for my family. So the fear of what could happen was the voice in my head that told me, 'Don't do that.'"

Joe stopped and looked at me. It was an intense moment. His wife, Eula, sat to his left, at their dining room table. I sat just three feet from him and noticed something different in the way he was relaying—no, reliving—this particular moment in his life. He told me how Papa had preached for years that if you were innocent, there was no need for worry. In this instance, there was simply nothing Joe could do but sit back and hope for the best, captive in a stranger's car

It had rained that morning and the streets of downtown were wet and shiny. Etherton continued to drive through downtown and then north, out past the city limits. Two miles out of town, with open fields on both sides of the dirt road they traveled, the car veered off into a pasture and toward an old, abandoned barn. Joe had never been to this part of rural Columbus.

The car stopped outside near the front of the barn and the engine was turned off. It was silent as the clouds gave way to partial sunshine. Cows roamed in a nearby pasture. No one else was around. There they were, two white men and three black teenagers. There were no witnesses and no one else to hear the screams that followed.

Peg Leg and Etherton opened their doors and the kids were forced out. As Joe and the stranger kid climbed out of the back seat into the still-wet low weeds and grass outside the barn, Peoples scrambled out on the other side. No one said a word.

The old barn stood witness, its doors long-since removed and its wood planks rotted by constant exposure. The men led the boys into the barn and lined them up on the musty dirt floor. Inside, they began to talk and asked pointed questions.

"Where's the money?" was asked repeatedly.

Peoples continued to deny any involvement. Joe and the stranger kid never said a word. As the two of them stood inside the barn, Peg Leg and Etherton told Peoples to get outside near the car. After he took the few steps into the sunlight, Etherton instructed him to take off all his clothes, including his socks and shoes.

"I was 15 and I can see it as if it was yesterday. It was like a terrible movie that played out in front of me. They beat this boy unmercifully. It was atrocious. I decided, 'Well, if it's gonna happen it's gonna happen.' I didn't do anything and there was no use being frightened about it."

Joe was implicated based on color.

One of the men yelled at the naked boy to get on his knees and elbows. It seemed to play out in slow motion. The men tied him with rope at the wrists and ankles, and placed two sticks to immobilize the teen. One stick went under his chest, the other behind his knees. The boy couldn't move.

Peg Leg and Etherton both walked to the car and opened the doors. They reached in and each pulled out a leather strap. They then walked back to Peoples.

The beating began.

"How long did it last?" I asked.

"At least an hour."

The two men continued yelling at Peoples, repeatedly calling him a nigger.

"Nigger! Nigger!" they screamed.

Periodically the whippings stopped and Peg Leg asked again where the money was. Peoples continued to deny any knowledge. The beatings resumed. Joe and the stranger kid watched from inside the barn just a few feet away. It was reminiscent of slave owners beating a slave.

"It was merciless. He was bleeding. His skin looked like how it does if you took a wet potato and rubbed its skin off. I thought I was next. I knew I didn't have anything to do with it but I also knew that these men didn't care."

Peoples never lost consciousness. But he did scream and cry. Even so, Peoples never cried out for help because he knew the other boys were powerless.

Joe never thought to try to stop the beating. He assumed Peg Leg had either a gun on him or at the very least, inside the car. As the hour dragged on, the men took turns pounding the leather into the boy's flesh. The smacks of the leather onto bloody skin got louder as more blood began to flow out of his body. It was brutality and an example of man's inhumanity to man.

As Joe stood in the barn, witness to the worst thing he had seen in his lifetime to that point, he recalled an incident several days earlier that clarified, to an extent, why he was in the position he was in now. Several days earlier, Joe and two friends who also worked at the nightclub were walking to work. Their route took them in front of Etherton's Meat Market just before they cut across the Tombigbee River and on to the nightclub.

On this particular afternoon, they saw a delivery boy. It was Peoples and he worked at the market. In the front basket attached to his delivery bike sat a greasy paper bag.

"What's in the bag?" Joe asked at the time.

"Just a delivery," Peoples said.

It seemed odd to Joe that a delivery from a store would look so dirty and grimy. Peoples rode off and the three continued walking to the nightclub for their shifts. Joe never thought twice about the bag.

This scenario played out in Joe's mind as he stood in the barn. Was that greasy bag full of stolen money? Was Peoples guilty? Did his crime fit the punishment being carried out in the middle of nowhere?

As the beating continued, a small single-engine plane flew over the field. Both Etherton and Peg Leg laughed. They told Peoples that whoever was in that plane was probably laughing as they looked down at the field below.

After an hour, the beatings stopped.

Peoples spoke up and told Peg Leg and Etherton he would take them to get the money. The teen collapsed in pain. As Joe and the stranger kid watched, Etherton yanked Peoples up from the ground and told him to put on his clothes and get in the car. They drove away.

Peg Leg came into the barn.

"He began to talk to us and the stranger boy said to the sheriff that he didn't have anything to do with this. He knew nothing about it. He motioned to me. So he must have known something about the money but after what we had witnessed, he was good enough and frightened enough to tell the sheriff that I didn't know anything about the money."

For the next 30 minutes, Joe wondered what was happening with Peoples. Every now and then, Peg Leg broke the silence and asked another question but he heard little new information from the stranger kid. Finally, they saw the car pull across the field and toward the barn. Peoples was in the back seat. The boy got out of the car and his pants were wet, halfway up to his knees. Joe wondered if they had been looking for the money in some sort of wet hiding spot. Etherton's pants were wet as well. When Etherton told Peg Leg there was no money, Joe knew there would be additional beatings.

Round two began.

This time, Peoples was put on the ground in his clothes and Etherton beat him again. Peg Leg stood nearby as he watched the leather strap pound the boy repeatedly. After a few minutes, both men seemed to realize this wasn't going to get them any of the money, so they put all three boys back into the car and drove back into Columbus.

The car ride back was again in silence. Peoples was bloody and in pain but didn't make a sound. Etherton made his way back to the black neighborhood in Columbus and stopped in front of Peoples' home. The boys were let out on the dirt road and when the doors were closed, the boys stood there. Etherton pulled out and drove away as bits of gravel and dust kicked up behind the speeding car.

Seconds later, the boys saw red brake lights. The car started to back up and headed toward them again. The boys stood still as the car came to a stop. Joe's beating was surely next. He thought, as he stood on the side of the road, he might not survive his beating. Fighting back was not an option, he told himself.

The car stopped and Peg Leg looked at them from his window. He yelled out that if he ever found out they had any knowledge about the money, there would be hell to pay. Joe remains surprised the men didn't beat all three of them. With the admonition, they drove off and Joe never saw Etherton or Peg Leg again. Joe never saw Peoples or the other boy again, either.

The boys went their separate ways and Joe walked home. The incident played over and over in his mind. It was the most traumatic incident of his life, save for losing Mama in 1940.

"It was never about the money in this case. It was about power," he told me.

The men knew they had total power over the black community.

"*Total.* There was no middle ground. It was total power. If they wanted justice to be done, they would have taken Peoples to court. But that's not what they wanted."

Somehow, Joe slept well that night. He never feared Peg Leg might someday come back and pick him up and amazingly, Joe never said a word about the incident.

"So many years later, though, I can still hear the pain," Joe said softly. "I can."

Papa never knew.

Peoples had lifelong scars but went on to serve in the Army during WWII. He was honorably discharged.

EVERY FEW WEEKS DURING OUR INTERVIEW SESSIONS, I asked Joe why he was not filled with hate. Why didn't he hate whites? Why not hate me for the race I represent?

The answer never varied.

"I really think it's hard for other African-Americans—and whites as well—to understand why I don't hate. I just don't. With the ethics I was taught, you just don't hate people. It makes no sense but it gives me a lot of pride. Let me tell you, as God is my witness, I do not hate those men—Peg Leg and Etherton. I credit my father because I think that happens because someone teaches you. You're not born with it. However, even though there's been great progress and we are light-years away from where it was when I was a boy, there's still a lot to be done."

Eula has yet to understand how her husband isn't full of hate.

"I don't see how he can't hate some things that happened to him. I don't understand that. I don't understand why he doesn't hate. I would," she told me.

Joe continued working at the nightclub, which was owned by two brothers—Mr. Emerson and Mr. Anderson.

"The owner, despite what I saw, was overall a decent man to *me*. Anderson wasn't a racist at all. One day, though, I was out in the back in a small warehouse and was loading up soda pop to bring in. We were usually busy at night with most of the business from the Columbus Flying School nearby. Emerson called me and I didn't answer because I couldn't hear him. When I came in, I heard him say to the other guy, 'Where is that yellow son of a bitch?'"

Yellow referred to Joe's color as opposed to *black* because the teen's color wasn't dark, but yellow was just as ugly and derogatory as being called a nigger. Emerson frequently called his employees *niggers, coons,* or *sons of bitches* as part of everyday dialogue.

One evening at the beginning of his shift, Joe was getting tables ready with silverware and napkins. Emerson stood nearby, in conversation with another white man. Joe was focused and paid little attention to what was going on in any other part of the room. Then he noticed it. His co-worker, also a black teenager, was making quite a bit of noise as he placed glasses on nearby shelves.

Emerson apparently didn't like the noise because he stopped his conversation, walked over, and hit the teen in the face with a closed fist. Then he went right back to talking with his friend as if nothing happened.

Years later, Joe returned to Columbus on break from college. He was downtown near the corner of College and Main Streets when he saw Emerson standing near the town clock. It had been years since they'd seen each other and they talked for a few minutes.

"I felt good about myself because I had no hate for this man despite all the things I saw and specifically watched him do to other blacks. On the street corner, my father's words echoed through my mind. He'd say, 'This society can control what happens to me as long as I live in this town but no one can control what I think.' I will be forever grateful that what my father thought and taught us was to look for the good in people, not their faults."

B ACK HOME, PAPA CONTINUED DOING ODD JOBS AROUND the area and next door. Ira and Josephine continued to expand their family with the addition of sons Ira Jr. and Bobby. The couple had three children altogether with the addition of a daughter named Shirley. Suddenly, Ira became critically ill and less than three months after Josephine had given birth to their daughter, Ira passed away.

Ira LaNier had been sick and went in for an operation in 1942, and when he came home he never fully recovered. He went back to the hospital and died a few days later—December 15, 1942— at only 26-years-old. Joe was on the job at the nightclub when a black-owned taxi pulled up the dirt road and into the gravel parking lot. Joe knew what he was going to hear: his brother was dead. Joe cared about him and loved him but they were never that close.

"This tall, dark, handsome man—my brother—was no more."

Ira was buried next to his mother, Savilla, in the cemetery on the outskirts of town. It was the first time Joe returned to the cemetery since Mama died nearly two years earlier. In their culture they preached, "Let the dead bury the dead."

A T 16, JOE LEARNED OF AN OPEN RED CAP POSITION AT THE Columbus bus terminal. He applied, dazzled the owners in his interview, and got the position and its salary of $17.25 every week. It was a big jump from the $9.00 per week at the laundry. Joe kept busy at the bus terminal until he entered the service two years later.

Even with the segregated society, there were certain whites who treated Joe with dignity and respect, despite his age and color. Mr. and Mrs. Daniels were Joe's bosses and together they ran the Continental Trailways Bus Company—or Tri-State Trailways—in downtown Columbus.

"Even though they had to run that bus station by the laws of the city—a segregated bus station with whites here, blacks there, in different waiting areas—those two people never made us black Red Caps feel second-class. I was a human being. In almost any other case, whites made us feel at best like, 'This is my boy.' It was almost, in good situations, like a parental relationship. We weren't equal."

Joe worked the day shift and started about 8:00 a.m. His uniform consisted of khaki pants and shirt, and a red cap. He wore it proudly.

He cleaned restrooms, tidied the waiting area, and took care of anything that needed attention, with particular focus on the "whites only" areas. Joe felt a greater sense of urgency to have those areas clean and as close to perfect as possible. Upkeep was important. If things were broken, they'd be fixed right away, except in the black areas where things often remained broken.

There were separate ticket counters for whites and blacks, and separate waiting rooms where people sat and waited for their outbound bus. The same white employee would sell tickets to members of both races but blacks were always forced to wait until all the white customers were ticketed. Blacks were also seated last and forced to enter the bus and shimmy down skinny aisles past the whites, already in their seats. It was humiliating for many. They had no choice but to follow the rules to get to their destinations.

Joe remembers the mail delivery—whether at the bus depot or any other Columbus address—was handled strictly by whites. There were no black postal employees in town. Only whites were allowed to handle and deliver.

As a Red Cap, Joe's primary duty was getting outbound luggage checked and stored in the undercarriage of each bus. Inbound busses were unloaded and if bags were checked to another destination, Joe was responsible for the successful transfer. Most of the travelers were white; however, he worked the shift with one other black teenager, about his age. There was also an older, uneducated man who did shift work.

Busses usually came into the bays one at a time, with an occasional overlap in schedules. Joe was always busy. If he was outside, he handled bags. Inside, he cleaned the tile floors and since there was no air conditioning, he also cleaned and adjusted fans. Onboard, he went row-by-row, seat-by-seat, picking up trash before the next passenger load.

He also had relationships with certain bus drivers; in Joe's eyes they had a career full of adventure and intrigue. The bus drivers liked Joe because he was a hard worker and was always there when they needed him. As a reward, on his days off he might hop a ride from Columbus to Memphis on what was known as a "special" or a chartered nonstop. Joe would still have to sit in the back in the colored section. But when they deadheaded back and the bus was empty, he could sit up front. On Joe's first trip to Memphis, the white bus driver liked Joe and let him sit up front, just the two of them. Even so, Joe still had to call him Mister. It was just understood. Since Joe had never been to Memphis, it was an early adventure and he was just glad to be going. Titles and seating arrangements were easily overlooked.

"The whole segregation thing boiled down to 'you're not as good as me.' But when there aren't other white people around to show that 'I'm better than you,' then we can have a conversation."

The Daniels even gave the now-17-year-old an important job, announcing stops westbound along Highway 82. It was unprecedented for a white family to allow a black teenager to be seen much, let alone heard.

They let him call the stops between Columbus and Shreveport, Louisiana—all over the microphone: Banks Plantation, State College, Starkville, Mathiston, Eupora, Tomnolen, Stewart,

Kilmichael, Winona, Greenwood, Greenville, and all points west. He was extremely proud to be the voice of Trailways' Columbus station. The fact Joe was allowed to do this part of his job shouldn't have come as a complete shock to him. He was affable, clean-cut, and intelligent, and despite his grades, he had an excellent work ethic and a clear, distinct voice for a teenager. He didn't push the envelope, though. He took what they gave but didn't push. It wasn't worth it.

Joe also saw soldiers come through the bus depot. They were often on their way to the Columbus Army Flying School north of Columbus and Joe can remember how troops from the North treated him differently than those from the South. It was a sign of the times.

He was making decent money but things at home continued to be strained. There was little food and no family dynamics for which Joe longed. It was at this point in his life he decided to join the Navy. When he volunteered for the service and left the station, the Daniels were proud. They talked with Joe about their pride in him for stepping out to serve the country.

O N AN EVENING IN LATE 1943, JOE WAS LISTENING TO THE radio in his Memphis Town home on North 14th Avenue when he heard a public service announcement about enlisting in the military. In between Billy Eckstine's jazz hit, *Stormy Monday Blues,* and other big-band tunes, the radio spoke to him. The Navy. Not too long after, he saw a newspaper ad featuring Uncle Sam—top hat and finger pointed directly at him—and Joe made the decision to join on his own without any family discussion. At just 17 years old, however, he needed his father's consent and more importantly, his signature.

Joe knew money was tight.

His approach to Papa was that he could give him an allotment of his service salary. At $37.00 every two weeks, Joe would make about as much as his father, though he avoided talking salary specifics.

"He never asked me for money. I just basically blew my money on clothes and junk food but he never said anything about that, either. I was the best-dressed kid in my neighborhood and I used to buy Stacy Adams wingtips and Florsheim shoes for $11.00 a pair. I also bought lots of Belly Washers and Hobo Squares—small cinnamon roll four-packs—and RC Cola," he laughed.

(For Joe's 86th birthday, I decided to buy him a brand new pair of Stacy Adams shoes. He loved them.)

Joe wanted nice things, even if he spent his last penny to get them.

"Of course, I was trying to make up for what I didn't have as a young child. Mama made my shirts, so I wanted store-bought shirts. I wanted more than one pair of underwear and no thermal underwear or 'union suits.' In the spring and summer we always went barefoot. I only had shoes in the winter and I promised myself I would never go barefoot again, like I did as a little boy. Maybe that's why today, I own 20 pairs of shoes."

The way Joe dresses today and the size of his wardrobe is a direct result of what he couldn't afford as a young man.

It was logical for Joe to make his decision about the military. This way, Papa never had to worry about him and could focus on the girls. Joe took care of himself. His small jobs gave him enough money to make it on his own.

Papa signed his son's paperwork at a small table in their Memphis Town home. It took just a few strokes of a pen in late 1943 to pave the way for Joe to enter WWII.

CHAPTER EIGHT

DUTY

JOE QUICKLY FOUND HIMSELF IN AN ELITE FRATERNITY, ONE of the fewer than 1,000 African-Americans serving on Iwo Jima. For all of the black Seabees in the 23rd, the monotony quickly set in as they were at best grunts, amidst what would be the most-publicized Pacific battle of WWII. While death was all around them, their war world was comprised of just a few hundred yards. They carried out orders as they were handed down, unloaded ships, battled thirst, and sweat through the blazing sun in the middle of the Pacific. On the north side of the island, Marines continued the advance to gain control of "Sulfur Island" (the Japanese name for Iwo Jima) against American-educated, Japanese General Tadimichi Kuribayashi. To the southwest, Joe's segregated unit went about their daily routines, despite the certainty the enemy was still scattered within Mt. Suribachi, filled with undetected tunnel systems.

Previously classified Japanese Defense Sectors, Iwo Jima.
(U.S. Department of War)

On the other side of the small island, evidence of the carnage and chaos of D-Day's early hours was still littered along beaches, all within walking distance of Joe's unit. He was unaware of the charred bodies, the remains of the Higgins boats along the coastline, or the Jeeps stuck deep in sand. Amazingly, Joe's unit never lost a man and none of them were injured on Iwo.

"First, you have a power structure in the service that doesn't see you as a group that's making a contribution to the fighting of this war. You are the guy that picks up the cans—you're ancillary. Second, the mechanism for getting people information was not instant the way it is now. It would be days before information would get out from certain areas. Plus, I don't think they felt it was necessary to give us all the information as to what was happening," Joe said. "It's an indication of what the 'powers that be' thought of us as a unit."

Two officers ran sickbay within the plateau camp. Joe visited once, when he had to go for a routine checkup. Other than that required visit to get another inoculation, he remained healthy and on just one other occasion would he visit medics during his time on Iwo.

EVEN WITH THE TIME LOST ON THE MEN FIGHTING AND serving on Iwo, many of them remember the days surrounding April 12, 1945. Joe and his men listened to a radio broadcast and learned President Franklin Roosevelt had died. The country was still at war, they were all thousands of miles away from home, and now they had lost a wartime president, their commander-in-chief. The unit was informed in a timely manner, in a group setting.

When Joe found out about FDR, he was saddened. While many blacks in those days were Republican because Abraham Lincoln had freed the slaves, Joe is still proud to say he remains a Roosevelt Democrat.

By mid-April, the flag over the 5th Marine Division cemetery, about two miles from Joe's camp, flew at half-staff in tribute to the late president. Row after row of meticulously placed white crosses rested at the top of freshly turned dirt, piled a foot high and eight feet long. While Joe's encounters with death were limited, other blacks on Iwo were charged with filling mass graves with the dead. Mass graves were usually filled 20 at a time, the heads on bodies pointed in the direction of the American flag.

★

ON THE PLATEAU, THE SMALL TENT CITY OPERATED AS planned. It was here Joe was assigned a new job, as an assistant inside the carpentry shop. As a gopher, he would haul 2x4s, 2x6s, planks, wood, and other imported construction material around in the crude lumberyard. The 23rd Seabees were tasked with constructing makeshift structures, while others in the unit were stevedores, responsible for unloading ships, working the docks, and transporting goods.

It was on the plateau where Joe noticed the flies. They were much bigger than ones he'd seen at home. These were big, green flies—bigger, Joe surmised because of the death on the island. The carnage was everywhere and a putrid smell consistently filled the air.

They spent four months in this new, sandy, dusty plateau area up from the beach. Joe and a fellow Seabee shared a canvas tent, about 8x10 feet in size, with a slit for an entrance. To enter, they had to stoop down and walk inside.

The days were long and arduous and during normal work hours, they left their carbine rifles and .44s by their cots and went about their duties in the secure sector of the island. Each Seabee tent had two cots but lacked even basics like tables and lights. Wool blankets were issued but because of the consistently warm temperatures, the men usually slept on top in their shorts. When it came to personal hygiene, it was up to each man to decide how they would use their two canteens of water per day. Shaving and teeth brushing had to come from this precious supply of water; the result was constant, itchy stubble or full-grown beards. On the plateau, the Seabees built a shower system comprised of half-barrels that tilted and spilled water but bathing was extremely infrequent. As the front expanded on the north side of the island, American troops took over Japanese-built water purification systems. Slowly, water became more readily available.

Six segregated African-American soldiers on Iwo Jima March 11, 1945.
(National Archives)

When time permitted, the men would gamble in their tents and tell stories of back home: girlfriends, mamas and papas, the best food, and favorite sports. Dice were prevalent, carried easily in a uniform pocket, and several decks of cards made their way around camp for poker games. Joe played five-card stud and deuces and in most every game, one-eyed jacks and a variety of other cards were wild. It was common for guys to win with five aces, which caused laughter and anger within the same game.

Most everyone on Iwo had their paychecks withheld but if they took a draw off their monthly salary, the Seabees were paid in Japanese currency. It was quite a sight to see those poker games inside the tents, with the pot of money piled high in paper yen and sen. The men gambled with Japanese money and really didn't know what they were winning or losing because the currency—which looked like newspaper clippings—made no sense to them.

Joe hated losing, so he didn't gamble as much as others in his unit. Some men lost their entire paychecks in card games and that was just too rich for Joe's blood. Despite not physically carrying cash, Joe had more money than at any other time up to that point in his life and he knew a part of his earnings were going back—with a government contribution—to his father.

On the rare occasion when Joe did take money out on Iwo, it was for an occasional card game or to buy small items like cigarettes and candy from the makeshift PX. By this time, he smoked a pack every two to three days; the habit set him back ten cents a pack.

Despite the iconic images of pinup pictures in B-17 cockpits and soldiers with pictures of their girl inside the top of their helmets, Joe didn't have a single memento of home. He had no pictures of any kind because back home they couldn't afford any.

There were occasions when the men of the 23rd were able to see newsreels from back home, right there on Iwo Jima. The Seabees, an ingenious bunch, would hang a sheet against a tent as someone manned the film projector. This was the only visual clue of the war's progression. However, they were able to hear the music from back home via the radio—via the enemy. Several radios were scattered about in tent city and many of the men gathered around the small devices to listen to the infamous Tokyo Rose.

Beginning around 6:00 p.m. every night, the sounds of Duke Ellington, Count Basie, Benny Goodman, and Tommy Dorsey could be heard coming from the tents, all lined up just a few hundred yards from mass carnage.

"Tokyo Rose would play the music and then come on and talk about your girlfriend or your wife in a real sultry, sweet voice. 'Jody' was the guy that didn't go into the service; Jody was the guy that was going to bed with your wife or your girlfriend back home.

She'd say, 'Jody is now listening to this beautiful music back home with your girl.' We sat there listening to this, and it was supposed to get you so riled up you didn't know what to do. It was stupid but that's what she did. And she told you via the radio how the Japanese were going to kill all of us. We heard how after the Japanese took the island, they'd be able to muster all the survivors and fit them in a telephone booth."

The broadcasts even periodically targeted segregated units on Iwo and reminded the black units they couldn't even enter a home in the U.S. via the front door. *The enemy is your friend,* she'd say. Despite the serious propaganda, the black Seabees were amused by the Tokyo Rose broadcasts and listened every evening—usually 75 minutes in length with 15 to 20 minutes of commentary scattered in-between the music.

The men came to the point where they actually looked forward to what she was going to say and what type of music she'd play. However, Joe noticed that on certain evenings, her psychological warfare succeeded. Many men would often stare off into the night, wondering if their girls back home still loved them and if they would live to see another day on Iwo Jima.

CARPENTRY WAS NEVER JOE'S CHOICE BUT HE DIDN'T really have one. His attempts to become a truck driver failed, though daily he would pester Brad, the dispatcher—a short, white guy with red hair who became part of Joe's unit only after he arrived on Iwo. Even though Joe had a good relationship with Brad, Joe' persistence to be a driver never paid off on Iwo and he went about his support role.

Without a construction background, Joe still performed admirably on his job. At times, under the open carpentry shop tent, Joe looked out to see trucks roll by down dusty, bumpy roads. Occasionally, he would see flatbed trucks full of Japanese prisoners. Sometimes the trucks would stop and the Japanese would file out under strict guard and clean the area of debris. Joe watched the men under supervision and took notice from what he witnessed that they were all treated humanely. Japanese prisoners, however, were rare to see. They were told to kill themselves before being taken prisoner. *Honor.*

The weeks dragged on at times and the death toll diminished rapidly but the damage had been done. More people died per square foot on Iwo Jima than any other battle in the Pacific Theatre. From February 19 to March 26, 1945, the United States' losses totaled nearly 7,000 with more than 19,000 wounded. The Japanese' losses were staggering, with more than 22,000 killed. Countless Japanese soldiers killed themselves in order to avoid capture, reflected in the fact that U.S. forces took just 216 Japanese prisoners of war.

THE CONSTRUCTION SHOP ON THE PLATEAU WAS NOTHING special. It was a busy place and ran on a tight schedule of projects but the crew was limited in the amount of work that could be done in a war zone. One day as Joe stood by, an officer came in under the tent to talk with the carpenter. The officer walked past the table saws, workbenches, and stored materials, paying no attention to Joe. Unbeknownst to the whites on Iwo, the black men had a code word for them: *Headquarters.*

Joe stood to the side as the fast-speaking LTJG spoke and didn't let the carpenter get a word in edgewise.

"Finally, he realized he wasn't letting the carpenter respond and he paused and said, 'Boy, I'm talking like a nigger.' He instantly looked at me when he said the word. I walked away. A bit later, I asked him for some time to speak with him in his office."

Joe took a huge risk. Here was an uneducated teenager from Mississippi, on Iwo Jima, requesting a meeting with a superior naval officer so he could relay his feelings about hearing the word "nigger."

The following day, Joe made an appointment to see the white officer at headquarters and to his surprise, the LTJG knew the context of the meeting. When it came time, Joe walked across the tent city and into an extremely vulnerable position. The mild-mannered Joe LaNier, the loner, the young man who didn't think much more than a few minutes ahead, was about to have a confrontation over a racial slur.

He went in and told the officer how he felt. The tone was respectful and Joe kept his emotions in check.

"I told him I felt awful about him using that term. Here we were doing our part to help win this war and to hear him say that was derogatory. I told him this was just terrible and I was insulted he would say that when we were all trying to make a real contribution to this war. I was really hurt when he said that. Why would you say that?"

The LTJG apologized.

Joe told me he truly believed his superior was sorry. He never saw the man again after Iwo.

As such, Joe never referred to the enemy as "Japs." Other members of his unit, particularly his superiors, consistently used the term. This has been the case with many of the veterans I have worked with over the years and some hold deep-seated resentment that is now decades old. Some of these Iwo survivors have spent years full of resentment toward the Japanese enemy: no Japanese-made cars, televisions, or friends.

"I understand what referring to them as *Japs* meant because I know what that feels like. It has a lot to do with 'nigger.' It's an interesting parallel but I have a different philosophy," Joe said.

He spent two months in the carpentry shop before he was transferred to the kitchen area.

THE IRONY FOR JOE AND MEMBERS OF THE 23RD IS THAT their color likely saved their lives. The odds of getting killed or injured on Iwo Jima were nearly fifty-fifty and other white Navy Seabee units took on casualty rates of as high as 75 percent. Joe came to realize that being segregated in war might have actually saved his life.

Joe remains a proud American and seven decades later still takes pride in his service, despite the military racial inequality he experienced from the moment he enlisted to the day he was discharged. He swears he never once questioned why he was fighting for his country, despite the racial divide.

Though the black Seabees were insulated from frontline combat, they could sense the tide of the battle was turning. Loud artillery fire would ring out occasionally at Joe's end of the island but when it was quiet, it was a matter of strict routine. The intensity level had dropped considerably where they worked, ate, and slept. The American flag flew proudly on Mt. Suribachi. Many of the ships—more than 450 off the Iwo coast during the initial stage of the invasion—had left to fight other battles and the talk among soldiers, Marines, and within the Seabees surrounded what was next in the war effort. After Iwo Jima, the next logical step was an invasion of Okinawa and Japan.

Joe was actually a bit upset when the war ended because in his mind he had visualized going to Japan.

"We needed to cut off the head of the snake. It never occurred to me the death that had already happened or the death that would ensue but I was ready to go because I wanted to see it."

AT THE CHOW HALL, JOE WORKED A FULL DAY SERVING fellow blacks and white officers breakfast, dinner, and supper. Joe had flashbacks of his previous food-service work and felt it was demeaning to be a server. When he was 14, he worked at the Straight Eight Café in downtown Columbus: seven days a week, 12 hours a day for $3.50 a week, plus a meal. He was there a month when he asked the owner, a large woman named Ms. Mary, for a raise. Joe's co-workers were making $5.00 a week and he wanted equal pay.

She fired him on the spot.

On Iwo Jima, apron around his torso, Joe set up food lines with different items and served hundreds of meals a day, plus desserts. There was no fresh fruit. They drank water and powdered milk, which Joe despised. Daily menus were set and the staple was Spam. There was Spam 'n eggs for breakfast, Spam 'n beans for dinner, and Spam croquettes for supper. Needless to say, Joe hasn't tasted Spam since the war.

He scrubbed dishwashing equipment and again developed a daily routine. It was monotonous and he lost that feeling of importance in serving his country.

As he turned in for bed one night in the spring of 1945, something happened that sent the teenager into a fit of sheer terror. An air-raid siren began its low, distinctive howl and the camp went into defense mode. The moon was full as a squadron of Japanese planes opened fire on the island and ships below.

"I heard the siren go off. My tent faced the west. All of a sudden, as we were getting out of our tents, I heard antiaircraft fire. As I climbed out, the sky was filled with bright, fast-moving tracer bullets. The weapons were firing down by the beach because Japanese fighters were going after our supply lines and our ships. It was like the Fourth of July. I was scared but not the kind of scared I experienced when San Francisco dropped behind the horizon as our ship left the U.S."

Joe's naiveté of war was never as obvious as that night in mid-May, 1945, on the island of Iwo Jima.

"I knew on an airplane, the tips of its wings had red lights on them. So when the glowing, spent tracer bullets fell to the ground, they floated back. People were out frantically taking positions, the siren was wailing, and I looked up as two lights were falling straight at me. I had never seen that before. I thought a plane was about to crash right on top of me. It was the first time I had seen any tracer bullets in all my months in the Navy. So I took off going in the opposite direction, running in my white underwear, and all of a sudden, I realized I didn't know what direction I was going. I had left everything in my tent and I was gone like a bat outta hell," he laughed.

"Then I realized where the camp was and I had to get back. What's funny is that earlier we had said, 'We might get attacked tonight—there's a full moon.' It wasn't too comforting. It was really the only time in two years in the service—in a combat situation—that I was frightened. It scared the hell out of me. To the point of, 'I could die.'"

Bullets and explosions were all around Joe. *This is like the movies,* he thought. Several hundred yards away, a Japanese plane was hit by antiaircraft fire and whistled and whizzed into the ocean in a ball of flames. The action was intense, and it was close.

U.S. batteries with high-caliber weapons opened fire up into the moonlit, Pacific night. Heavy guns mounted both on Iwo and on warships off the coast blazed during the 20-minute air raid. At times, the planes seemed to peel out of the moon itself, from east to west and then headed north. Joe guessed 15 to 20 Japanese Zeros were involved in the raid. Antiaircraft fire shot down just one that night.

When it was over, Joe walked back to his tent, over its plywood floor, climbed into his cot, and slept soundly. Two weeks later, another Japanese plane came in over Iwo but this time the men of the 23rd Seabees stayed calm and watched from a distance as Zeros tried to attack U.S. ships protecting supply lines. Once again, tracers and antiaircraft fire lit up the night sky.

Over the course of his final two months, Joe continued his work in the chow hall and in his downtime he started to write Papa a bit more frequently. His tone was casual and he never indicated how he longed for home or how he was in harm's way. The information was generic because the men sending letters out from the war zone knew the military censors would eventually go through every word of their correspondence. Every now and then, a letter would come from home but predictably the information was long outdated by the time it arrived on Iwo Jima. Joe wrote perhaps ten letters in the service and in two years received even less.

The plateau camp continued to run smoothly. By now, most of the Japanese were dead. The daily fighting had stopped and the Marines had deemed Iwo Jima "secure."

The Seabees camp was adjacent to an all-white Army post and due to the segregated compounds, Joe and his fellow sailors saw little of their white counterparts. A barbed-wire fence ran between the two camps, attached to wooden posts pounded into the ground every few yards. Both outposts faced the ocean, northwest toward Japan. There was an elevated submachine gun positioned inside a circle of sandbags near the coast bordering the two camps, with two white soldiers on guard around-the-clock.

By this point, Joe felt more comfortable about taking his routine walks down to the ocean. The walks were longer and the time near the ocean's edge lasted a bit more on his days off. On these walks, he would occasionally see body parts coming out of the sand and along dirt roads—an arm here, a leg there. Even so, he would daydream as the surf rolled in and out, his head full of random thoughts.

ONE AFTERNOON AS HE MADE THE RETURN TRIP BACK TO camp, he saw a man to his north. The man continued to move up the plateau, toward the two compounds.

It was a Japanese soldier, dressed in a white uniform with a white sash adorned with hundreds of red stitches, tied around his waist. It was a *senninbari-haramaki,* a traditional strip of cloth—a good-luck charm—likely stitched by the man's loved ones back home on mainland Japan. Thousands of these cloths were made for Japanese soldiers and the majority of them were stitched with the slogan *bu-un cho-kyu* or "eternal good luck in war."

The enemy took a few more steps toward the U.S. compounds and then the distinct, loud, cutting sound of machine gun fire filled the afternoon air. The soldiers waited until he got just a few yards away and unloaded.

"Gone. I saw them cut him down."

Joe watched the man fall to the ground and die instantly. The enemy was armed and was not trying to surrender. Within five minutes, Joe walked down to the dead Japanese soldier and was met there by the two white Army soldiers who had opened fire.

No one said a word as they all stood above the body. Despite the machine gun death, there was surprisingly little blood.

Joe turned from the body and didn't look back. He walked back to camp and prepared for dinner. That night, there were no nightmares. They never came. Joe never shed a tear in two years in the Navy, yet that sunny afternoon remains an image he still carries with him today.

"Looking back, it does make me sad so many died that didn't need to die. But freedom is not free. Somebody has to pay for that. Sometimes I wonder, 'Why was that not me? Why was I fortunate?'"

Joe never prayed on Iwo—not one time, even though he still possessed that Navy-issued King James Bible, the same one he had in his sea bag as he climbed down the rope ladder on February 23, 1944. Yet within his outfit, two Seabees took it upon themselves to act as preachers. They would proselytize anyone within earshot and they also talked about their congregations back home. In their home pews, they battled a common enemy in Satan but here in the Pacific they fought another powerful enemy in the Empire of Japan.

There was no way for any soldier, sailor, or Marine on the lines to have the knowledge that as every day that passed, the United States was a day closer to dropping atomic bombs on Japan. The airfield in the middle of Iwo was now secure and busy with Army Air Corps activity—the smaller P-51 fighters and B-29 "Superfortress" bombers were parked wing-tip to wing-tip across the landing strips and tarmacs. Large, thick plumes of black smoke were often seen rising from the airfield due to crashes and emergency landings. Motoyama Airfield #1 was to the east of the plateau camp.

"We were almost in the flight lines. You would know when there had been a successful raid because the P-51s would fly over Iwo Jima, then fly straight up in the air for what seemed like forever and then come straight down and peel off. Showboating. You would feel..." Joe paused. He then resumed after briefly collecting his thoughts.

"You would feel so safe. You would feel so safe with those kinds of maneuvers taking place."

He was fascinated by the twin-fuselage P-38 "Lightings" he would see flying above. Despite being so close, the blacks of the 23rd were never allowed to go near the airfield. Joe watched the big B-29s as they came in for landings after long missions and it was obvious when there were accidents at Motoyama. The sight of smoke in the air was never a good sign.

Joe was also able to identify the B-24s, the P-61 Black Widows, the P-51s, and B-29s. When they came in over Mt. Suribachi and the plateau camp, they landed to their northeast.

THE WEEKS ON IWO JIMA HAD NOW TURNED INTO MONTHS of living on that dusty, acrid island. In mid-July, the LTJG gathered the men of the 23rd to inform them they were moving on to another "destination unknown." Joe didn't need an explanation. He wasn't eager to leave Iwo Jima but wasn't connected with the place, either. The fact remained—Joe LaNier was better off socially and economically in the Navy than he was back home in Mississippi and the same could be said for the rest of the 23rd. Their time on Iwo was coming to an end and they began the organized teardown of the tent city, while on other parts of the island, cleanup and operations continued.

Over the course of the next two weeks, the tents came down, the dump was cleared out, and matériel was packed in crates headed aboard LSTs (Landing Ship, Tank). Trucks and ammunition were loaded back up and the Mt. Suribachi sector of the island was again bustling with activity. The stevedores, maintenance workers, construction specialists, ensigns, chaplain, and even medical and dental officers all prepared to leave Sulfur Island. Sweaty, dirty men went back and forth countless times from the plateau to the shore, loading and unloading trucks full of supplies. Joe had never seen trucks like these in Mississippi and was fascinated by the size and power of the ones used in transport. He quietly continued to hope someday, in the near future, he would get his wish to drive one. He watched as his home on Iwo Jima disappeared—every bit dismantled and loaded up for the next destination.

It was finally time to leave.

According to previously classified documents, on July 31, 1945, the 23rd received orders "to proceed to IsCom (Island Command) Okinawa for duty."

THE 5TH MARINE DIVISION, OFFICIALLY ACTIVATED JANUARY 21, 1944, at Camp Pendleton, north of San Diego, had come to Iwo Jima from Guam on D-Day, February 19, 1945. As the Marines stormed the northeast Iwo beaches, Joe and the Great Lakes boys were sailing in from the northern Marianas. On Iwo, the 5th sustained 1,098 killed in action and nearly 3,000 wounded; by number, the highest casualty rate among Marine divisions involved in the invasion. On March 21, the 5th Marine Division cemetery was formally dedicated on Iwo Jima as the fighting continued for another five days.

F OR JOE, THERE WERE NO FEELINGS OF EATING A LAST MEAL or taking a final walk near the surf before he headed again to an unknown destination. As his LST transport ship waited at the water's edge, he walked down through the same black, volcanic-ash sand; up a large ramp; and aboard the ship.

He never looked back.

"It was not San Francisco. I was a veteran now. I was ready to go some new place I'd never seen before," he said.

The ships all steamed north, headed toward Japan and the island of Okinawa.

CHAPTER NINE

OKINAWA

THE 23RD SEABEES SAILED AWAY FROM IWO JIMA IN AN enormous flotilla, much larger than the one that brought them to the island. The LST was powered by two large diesel engines and reached speeds of about 12 knots, or about 14 miles an hour. The 23rd was once again segregated below deck where trucks, tanks, ammunition, and provisions also took up valuable space. The LST was more than 300 feet long and carried about 200 passengers and crew, protected by a 76mm cannon, six 40mm Bofors antiaircraft guns, six 20mm guns, and six machine guns.

U.S. Navy ships were everywhere—literally as far as the eye could see. They all moved in unison, spaced evenly over miles of wide-open ocean, and traveled at the same, slow speed. Joe's LST was on the outer edge, with the horizon ahead of them covered with everything from frigates to LSTs to battleships and destroyers. Once again, they were passengers and for many, crossing the Pacific in this enormous convoy made them feel safe.

Joe, at six feet, was still sporting his scrawny, 130-pound frame as he settled in again aboard a transport ship, off to another part of WWII and the Pacific Theatre. This trip, he avoided the seasickness that had ruined so many days of his early journey out of San Francisco Bay.

The men passed the time by doing their own laundry. They would take a rope and tie their clothing to one end. Then, from the ship's top deck, they threw their items overboard and let the natural agitation of the ocean clean their clothes. It never really dawned on them that if someone fell into the ocean, they would likely drown or get eaten by sharks known to swarm this area of the Pacific. Sad was the story of the man who fell overboard during transport, only to be left behind. For those unlucky souls, it was simply a matter of how long they had to live and in what manner they would die. Convoys could not and would not stop. For Joe and his shipmates, this was a non-discussion. They pulled the ropes back up, wrung out the items, and laid them flat on the deck to dry. In the process, Joe never lost a single piece of his government-issued clothing.

The ocean journey north was similar to his previous seafaring, in that he had no idea where they were headed or how long the trip would take. The flotilla was limited in its speed and with the elements, threat of attack, and the distance to Okinawa, it was again about a month-long ordeal.

Below deck, the black men from Great Lakes, relegated to the role of passengers, did not have assigned duties. To pass the time, they again smoked, played cards, rolled dice, and slept on tiny cots, all in tight quarters. There were never updates from senior officers, and war updates or word of the Allied progress was never passed down. Above deck, trucks, flatbeds, small tanks, and crates filled every square inch of space. Tarps covered most every item to protect from the elements. Finally, weeks in, they saw land. The island of Okinawa came plainly into view and the LST slowly advanced on the eastern part of the island.

In a move similar to what happened before they disembarked and landed on Iwo Jima, the XO called the men below deck and gave them a speech. Once again, it was stressed they avoid picking up anything as a souvenir. They were told that the difference between Iwo and Okinawa was that the embattled Japanese island was much larger and the southern end of the island was not completely secure.

Soon after the lecture, it was time to land.

The LST came to rest on a beach where the large steel doors opened onto foreign soil. Once the 30-foot bow of the ship was unlocked, a ramp, lowered by large metal chains, came down to assist in exiting. The *passengers* transformed back into their active military status and then assembled onto designated, flatbed trucks that took them to their new camp.

The 23rd Naval Construction Battalion was still attached to the 5th Marine Division and once more the sailors lived in rows of tents, already assembled but this time with up to three people inside.

★

SHORTLY AFTER THEY ARRIVED ON OKINAWA, THERE WAS A large, daytime explosion that echoed through one of the dumps near Joe's camp. He felt it was sabotage but being of his low rank and black, he was never told. Ammunition was blown to oblivion; luckily, no one was hurt. Guard duty around the dump was increased and security tightened.

Joe still had a burning desire to drive a truck.

The truck shift supervisor knew Joe from his numerous requests to drive on Iwo and decided to finally give him a break. Joe was given the keys to a stick-shift, green Jeep and allowed to drive officers to various parts of the island. It was the first time since his carpentry shop position on Iwo Jima that he did anything of significance and that didn't involve food service. He felt he was a gopher but with keys to an important transport.

The Jeep job went off without a hitch. Joe was prompt, efficient, and pleased his superiors enough that his wish came true: he finally got keys to a *truck*.

He was told he could drive a truck once, as a trial. It was about the size of a modern-day dump truck and the route was back and forth between Camp I and the LSTs parked at the docks.

After a successful trial run, the man whom Joe had pestered the past six months finally gave him an official job upgrade.

Okinawa was under a blackout and Joe's truck-driving shift was at night. There were no headlights; instead, just small slits of light at the front of the vehicles. Headlights proved to be nothing more than targets for Japanese sharpshooters. Road recognition was extremely difficult, even over the relatively short distance between the dump at Camp I and the docks. Joe would pull up to the LSTs where another black Seabee crew would place his load in the back. He never knew his contents.

ONE MEMORABLE NIGHT, HIS BIZARRE SHIFT BEGAN WITH another run to the docks, where an LST was being unloaded and its contents transferred to waiting trucks. Joe was parked in a dirt lot that ran down to the beach. The truck's rear end faced the ocean.

As Joe sat in the musty cab, two strangers approached.

"It's dark. There are no lights. I'm sitting in the cab alone when I notice two guys come up and stop about five feet from me. I never saw their faces but I hear, 'Hey Joe, how do I get to Yellow Beach?' I could see enough to know they wore U.S. Army uniforms, so I told them how to get there. I told them to follow this road down here and pointed to where Yellow Beach was," he recounted.

The Japanese spies spoke perfect English.

The irony of the run-in was the way they addressed the 19-year-old. "Joe" was of course colloquial, as in "G.I. Joe," but it just so happened these two spies got lucky, running into Joe. He never did ask for a password.

"Twenty minutes after I saw them, word came down that they had been captured. That's when I recognized those were the guys that had passed me. It didn't occur to me until later what could have happened to me. I was just trying to help out my fellow soldier," he said.

Joe never told a soul until after the war.

The spies were deep into the U.S. base and were taken into custody near ammunition storage facilities. It was never known if they were responsible for the daytime explosion that destroyed the ammunition in the earlier incident or how the Japanese managed to get their Army clothing.

On another night shift, Joe's truck was loaded with ammunition with orders to take his contents to a new area, up on the frontlines.

Driving alone, he passed an empty Marine sentry and kept rolling. Within seconds bullets began hissing and whizzing across his truck, missing him by just a few feet. He was dressed in his normal clothing, without body armor, save for his helmet. After he rolled about 100 yards into the danger zone, Joe decided to get out as quickly as possible. He slammed the truck, already weighed down by the ammunition load, into reverse. As he traced his route back, he again came upon the sentry location. This time, someone was there.

"So I asked him, 'Why didn't you tell me I was going in the wrong direction?' He told me, 'I figured you'd find out when you got up there.' And I consider that to be American humor. Ol' truck driver Joe got shot at," he chuckled.

In the end, Joe realized he had made a wrong turn that night. He didn't know it but his truck driver career in the U.S. Navy was about to come to an end.

On yet another dark, steamy night on Okinawa, Joe was again alone in the cab doing his trek from the dump back to shore. Because the roads were temporary, they cut through normally saturated fields and coastal areas. During typhoon season, the roads would wash out and even in the best of conditions, would be full of ruts, bumps, and hazards. Bushes, shrubs, and trees lined the military roads and top speeds were never more than perhaps ten to twenty miles an hour. The trucks were weighted down with wooden boxes, canvas bags, equipment, and contents unknown. He would haul things up to five miles and averaged up to four trips per night shift.

He moved slowly along the route, when suddenly the truck listed to the left. It never flipped over but it became stuck in dirt that had been pushed out of the way to make the new road. The teenager was stranded in the middle of potentially hostile territory, in the pitch-black of night. He hoofed it back to base dressed in cut-off pants, a shirt, wool socks, and leather boots. When he finally walked in to the dispatch center underneath a canvas tent, there was some explaining to do. Brad, the dispatcher, sat at his paper-filled, makeshift desk and learned about the mishap. Joe turned in his set of keys and it wasn't long after that he was relieved of his truck duty. Joe never again drove a truck in the military and was later sent to a different camp, but he laughs about it today.

When Joe received all of his personnel records for purposes of this book, he found out he had scored a high of 3.0 (good) and a low of 2.5 (passing) during his truck driving tenure. He received a 4.0 (excellent) rating for his conduct up to the summer of 1945.

T HE BATTLE OF OKINAWA HAD JUST FINISHED PRIOR TO JOE'S arrival on the island, south of mainland Japan. It represented the highest number of casualties anywhere in the Pacific Theatre. From April 1 to June 21, 1945, the intense fighting left more than 12,500 Allied forces dead and nearly 40,000 of them wounded. Japanese losses totaled nearly 100,000 and estimates of up to 150,000 civilians were killed. The numbers were staggering, considering the proximity to Tokyo and perhaps indicated to Washington just how deadly a Japanese invasion would prove to be if U.S. forces tried to take the country from the ground, air, and sea.

Demolition crew from the 6th Marine Division destroy a Japanese cave on Okinawa, May 1945. (National Archives)

While Joe and members of the 23rd spent their final months on Iwo, Okinawa was being blown up and occupied by U.S. and British forces. The Navy engaged in fierce fighting with Japanese kamikazes, as more than 50 vessels and 17 aircraft carriers floated off the coast. Japanese coastal positions fired around the clock, trying to protect from invasion. The battle on land lasted more than 80 days as Army soldiers and Marines moved inland in some of the most hellacious conditions of WWII.

During the Okinawa campaign, word spread during the first part of May 1945, that Allied victory had been declared (V-E Day) in Europe. The fighting on Okinawa would rage another six weeks. The U.S. dropped atomic bombs less than two months after the fighting on Okinawa had subsided.

To this day, Joe appreciates his good fortune on Okinawa. He missed full-fledged action by no more than two weeks and no one in his unit knew of the carnage that preceded them. There were no briefings, especially to those in a black unit.

After the stuck-truck incident, Joe and a few members of the 23rd were transferred from Camp I to Camp II, 20 miles away on the western side of the island. At Camp II, Joe once again found himself serving food in the chow hall, serving his fellow black Seabees. He did that for about a month. From August to December 1945, Joe was assigned to the officers' mess, where he served senior white officers three times a day. When the food was ready in the kitchen, Joe would bring the trays of food to his assigned tables.

"It bothered me from a general point of view. I was among the first black seamen; I had two stripes on my sleeve. I was very proud of that, especially because my predecessors were only able to be in essence, servants. Serving the officers, I felt like a stewards' mate. It was demeaning to me. I was so proud to be among the first blacks to be seamen. I felt like a servant and that's what I didn't like about it. This was telling me where my place was," he said.

Despite his new assignment, he was still proud to wear a Navy uniform.

Joe took orders from officers and then took orders to the kitchen where the meal was prepared. He was a waiter. His only "tip" was when he served at a party one evening. A lieutenant, Foley, ordered a drink, then immediately told Joe (tongue-in-cheek), to "throw it out." What he was trying to do was to get Joe a scotch to enjoy for himself. Not wanting to do anything but what he was told, Joe threw out the drink. Later, Foley asked Joe if he'd liked the drink and when each realized what had happened, they shared a laugh.

Joe received his three meals a day on the job, the 8:00 a.m. to 4:00 p.m. shift, and there he learned a few things. He also gained eight pounds.

"Talk about how things and your environment from long ago can shape you—one day we had butterscotch pudding for dessert. I'd never had that before and didn't know what it was. I'd never heard of regular pudding before and one batch had been scorched. So I thought it was really called butter*scorched* pudding and I liked it!" he said.

Joe had never heard of pancakes, either. They were not a staple in Mississippi but he learned to like them. Officers in Camp II loved to eat pancakes with jam and a side of eggs.

He slept well on Okinawa, even though he had two tent mates. During his downtime, he wandered the camp and again passed the time playing cards, dice, and hanging out with his friends. One activity that surely would have sent them to the brig was making raisin jack. Some of his friends became experts at stealing raisins from the food storage area. They would put the raisins in a container with water and hide the concoction in the forest, where after a few days in the hot sun, it would ferment.

"My immediate supervisor in the kitchen could never figure out why he kept running out of raisins. It was pretty funny because on our days off, you could go out into the woods and smell fermenting raisins all over the place. I actually tasted the stuff when it was ready but I never stole anything. I didn't like alcohol. Other guys we knew who worked on planes would drink 'torpedo juice' from stuff they collected but I never tried that."

The weather was similar to conditions on Iwo Jima but on Okinawa there was considerably more rain. A typhoon roared through while members of the 23rd were there, bringing torrential rain and wind like Joe had never experienced in his young life. The wind was ferocious and came at his back so strong, it was as if he was up against a wall. When the rains came, it was a deluge. He had heard of tornadoes, but never a typhoon.

BASED MOSTLY ON HIS UPBRINGING, JOE REMAINED A LONER. He didn't gravitate toward others, even in his close-knit unit. They never bonded over their trials and tribulations as black men in a white Navy; they never commiserated over their time on Iwo. Joe had lots of people he knew but they were nothing more to him than acquaintances. He was comfortable being alone.

One afternoon at Camp II, Joe took another walk. He followed a path through a wooded area and a few minutes into the trek, he had an unexpected encounter. It was an older woman with two teenagers gathering fruit from nearby trees. The woman was in her early forties, dressed in western clothing, a shawl, and a hat.

It was a friendly exchange, perhaps surprising in that neither expected the other. Joe said hello and they smiled back. He tried to speak with them but they couldn't understand English. They exchanged smiles and waves and Joe kept walking.

It never occurred to him that the situation could have ended differently, considering his run-in with the Japanese spies a few weeks earlier. The irony of the meeting didn't hit Joe until it was pointed out the native Okinawans, or *Ryukyuans*, were considered the "niggers" of the Japanese culture. They were second-class citizens in the eyes of many of the affluent and educated on mainland Japan.

JOE WAS NOT MUCH OF A READER. BECAUSE HE HADN'T completed the ninth grade and had been held back in the third grade, he was anything but a voracious page-turner. On Iwo, there was little free time even if he had wanted to sink into a book. But on Okinawa, he picked up several, among them one by Wisconsin native and author, Bucklin Moon. (In 1945, Moon became the first white writer to publish an anthology of writings by and about black authors in *A Primer for White Folks: An Anthology of Writings by and about Negroes from Slavery to Today's Struggle for a Share in American Democracy.*) Joe also read Mickey Spillane's *I, the Jury* on the island.

On Okinawa, Joe didn't write home any more or less; his family and friends back in Columbus knew he was at war in the Pacific, but they had no idea and could not comprehend how he was living and what he was seeing. It was during the summer of 1945 he corresponded for the first time with a pen pal back in the States. Soldiers in both the Pacific and in Europe randomly received letters from well-wishers; strangers they'd never met.

Religion was a big part of Joe's childhood but it faded during his war years. There was a chaplain assigned to provide spiritual guidance to the black men stationed on Okinawa but there was something missing in his delivery of the Word. They poked fun at Chaplain Roland Rainwater, a white lieutenant, and told him they needed more *Amen's!* and a heck of a lot more hellfire and brimstone, like they were used to back home. Chaplain Rainwater took it well, though he failed miserably at trying to change his delivery and his spiritual message.

One of the lighter moments in Joe's WWII service almost became a painful ordeal. As a child, his family had little access to medical care and he never went in to see a doctor, thus he had never been circumcised. During a routine health exam, a Navy doc on Okinawa told him to get a circumcision but Joe emphatically said no, and that was that. In this medical area of Camp II, Joe also saw nurses—the first women he had seen in a year.

On Okinawa, like on Iwo, bathing facilities consisted of homemade showers, built with those barrel-type devices and a chain to tilt the water down from above. Again, the men had to conserve water but the facilities in Okinawa were better organized and a bit more favorable. Latrines were readily available, with troughs and stalls set up inside.

JOE WAS ON OKINAWA WHEN THE ATOMIC BOMBS WERE dropped, just 634 miles north-northwest of his new location. Hiroshima was bombed August 6, 1945, and three days later, Nagasaki was targeted. Based on memory, Joe recalled one day in early August when he looked out toward the East China Sea.

"I was off duty and I saw a huge plume. I didn't know what that was. I just dismissed it. And later in life I have thought, 'Could that have been what they dropped on Japan?' I remember that, and I have always wondered what it was."

Joe may never know for sure but estimates from tests on other atomic bombs had the radioactive plume initially hitting 20,000 feet and then gradually increasing to 50,000 feet in the air—nearly ten miles into the atmosphere. Joe was closer to both atomic bombs than nearly every American alive today.

As the shock and awe of the atomic bombs overwhelmed the Japanese, negotiations to end the war began almost immediately. Japanese Emperor Hirohito agreed to the Potsdam Declaration, which had been set three weeks earlier. On August 14, the Emperor recorded his speech—the *Gyokuon-hoso* 大東亜戦争終結ノ詔書 or "Jewel Voice Broadcast"—on a phonograph and told his country Japan had agreed to surrender. Within the inner circles, it was officially called the *Imperial Rescript on the Termination of War.*

It was replayed the following day to the Japanese people and to the world:

After pondering deeply the general trends of the world and the actual conditions obtaining in Our Empire today, We have decided to effect a settlement of the present situation by resorting to an extraordinary measure. We have ordered Our Government to communicate to the Governments of the United States, Great Britain, China and the Soviet Union that Our Empire accepts the provisions of their Joint Declaration. To strive for the common prosperity and happiness of all nations as well as the security and well-being of Our subjects is the solemn obligation which has been handed down by Our Imperial Ancestors and which lies close to Our heart.

The speech continued, as millions around the globe hung on his every word:

Moreover, the enemy has begun to employ a new and most Cruel bomb, the power of which to do damage is, indeed, incalculable, taking the toll of many innocent lives. Should We continue to fight, not only would it result in an ultimate collapse and obliteration of the Japanese nation, but also it would lead to the total extinction of human civilization.

The Emperor addressed the men and others who died in fields of battle and the innocent civilians who died in the four years of war. He acknowledged the hardships of their past and the "long road" ahead. He concluded:

Having been able to safeguard and maintain the structure of the Imperial State, We are always with you, Our good and loyal subjects, relying upon your sincerity and integrity. Unite your total strength, to be devoted to construction for the future. Cultivate the ways of rectitude, foster nobility of spirit, and work with resolution —so that you may enhance the innate glory of the Imperial State and keep pace with the progress of the world.

Joe remembers the news and how it spread through Camp II that hot, muggy day. He remained in what he called "adventure mode" and actually wanted to head to Japan, but the surrender meant a celebratory change of plans.

I N THE U.S. THE NEWS ARRIVED AUGUST 14, 1945. THERE were victory celebrations in cities and towns, big and small, as families and farmers, industrial workers, and teachers, the rich and the poor, the young, the old and the middle-aged all gathered around their radios to hear welcomed news.

Bottles of Ballentine's Beer were raised in the Officer's Club at Naval Air Station, Beaufort, South Carolina. A soldier walked down a street in Washington, D.C., son clutched in his left arm as his wife read the headline in the newspaper. At the Naval Amphibious Base, Manus, in the Admiralty Islands, blacks and whites in the 22nd Seabees listened to the special radio broadcast coming from Tokyo.

Outside on the base, black sailors made an impromptu sign and held it high for all to see: *War is over! Good-Bye Pacific. Hello USA.* On Guam, Japanese prisoners of war stood at attention,

The War is over! Enlisted African-Americans aboard the USS Ticonderoga (CV-14) after hearing of Japan's surrender. August 14, 1945.
(National Archives)

some with bowed heads, as the speech was transmitted through barbed-wire fence. There were fireworks above Leyte Gulf in the Philippines. Men below deck broke out into spontaneous dance and screams of joy aboard the USS Bougainville (CVE-100) in the central Pacific. On cots below decks on the USS Wileman (DE-22) sailors were so happy they made sure to crowd in front of a camera to capture the moment.

In China, members of the U.S. Coast Guard celebrated with locals and drank rice wine in Area VI, while others attended a "peace" Mass. The U.S. Third Fleet readied to take positions off the Japanese coast. "Helldiver" bomber pilots pounded their planes with their open palms, ecstatic they would no longer plan for Japanese bombing runs. They lit victory cigars at Camp Pendleton. Newspaper headlines read "JAPAN GIVES UP." In New York's Times Square, a sailor grabbed a woman in a white dress, bent her backwards, and kissed her on the lips. Car horns honked on Main Street in Columbus, Mississippi.

WITHIN SEVERAL WEEKS OF THE SURRENDER, JOE WAS told with the war over, he could re-enlist and pick his theatre. After some thought, he walked down to a specific tent at Camp II to inform his superiors he had decided to make it a Navy career. He wanted to be sent to post-war France, though besides knowing his name was French he had no connection with the country, other than hearing about it while he was stationed at Pearl.

Joe walked into an administrative tent and talked with the person sitting at another makeshift desk. He explained his desire to be transferred to Europe but was met with a quick and resounding "no." Joe was disappointed. He didn't say a thing as he turned around and walked back out of the tent, dejected.

"I was going to make a career out of the Navy. What else was I going to do? I was only in the second half of the ninth grade and I was almost 20-years-old. So what was I to do? I was a country boy.

I was not an athlete, so there was no scholarship available. I wasn't a straight-A student, so no academic scholarships were available. I then remembered meeting the *Golden Thirteen* back at Great Lakes, and I could see myself as an officer. Boy, that uniform...." Joe mused.

He thought his education was over, yet he knew in order to advance in life he needed to complete high school. He knew there must be a better way.

After the disappointment, there was a glimmer of hope.

As Joe sat on his cot, thousands of miles from Mississippi, he contemplated what he would do when he got back home. Within a few days, word filtered down via a memo that men involved in WWII were eligible for the G.I. Bill—known officially as the *Servicemen's Readjustment Act of 1944.* More than a year after it had become law, the Seabees heard about it for the first time.

"They told us and I wanted to know all about it. I followed up. It was an opportunity. Without it, I would have gone back home and dug ditches the rest of my life. I went to HQ and they told me if I went back to school, I would get $90.00 a month and they'd pay for my books and tuition. I said to myself, 'If you don't take advantage of this, you've got to be dumb,'" he laughed.

The Japanese officially surrendered in a ceremony aboard the USS Missouri (BB-63) in Tokyo Bay September 2, 1945. As the world rejoiced, Joe was focused on the G.I. Bill. His final two months at Camp II on Okinawa were as routine as they could be in the weeks post-war, with menial assignments that filled the hours of the day. A month later, unbeknownst to them at the time—on October 29, 1945—their unit was awarded the "World War II Victory Medal" and authorized to wear the special ribbon.

IN EARLY NOVEMBER 1945, JOE DID SOMETHING OUT OF HIS norm, something that caused a Mississippi flashback. Dressed in cutoffs, he decided to join his friends from the 23rd at a nearby saltwater lagoon on a warm, sunny fall afternoon. His friends were going for a swim.

They all walked down to the calm water when in jumped two of Joe's friends. Joe was no more comfortable in the water than before but he had to be one of the guys, so he took off his shirt, socks, and shoes and went into the warm water. About halfway across, Joe had a Mississippi mud hole flashback and felt he wasn't going to make it. He eventually did but was the last one out of the water. Tired and scared, he quickly realized his swim trip was only half-completed. How would he get back to the other side?

Luckily, a local fisherman in his fifties was nearby, floating in a small, homemade skiff. They flagged him down and hitched a ride back across the lagoon with him. With one oar, he got them back to where they began. He was a godsend to the boy from Mississippi, who could still barely swim.

Joe climbed out, thanked the local, and put on his shoes and socks. It was the last time he swam in the war and he never went back to the lagoon again.

FOUR DAYS AFTER THANKSGIVING 1945, WORD FINALLY came: they would leave Camp II and head the 20 miles back to Camp I to spend their final days on the island. The directive to the Seabees was to pack up their personal belongings and head back to where they had started on Okinawa. The packing didn't take long since all their belongings were in one green sea bag.

Thanksgiving dinner had been served the previous Thursday in camp; the usual military holiday meal was presented in a low-key manner with turkey, potatoes, gravy, and dessert. Joe picked at the food on his plate and thought about going home.

"The future was out there," he reflected. "I was going to have to deal with it."

CHAPTER TEN

A HOMECOMING

T HE MORNING OF WEDNESDAY, DECEMBER 5, 1945, JOE AND members of the 23rd woke from their cots and packed up their bags for the final time on Okinawa. The early morning sun cut through the trees and cast shadows on the manmade dirt roads used for transport. The truck Joe stuck in the dirt berm several months prior was parked, its engine cold. The woman Joe came upon in the field was within a few miles, up early making breakfast for her family. The fisherman who helped three young black teenagers across the lagoon went about his business and prepared for another morning of fishing. The dishes, bourbon glasses, and the silverware inside the officers' tent were packed. Some 600 miles to the northwest, in Hiroshima, radiation continued to sizzle skin and the cells of those who survived the atomic blast. There on Okinawa, the birds chirped as dawn broke. Inside Camp I, the tops of canvas tents had a soft glow as the sun began to illuminate what had been home to members of the 23rd.

It was time to board ship and head back to the United States.

They had survived the Pacific Theatre and WWII.

Joseph Conklin LaNier II left Camp I in much the same manner he had left Iwo Jima four months earlier—he never looked back. They sat in familiar positions in the back of flatbed trucks, bags at their feet. They drove down bumpy, dusty dirt roads back to the harbor and there, they saw their transport back home. It was another converted merchant vessel similar to the one they boarded more than a year earlier, at both San Francisco Bay and at Iroquois Point, north of Pearl Harbor.

There was little talk. There was no celebratory mood. Joe remained the youngest person aboard and one of just a handful in his unit who had volunteered to enter the Navy. From Great Lakes through Hawaii, to Iwo to Okinawa, the vast majority of men were there because they had been drafted. Joe signed up himself.

Aboard ship, officers again offered no information and they all soon set off to another "destination unknown." This time, though, their destination was somewhere in the United States. They knew they were going home but would it be via Los Angeles? San Francisco? San Diego? Seattle? They didn't know and they certainly weren't told.

The merchant ship pulled out of the harbor and headed out east into the Pacific Ocean. Below deck, they settled in for their ride back and most men repeated what they had done so many times before. They had their three meals per day, slept on small cots covered in wool blankets, and passed the time with card games and talk of the future. Joe was focused on returning home to complete his ninth grade education. He planned to tackle college after that, supported by the G.I. Bill.

THE NEARLY 6,000 MILE TRIP BACK TO THE MAINLAND U.S. took half the time it took on the way out. The ship made it from Okinawa to the wooded, rocky shore of the Pacific Northwest, off the Oregon coast, in just about two weeks. At the mouth of the scenic Columbia River, north of Astoria, Oregon, Joe's ship headed inland. At first, they traveled east and then continued south, past wooded riverbanks and small river towns. To sail into Portland, they turned right and followed the Willamette River to their destination. The number of pine and spruce trees overwhelmed many of the men from the South, many of whom had never been west of their own states back home.

The men were not aware they were headed into Portland, Oregon.

Joe had never heard of it and was equally in awe of their route back to the United States. He never dreamed a big ship could navigate a river and he had absolutely no idea where he was.

On a cloudy, chilly afternoon, they sailed into a terminal at the Port of Portland. Despite being an inland city, its yards produced more than 450 ships during WWII and employed 150,000 people by 1944. Most lived near the port in government-built housing as they contributed to the war effort.

Joe stood on deck in his dungaree denim jeans as he took in the new sights and adjusted to the stark climate change. The men hadn't touched land since they took their final steps off Okinawa and were ready to return to American civilization, but they were immediately quarantined for two weeks inside a warehouse along the river. Rows and rows of cots lined the huge warehouse floor in the area officially known as the "receiving barracks." They weren't locked in but they all knew they couldn't leave.

Liberty was still 14 days away and in that time frame, the 23rd received booster shots every few days to prevent the possible spread of illness the men may have brought back with them. Similar to Great Lakes and on Iwo, white doctors administered the shots.

They passed the time as best they could with three meals a day, idle conversation, and card games but there was no P.T. The unit remained bored for two weeks and they were all anxious for liberty. For those two weeks, they never left the building. *Get it over with,* Joe thought.

The dissemination of information was once again kept to a minimum and for all they knew, they could remain in the warehouse another month. It was really nothing more than a holding pen for the men who were still thousands of miles from home; to make matters worse, it was just days before Christmas.

Inside the warehouse, there was no Christmas tree or sign of the holiday. The "holiday" meal was a little better but that was the extent of Christmas 1945 in Portland. There was no Christmas party. It was just another day.

WORD FINALLY CAME THAT THEY HAD CLEARED THEIR quarantine and could leave the warehouse on liberty. Joe wanted to experience Portland.

"Late one afternoon, just before sunset, in my dress uniform, I walked out of the warehouse and caught a bus to downtown. I went alone. When I got there, I got off the bus and standing on a street corner, I looked up and saw the Royal Palm Café, lit up in blue neon."

Bespectacled as usual and crisply dressed, Joe was drawn to the restaurant as he walked up the sidewalk. The Navy had paid them back at the warehouse and inside his pocket Joe carried $130 in cash—the most money he'd ever carried, or had. The Royal Palm would become the first integrated restaurant he'd ever been in and the first restaurant overall since Hawaii. He had no clue as to the status of race relations in Oregon.

As had become almost second nature, he did a quick survey of his surroundings and looked for signs of any blatant discrimination. There were literally no signs and no separate entrances. Christmas decorations and lights filled the downtown area and the air was cold and clean. The city was lifeless, which was not surprising since it was the week between Christmas and New Year's. It was December 26, 1945.

Joe walked through the front door of the Royal Palm and into the empty restaurant and seeing no one, he took a seat at an open table. The kitchen door swung open and in walked an employee. She was an attractive black woman in her thirties and Joe felt at ease knowing there was no segregation.

"She came up to the table and said hello. I smiled, said hello, and I asked her, 'Do you have any buttermilk and cornbread?' And she told me, 'I think I could have them fix that.'"

Joe's order was a simple staple in the South, but he hadn't tasted the tanginess of buttermilk or felt the crumble of fresh cornbread on his tongue in more than five years. The last time he'd had the combo, Mama had served it at home in Columbus.

As Joe waited for his order, outside the sun was sinking low and darkness began to fall. It was peaceful and an unspoken holiday spirit filled the air. Then it was time to eat. Since it wasn't on the menu, Joe remains adamant the friendly waitress left the restaurant and went to purchase the buttermilk and cornbread offsite, just for him. After a long wait, it arrived in a bowl. He felt at home.

Many Portland residents at the time, particularly in the restaurant business, seemed to cater to those returning from war, especially if they were in uniform. As he ate, he told her where he was from and that he was on his way home from the war. He related that for some reason, he didn't want to be on the train New Year's Day but planned to leave after the holiday. They hit it off and she eventually invited Joe to stay with her and her husband until he left Portland.

Joe gladly—if not incredulously—accepted the offer from the complete stranger. She gave him her address, something that still baffled him as he recapped the story.

About 90 minutes after he walked in, he finished his bowl and conversation, and paid his half-dollar tab. He tipped well after the memorable post-holiday meal and took her information.

The waitress told Joe that her husband, Charles, was a drummer in a band at a nearby nightclub, in the black section of Portland. The man was crippled, with one leg shorter than the other. He was known in the city's black jazz circles as "Gimpy." With money in his pocket, he said goodbye, walked out of the Royal Palm, and headed down a few blocks to meet a new friend.

Joe turned a few corners and came up to the club. He saw people milling around the entrance and could hear music coming from inside. He blended in with the crowd and walked inside. During that time period, no one really thought twice about seeing someone in Navy dress blues walking around town. Once he was in, Joe stood near the back and caught the final number before intermission. Gimpy was the band's leader and was prominently positioned on stage, behind his drum kit. When the song finished, the band left the stage and a black comedian came up to entertain the audience and resume his role as the evening's emcee.

The comedian told jokes and poked fun at Astoria, Oregon—the small city Joe and the 23rd passed as they entered the mouth of the Columbia River. Joe can remember most of the punchlines in the jokes emphasized the "ass" in Astoria. The crowd laughed along with him. Joe liked the guy, particularly because he respected the service members on liberty who were there in the audience. The black band came back to the stage.

It was a mixture of races inside the club but most people were black. They were served alcoholic and non-alcoholic drinks at the bar and small, round-top tables were scattered in front. Joe just watched, never ordering a drink, and when the time was right, he went up to the drummer and introduced himself. He was warmly greeted by Charles and told he was welcome to stay with the family through New Year's. It remains a vivid memory—this family reaching out and helping a stranger who had just served his country thousands of miles away. It was as if this was their tiny contribution to the war effort.

Curfew approached quickly, so he said goodbye and made his way out and back to the bus line, then on to the warehouse.

The next day, Joe came back to downtown Portland and took another walk, this time down a different street. Holiday decorations were still inside storefront windows, and as he walked down the block, he saw a black man shining shoes on the sidewalk outside a barbershop. The man was the only black Joe could see in any direction and the two struck up a conversation. They talked about discrimination in Portland and Joe learned from the stranger that Nat King Cole had played nearby, before he became a household name. The old shoeshine man stood in front of his elevated chair, his tired fingers blackened by the years of dabbing polish. White people passed by as the their conversation continued.

Joe would later learn that the day he boarded ship in Okinawa, unbeknownst to him, the very city he would stop in next was getting ready to host a special night of jazz. At 240 N. Broadway in Portland, at the Dude Ranch jazz club, Coleman Hawkins appeared on sax, along with trombonist Roy Eldridge, Al McKibbon on bass, and a 25-year-old phenom on piano—his name: Thelonius Monk. Joe just missed the legendary performance—he missed it by the length of a trip across the Pacific. The *King Cole Trio* later played in Portland a few blocks away—something Joe would have loved to see, especially the performance of *Straighten Up and Fly Right.* It was a hit when Joe was just 16 and based on an old, black folktale.

He said goodbye to the shoeshine man, continued down the street, and went back to the Royal Palm Café to eat. Once again that night, he met curfew and slept well on his cot inside the enormous riverside holding area.

Joe repeated his bus trips back and forth to downtown Portland and visited the nightclub to enjoy music and talk with his new Oregon friends. One night he went back to the club to hear more music and learned the club comedian/emcee had been killed. The man got involved in some kind of brawl and didn't survive his injuries. The loss saddened Joe, who couldn't help but think of the irony that in his months on Iwo and Okinawa, the Portland funny man in his mid-thirties was the only one he actually knew who died.

A FEW DAYS AFTER CHRISTMAS, MEMBERS OF THE 23RD finally heard the most positive news since their return two weeks earlier: they would get a 30-day leave and have a month to report back to a specific camp for discharge. In his *Orders* letter drafted December 22, 1945, Joe was told to report once again to the officer in charge at United States Recruiting Station, Jackson,

Mississippi. He had 30 days' "authorized delay" or leave, and four days' travel time. The letter informed him to report no later than 1200 (noon) on January 25, 1946.

The letter contained standard Navy jargon within its seven paragraphs. In the sixth paragraph, a warning: *"You will not divulge any information whatsoever relative to the whereabouts or movements of any ships or naval information to any unauthorized person. You will not participate in any press conference or talk to reporters or over the radio except after consultation with or clearance of subject matter by a public relations officer. Failure to abide by the foregoing will render you liable to disciplinary action."*

LTJG D.L. Peterson, USNR—an Assistant Personnel Officer, signed the letter.

A T THIS POINT IN JOE'S TENURE IN OREGON, A FEELING drove him in his gut—perhaps a premonition. For whatever reason, he didn't want to be traveling by train on New Year's Day 1946. He's never been able to explain it. Possibly the thought of spending a holiday in the United States, after the chaos of war, was an appreciation of the security and stability of America.

Because of his plans and the self-imposed off-limits of New Year's Day travel, Joe took out the piece of paper with the kind woman's address on it. With his Navy-issued, green sea bag in tow, he made it to suburban Portland, about five miles from Rose City and into a well-kept black neighborhood. Once he found the house number, he stopped in front and looked at the two-story home. He walked up the steps to the home of two friendly people he had met just days earlier. At 19, it was the nicest home in which Joe had ever been. It was amazing to him, considering earlier in the month he had never heard of Oregon.

The family had two children, a young boy and a teenage girl, yet Joe never thought twice about accepting the offer to stay and he was overwhelmed with the hospitality. For the first time since 1940 when his mother died, Joe was in a home with a mother, father, and children. Once again, he was old enough to fill the big-brother role, albeit for just a few days.

They treated him like a war hero, with family dinners, laughter, and conversation. It was a family setting unlike perhaps any he had ever known. Joe's guest accommodations were upstairs in a cozy, furnished attic bedroom. The bed was comfy and as usual, he slept well. For three days, he blended in with this family and was made to feel at home at every turn.

During his final days in Portland, he connected with several of his friends in the 23rd ahead of their departures on trains going east. New Year's Eve he partied with them at a new nightclub downtown, which proved to be an eye-opener for the teen from Mississippi. A jukebox provided the soundtrack. After a night of fun, Joe went back to his temporary quarters and, as he closed his eyes in the upstairs bedroom of his host's modest home, he said goodbye to 1945.

New Year's Day was spent with the family.

Though Joe had been back in the U.S. for more than two weeks, he had yet to have any contact with anyone back in Mississippi. For several months, no one in his family knew he was out of harm's way. From the warehouse, he wrote his older half-brother, Clarence, in St. Louis, and informed him he was now back in the U.S. and would soon come through town on the train.

New Year's night, the Oregon family hosted a holiday dinner— in essence, the goodbye meal Joe never had. He knew it was his last night at the house with this incredibly generous family. They talked of keeping in touch and all went their separate ways to bed. Upstairs, Joe climbed under the covers and glanced at his train ticket on top of the nightstand. He departed early the next morning—January 2, 1946—on tracks that would eventually lead back to Columbus.

He fell asleep at ease and with a full belly for the last time in Oregon.

JOE WOKE THE NEXT MORNING AND GOT READY. HE PUT ON his uniform, tied his shoes, glanced at his reflection in the bathroom mirror, and then walked downstairs into the kitchen to a goodbye breakfast.

"It wasn't emotional but I had such gratitude. After we ate, we hugged goodbye and I thanked them for everything they'd done for me. It wasn't all that hard to leave because I wanted to go home and see my dad."

Joe left the house in his Navy uniform, bag slung over his right shoulder, and walked down to the street.

He didn't look back.

UNDER CLOUDY SKIES, HE WALKED DOWN THE ROAD A BIT and caught a bus to the train depot. The sleek, City-of-Portland train was getting loaded with luggage and food as Joe arrived back downtown, near the Willamette River. The engines, painted with striking Armour yellow and light gray with red trim, cut through the drab of a cold, Oregon morning. He walked through the train station and then out onto the platform, where men stood in suits and hats. Mothers held their children's hands. Joe was unaware of the route he was about to take but unlike his last train trip to California, this was a regular passenger train with civilians. The train boasted a Portland-to-Chicago journey in less than 40 hours, with powerful locomotives able to pull baggage, coach, sleeper, and dining cars with ease, east through western Oregon, south-central Idaho, southern Wyoming, and into northern Colorado. His final destination was Columbus, Mississippi, but the first leg of trip would end in St. Louis, where he planned to get off and visit his older brother for a few days.

For the first time in Joe's life, he was no longer segregated on the rails. He looked at his ticket and climbed up into the train through a small entrance, near the end of one of the cars. The government didn't pay for a sleeper car ticket, so he took a regular scat by thc window. He saw other military members on the platform and inside the train but he didn't recognize a soul. He settled in and as usual, kept to himself. Because of the scenic route, the Union Pacific Railroad scheduled departure times to maximize daylight through the Cascades and parts of Idaho, before the less-scenic areas into Cheyenne, Wyoming. Joe was in a prime position to continue his adventure by at least seeing the beautiful country-side roll past his window.

As the train started to slowly roll away from the platform and down the tracks out of Portland, Joe patted his pant pocket. Tucked inside his Navy uniform, he still had most of the $130 from his payday, days earlier.

Joe didn't know it but the train's next stop was Denver, yet another place of which he'd never heard. And it would change his life.

CHAPTER ELEVEN

RESTLESS

THE UNION PACIFIC TRAIN HEADED SOUTH INTO COLORADO after several overnight hours rolling through rugged Wyoming country. Joe reclined in his train seat, his eyes fixed on the vast open plains until sunset; his mind focused on getting back to Mississippi. He was on a 30-day leave and had to make it back to Millington, Tennessee, for official discharge from the United States Navy in early February.

It wasn't clear where they would stop along the eastbound route but Joe's ticket informed him of his route and final destination: Portland, Oregon; to St. Louis, Missouri; to Columbus, Mississippi. He planned to get off in St. Louis for a few days and spend time with his brother, Clarence; his wife, Mary; and other nearby relatives. As the plains rolled by, Joe's train was now headed south and into Denver, a place he had never heard of before the conductor informed them onboard.

The train slowly came into Union Station in downtown Denver just before noon, Thursday, January 3, 1946. Outside, the dull, low, monotone hum of the engines was interrupted by an occasional hiss, as Joe stood from his window seat and waited for the people around him to get down the aisle to an exit. He left his bags near his seat as the conductor informed passengers their stop in Colorado involved a three-hour layover. Joe put on his wool Navy pea coat—fastened some of its oversized buttons—and went out into the cold, Rocky-Mountain air. There was no snow on the ground but it was frigid, the kind of cold that fills your nose and slightly stings the lungs.

He stepped onto Colorado soil in his Navy-blue dress uniform, the same one he had put on the day before in the upstairs spare room in Oregon. On both his collar and his wool sleeves, his stripes indicated his Seaman, Second Class rank. He could see his breath as he followed exit signs to the terminal and then out into the city. He was the only black man who got off the train in Denver, and he had three hours to kill.

Joe walked south out of Union Station's double doors into the brisk air. In front of him, he saw a drugstore across Wynkoop Street, and inside, he knew there would be the standard ice cream counter and a soda fountain.

There was little traffic as he crossed the street and headed toward the Dwight W. Duke Drug Store. As he walked across, he noticed a man operating a street sweeper about 50 yards away. It was something Joe had never seen. It was mechanical and sprayed water as large whisk bristles rotated and cleaned the asphalt. He kept walking and stepped back up on the sidewalk in front of his destination.

There were no signs that indicated "colored"—there was nothing outside that led Joe to believe he couldn't come in through the store's front entrance.

He put his bare hand on the cold metal doorknob and opened the door to the small drugstore. It smelled good inside. The soda fountain, with its upholstered stools and shiny countertop, was to his left; booths were against the right wall. The prescription counter was toward the back of the store and the place was empty, except for a young white woman in her late teens wearing an apron, working behind the fountain counter. She was attractive, with short dark hair and about Joe's age.

In another part of the country, just a few years earlier, Joe would have turned around and got out of the potentially dangerous position as quickly as he could. He had no idea of the race-relations in Colorado and though he knew this wasn't the South, there were so many things that could go wrong. He could be accused of something and it could come down to his word against that of a young, white, female teenager. It was exactly the type of situation his parents told him to avoid as he grew up in Mississippi.

With a bit of trepidation, he walked up to the counter and ordered an ice cream cone.

The teen looked at him, heard his order, and walked over to the waist-high, slide-top freezer and scooped vanilla into a cone. They didn't talk. She gave it to him and he paid a dime.

Then it got uncomfortable.

He stood there and didn't know what to do. Could he sit? Would he be kicked out, ridiculed, or worse? He scanned the store and saw no signs for "blacks" or "whites only."

The teenager watched Joe as he stood near the counter, in his Navy uniform covered by his long, blue wool pea coat. She sensed something was wrong and knew he wasn't from Colorado. He didn't know what to do. Does he sit and eat it? Does he get his cone and immediately leave?

And then she spoke.

"Why don't you have a seat and enjoy your ice cream."

It was more a directive, not a question.

Joe looked at her.

A million things went through his mind as he contemplated her suggestion. His response seemed to be suspended in air. He finally spoke.

"Thank you," he said softly to the young woman.

At that point, Joe felt the weight of the world lift from his shoulders. He had just spent two years in the Navy. He was only 19-years-old. He had smelled death, seen people shot, been shot at, survived two months in a foxhole, and driven night routes in hostile territory. He had been called a nigger and heard the term countless times throughout his life. And as he stood there inside a drugstore—vanilla cone in his hand—he felt a sense of belonging in a white, vanilla world.

Joe walked a few feet and sat down inside a clean booth, with its napkin holder, sugar canister, and salt and pepper shakers neatly aligned toward the back wall. As he sat in his booth, he realized this was a completely new experience.

Joe can remember the moment like it was this morning.

"It was just…," and his voice trailed off.

"I felt so comfortable. Comfortable in knowing I could sit. The only explanation I can give for feeling that way is that my mind would automatically go back to where I grew up in Mississippi, where the consequences could have been dire if I had made the wrong decision. For some reason, that was going through my mind."

It was a monumental moment in his life—right there across from Union Station, in the downtown area of a city he didn't know.

The teenage girl never said another word to Joe.

She continued to clean and organize behind the counter. He ate his ice cream, quietly and alone in the booth. His mind raced. In Mississippi, he would have been *persona-non-grata* yet here— in this place called Colorado—he was seated at a booth inside a white-owned drugstore.

He finished his ice cream in about ten minutes, then got up, casually said thank you, and walked out into the cold. He never gave an outward hint that what had happened was perhaps the most significant moment of his entire life.

"It was big. That particular incident, coupled with the sweeping of the streets—the place was clean! I'd never seen a city clean this way. In just the little area that I could see, it was so clean it was like people just sweeping up the problems and disposing them in their place. And I saw them do that. Then, I decided to go to the movies."

Joe still had time before his train departed for St. Louis. He didn't have a watch but he knew there was still the better part of two-and-a-half hours to go. With hands in his coat pockets, he walked one block and took in all the sights of this new city. He walked until he saw the Tabor Theater and went up to the ticket window. Thirty-five cents later he was inside an integrated theater about to see a movie. He knew there was no separate seating and no need to worry he was seated in a 'whites only' section. Joe took an aisle seat. The movie was already underway.

Once inside the lobby, he told the white usher that he had to catch a train and would he mind telling him when he needed to leave. An hour later, the usher came in, tapped Joe on the shoulder and said, 'It's time.' The usher followed through on his word, exactly as he said he would.

The street sweeper. The ice cream cone. The usher.

It all added up.

"At that moment, I decided, 'This is where I want to live. No question.' It never changed. I made the decision right then. It was these three incidents that came together."

So it was settled in his mind. Though he was a bit less than three months from turning 20, he still needed to finish the ninth grade. High school and college loomed. Joe had no clue what he wanted to do with his life or where the G.I. Bill would take him but after less than three hours in Denver, he knew where he wanted to reside.

Joe thanked the usher and retraced his steps back outside the theater, down 17th Street, and crossed back over Wynkoop to Union Station. There were no blacks in sight as he walked back into the station and past the high-back, golden-brown wooden seats. The room echoed. He proceeded down the tunnel, then up onto the train platform, and arrived with plenty of time to spare. When he climbed aboard and walked down the passenger car, he again took his window seat.

The train whistle blew and the conductor made the familiar *"All aboooooooard!"* announcement. The engines kicked up their hum, the wheels began to turn, and the Union Pacific train started to roll out of Denver.

This time, Joe looked back.

He *knew* he'd be back.

THE TRAIN CUT THROUGH COLORADO'S EASTERN PLAINS and out onto the prairies of western Kansas. The cars rolled through Salina, on past Kansas City, and into St. Louis the next day. On January 4, 1946, Joe's first leg of the journey was over. The Mississippi River rolled on past as an occasional barge floated by, perhaps headed to New Orleans and the Gulf of Mexico. It made the Tombigbee River back in Columbus look like a small ditch with but a trickle of water.

At St. Louis Union Station, the train again came to a stop with hisses and belches from the multiple engines. The typical rustling of passengers filled the train cars again as Joe watched the ground outside finally come to a stop. As people exited, Joe got up from his window seat and grabbed his green sea bag. It was his first time in Missouri.

He stepped out onto the platform and was met with another cold morning as he made his way into the station's grand hall. The ceiling stood 65 feet above him, complete with archways, fresco, and gold leafing detail and the station's trademark "Allegorical Window," handmade with Tiffany-stained glass. It was a bit overwhelming, considering where he had been over the past several weeks.

There was no one to greet Joe as he walked through. He wasn't expecting a hero's welcome back, even though there were hugs and greetings all around him while others bustled to make their next train. Voices echoed up into the tall, open space as he continued out the front doors. He knew where he was going as he climbed into a cab and instructed the driver where to go. A letter sent weeks earlier from Oregon informed them of the impending visit.

After a 20-minute cab ride, Joe pulled up to his half-brother Clarence Roberts' home on Page Boulevard. His brother actually rented one of the rooms in a nice, two-story residence and shared it with friends. Like in Oregon, it was located in a well-kept but predominantly black neighborhood. In this Missouri city, Joe knew he would experience many of the same things he did in Portland and Denver. These were integrated cities, unlike his final destination where he would again have to sit in the back of the bus or enter through 'colored only' doors. Joe viewed St. Louis as a place free of segregation and white strangers didn't have to be addressed as 'Mr.' or 'Mrs.'

With 13 years difference, Joe didn't know Clarence all that well, though he looked up to him from afar. When Clarence left Columbus, he settled in St. Louis where he met his wife, Mary Willie Allen. She knew how whites lived "the good life" as Joe called it. In turn, she kept a clean house and focused on smart clothing and home-cooked meals. Clarence went along with it. The fact they lived on a boulevard was a big deal, a small sign they were—at least among their fellow blacks—middle class. The neighborhood was nice with small lawns that were kept up and sloped to the street. These brick homes, with their tuck-pointed facades, greeted anyone who came to visit.

Joe walked across the sidewalk and up a few stairs to the front door, expecting to see a familiar face. With his sea bag at his feet, he rang the doorbell and instead of family, a stranger answered and he explained who he was. The landlord named Lula welcomed him in but she told Joe that Clarence was at work at a construction site, and Mary was working at the Wiesaw family estate in nearby University City. Mary was a maid and led a life similar to the women highlighted in the novel *The Help.*

The Wiesaws owned a successful St. Louis button factory and Mary took care of their household duties and cooking for parts of multiple decades. Clarence was blind in one eye, the result of a construction accident after he came home from the war.

At the home on Page Boulevard, Clarence and Mary had the back second bedroom on the first floor. Lula led Joe to a small room with a cot, adjacent to his brother's room. The multi-family dwelling shared one common kitchen on the first floor, while another family lived upstairs with their own kitchen and amenities.

Joe passed the time until sundown talking with Lula about various topics, sans war, and relaxing in his room.

As evening approached, Clarence and Mary came home. They had been married almost ten years and were the first family members Joe had seen since he said goodbye to his father in February 1944. It was a pleasant, welcomed homecoming. There were brief hugs, handshakes, and small talk.

It was then time to eat.

Joe was fascinated by Mary's cooking. She was used to cooking for wealthy white people and took pride in making what Joe considered the best food he had ever tasted. Two of his favorites were her fried chicken and her coconut cakes, something she made for family for decades—in fact, almost up to her death at 96. This particular homecoming represented the first home-cooked meal Joe had with any member of his family in more than two years.

With his stomach full and satisfied, he said goodnight and walked back to his small guest bedroom. As he fell asleep that St. Louis evening, he was happy to be "home"—home in the sense that family members were just a few feet away in another room. He closed his eyes and slept well.

The next morning, they shared breakfast and Clarence and Mary went to work. Joe decided to visit Robert and Sally Barnett, his aunt and uncle, who lived nearby. He also saw his cousin, Louisa, named after his grandmother, and visited Minnie, another aunt. Amazingly, no one ever asked Joe about his two years in the Navy or what he had experienced in the Pacific. That, combined with his lack of desire to rehash what had happened meant no one really knew what the 19-year-old had been doing since 1944.

CLARENCE ROBERTS HAD BEEN A PRIVATE FIRST CLASS IN the Army, part of the 1st Platoon, Company A of the 614th Tank Destroyer Battalion. The battalion was comprised almost exclusively of blacks from across the South, first fighting in parts of France—including Normandy—before they were transferred to England in the latter portion of 1944.

In fighting at Climbach, France—five miles from the German border—Roberts' black military brethren in the Third Platoon came under fire and lost more than half their men. During the battle, a seriously wounded Captain Charles Thomas led his remaining troops and Company C held its ground against the Germans. Thomas received the Distinguished Service Cross in 1945 and his 3rd Platoon received the Distinguished Unit Citation, the first black unit to receive such an honor. Nine in the unit were awarded Bronze Stars and four received Silver Stars.

Five decades later, seven black heroes who had received the Distinguished Service Cross in various WWII battles were instead presented Medals of Honor. The upgrades were determined to be the direct result of racist behavior within the Army in the 1940s. Captain Thomas was awarded the Medal of Honor—posthumously—in January 1997. (This type of blatant racism also presided in the United States Air Force in 1949, when a team of African-American fighter pilots—Tuskegee Airmen from the 332nd Fighter Group—took first place at the inaugural Top Gun fighter competition at Las Vegas—now Nellis Air Force Base in Nevada. They dominated the competition in their propeller-drive P-47N Thunderbolts. However, from the time of the contest until April 1995, the black team was never recognized as the winner. The trophy was actually hidden for decades and the annual Air Force Almanac consistently listed the 1949 USAF Fighter Gunnery Meet Top Gun winner as "Unknown.")

Upon his death October 29, 1970, Clarence was buried in the Jefferson Barracks National Cemetery, along the banks of the Mississippi River. Among the graves, were soldiers from the Revolutionary War and several Medal of Honor recipients.

"We never talked about the war, except when Clarence told me he saw a snake in France. He also told me in England, British troops would often sing 'Old Black Joe' around them and the blacks told the Brits to stop. The blacks let them know that was a derogatory song to us and they quit using the word 'black.' So, instead, they started to sing it as, 'Old, Old Joe' to fill in the space."

Stephen Foster wrote "Old Black Joe" in 1853, inspired by a servant in his father-in-law's home in Pittsburgh:

Gone are the days when my heart was young and gay
Gone are my friends from the cotton fields away
Gone from the earth to a better land I know
I hear their gentle voices calling "Old Black Joe."

(chorus)

I'm coming, I'm coming, for my head is bending low:
I hear those gentle voices calling, "Old Black Joe."
Why do I sigh that my friends come not again
Grieving for forms now departed long ago.
I hear their gentle voices calling "Old Black Joe."

(chorus)

Where are the hearts once so happy and so free?
The children so dear that I held upon my knee
Gone to the shore where my soul has longed to go.
I hear their gentle voices calling "Old Black Joe."

Just two days after he arrived in St. Louis, Joe was ready to get back on another train and finally head home to Columbus. Mary packed him as much food as he could carry on the trip south and her food brought comfort and care. The goodbyes back on Page Boulevard were not long and drawn out; instead they were quick with hugs and handshakes. He walked a few blocks and caught a streetcar to St. Louis Union Station.

As he again settled into his train seat, the engines fired up and the train pulled out of St. Louis on a non-stop journey to Mississippi. Black laborers, decades earlier, had laid the very tracks he rolled over on his way into the Deep South, from the Midwest. They battled deadlines, temperature changes, and the elements to complete their task at hand, connecting small towns with big cities, the previous century.

The train rumbled south and most folks kept to themselves but Joe kept noticing a black woman near him. She was middle-aged and dressed in her Sunday best, though he could tell she was uneducated. A black conductor, unusual for the time period, returned to the woman's row several times during the train trip to give her claim checks for her luggage. Joe had no way to confirm but he suspected the woman was intentionally trying to lose her luggage in order to collect money from the train's operators. After all, most blacks in the South made no more than $6.00 per week.

The train stopped in Artesia, Mississippi, 40 miles southwest of Joe's hometown. He transferred trains, from steam engines to a diesel, and took the short trip into the tiny Columbus train station. The black woman with claim check issues also made the transfer. The train rolled out of Artesia and soon crossed the familiar Tombigbee as it rolled past trees covered with kudzu vines, dusty dirt roads, and farmland. Joe thought about Colorado.

"Co-lum-bus is next!" yelled the porter.

When his train stopped, Joe grabbed his sea bag and stepped off. Home.

Two years after his father agreed to sign entrance papers, the 19-year-old was home from war and he stood for a moment in his Navy uniform, not far from his birthplace. Joe wasn't able to call ahead and let his father know he was on his way; Papa didn't have a phone.

As had been the case in St. Louis, no one was there on the Columbus platform to greet him. The Columbus station was a few miles east of downtown and was really nothing more than a collection of railroad buildings. It was nothing like the beautiful, grand stations in Portland, Denver, or St. Louis. No one in his family back in Mississippi even knew Joe was on his way back from the Pacific.

After waiting a few minutes that afternoon, a Sykes cab pulled up to the train station. The woman with the claim check problem was also standing at the depot and they agreed to split the cab. The cab company was owned and operated by two brothers from a prominent black family, who also owned the funeral home at 422 12th Street in North Columbus, the one most blacks used.

Joe put his sea bag in the trunk of the cab and sat in the back seat with the strange woman. Familiar streets rolled by; his hometown looked the same. At times during the war, he thought about this moment and considered at least the remote possibility he would never see Mississippi again. Would he find himself in the crosshairs of a Japanese rifle? Would he step on one of the tens of thousands of landmines? Would a Japanese sub come up from the depths and sink his transport ship? Those fleeting thoughts were now history and the reality was sinking in that he was back in familiar territory.

A few miles into the cab ride, they pulled up to the woman's home. What happened next was right out of a USO comedy sketch. The cab pulled to the curb, the driver put the woman's bags on her porch, and she went inside to get money to pay her fare. Within seconds, another woman in a nightgown busted out the front door. The crazy claim check woman came running out behind her wielding a stick. She had apparently come home early and caught a stranger in bed with her husband.

Joe watched the event unfold from the back of the cab. Moments later, the chaos had died down, the cab driver was paid, and he continued on to Memphis Town as they laughed.

AFEW MILES LATER, THE CAB CAME DOWN A GRAVEL ROAD and stopped in front of Joe's childhood home on North 14th Avenue. They shared a final laugh about what they had just witnessed; he paid the driver and climbed out of the back seat. He stood in front of the modest house, sea bag at his feet. He looked at the outside and surveyed the neighborhood before he took his first steps forward. The mess-producing Chinaberry tree his father planted was a bit bigger and spread like a canopy over the small front yard. A peach tree thrived in the side yard. It was ungodly hot. Joe stepped past the mailbox, went across a small bridge perched above a dirt drainage ditch, and made his way up onto the front porch and the door. He knocked. He didn't have a key.

Joe stood for a moment and waited. His mind and heart raced a bit. From inside the home, he could hear the footsteps.

They grew closer to the front door, and it opened.

It was his father.

They stepped toward each other and hugged briefly but neither man showed much emotion after their initial embrace.

"I don't ever remember him telling me as I grew up that he loved me. He never used those words. But I knew he did. He just was not an emotional man. I saw him cry once and that was when my mother died. It was a different mindset in those days about men. You know, you hug women, not men."

Joe walked back into the modest, yet familiar surroundings. On the right was a room that served as his father's bedroom. A wood-burning stove was stationed to the left of a bed; the heater's pipe ran up through the roof for exhaust. There was electricity but it consisted of one wire attached to one single light bulb that hung down from the ceiling. For years, when darkness set in, the family's lone kerosene lamp provided poor lighting inside. The home had no indoor plumbing or running water; an outhouse stood in the back of one of the two LaNier lots. The *Sears Roebuck and Co.* catalog served as their toilet paper. The Moss Tie Company supplied the water for the community and every few days each family would go to the tap and fill containers for later use.

Across the room, past the front door, on the left side of the house was another bed, where Joe's sisters slept. A small closet was just through a doorway into the kitchen area. The LaNier home had no enclosed walls and the studs were visible in each room. There were cracks throughout, which offered a peek to the outside from nearly everywhere in the house. They had no money for windows, so Papa built shutters instead.

Papa added an addition on the west side to accommodate Joe's brother Ira, who moved back in with his father years earlier. That bedroom was built with a chimney inside, which provided much needed heat for the drafty residence. Joe's two younger sisters, Ruth and Gladys, were also in the house and though they hugged him, they had no concept of what their big brother had been doing the past two years.

The LaNier family was fairly close but the times were still extremely tough. Papa still worked hard in the fields and had little time for anything other than rising before the sun came up and going to bed after it set for the day. He never acknowledged his son's financial contributions during the war years, yet like clock-work, Joe saw to it the government was sending home the proper allotment of money for his Papa.

"He didn't thank me but it wasn't necessary. In fact, I never even talked to my father about the war. No debrief, nothing. He never asked me a single question about what I did or where I went. My sisters never asked me, either," Joe said without emotion.

Throughout our interview sessions, it constantly amazed me to find such important pieces of Joe's life—so graciously shared with me—were unknown to his family.

Papa went to his grave never knowing his son served on Iwo Jima.

Joe's first meal back in Columbus was served at a table just down the road in Memphis Town—three different restaurants were on 14th Avenue, which ran in front of his father's home. Ms. Fannie Mae Miller had a place; so did Ms. Susie Gregory and Ms. Georgia Mae—all within three blocks. Ms. Fannie Mae warmly greeted Joe, like a child who had been away from home too long. After dinner, Joe walked back down the gravel road and went to the house next door to his childhood home. Ira's widow lived there with her three children. Joe wanted to see her and visited for a while, and once again he wasn't asked a single question about the past two years.

After the two had exhausted the conversation, Joe went back next door and went to bed in the spare area, on the east side of the house. It also served as the family porch. Papa slept in the front room, while Ruth and Gladys slept in the other bedroom a few feet away. Joe's mother died in the room at the south end of the house a little more than five years earlier.

For the next 25 days, Joe settled in as best he could—but he was restless. Thoughts of Iwo Jima, Okinawa, and his Navy service often swirled in his mind. There were no nightmares, night terrors, or any regrets. He had done it. Within two years' time, he had been in Chicago, San Francisco, Honolulu, Portland, Denver, and St. Louis—all big cities with bustling nightlife, busy streets, and new faces. Columbus was anything but thriving.

Originally known as "Possum Town" when it was founded in 1821, Columbus served as a hospital location for both Union and Confederate soldiers during the Civil War. After the deadly Battle of Shiloh in southwestern Tennessee, so many casualties flooded Lowndes County, Mississippi, that buildings were turned into makeshift hospitals and treatment centers. The battle in April 1862 left nearly 20,000 soldiers dead or wounded. Joe's grandfather was ten-years-old at the time.

H E CAME BACK HOME TO THIS SLEEPY, SEGREGATED CITY with a population of less than 10,000 and a county of no more than 36,000. More people had died on Iwo Jima than ever lived in Lowndes County. They were at least 100 miles from the nearest big city and upon his return, it was clear to Joe he had outgrown his small town. Though he was back, he knew he'd never live there again.

Joe visited his old teachers and in particular, Ms. Grace Harris at Union Academy Grade School. He wore his Navy uniform and Mr. Hunt, the principal, warmly greeted him.

Joe still had the better part of a month to kill before he was officially discharged from the Navy, not in Jackson as was the original order, but instead in Millington, Tennessee. His discharge date had also been extended, from January 25 to February 1, 1946. He passed the time visiting friends and family—proud of his service but giving little detail as to what he saw in the Pacific. On occasion, someone would make a bigger deal out of his military time than others and it made him feel good. He enjoyed the status and recognition, especially considering there were so few times in his life to that point where he had been the positive center of attention.

By the end of January 1946, he had seen all the people he could possibly visit and his antsy spirit led him on several occasions to the Columbus bus station where he had fond memories of his Red Cap days.

He was restless.

At times he would buy a bus ticket just for the sake of riding to a place he'd never seen. He'd visit Meridian, Jackson, and other small towns—alone.

Real adventure was just a dozen miles north, at the Columbus Army Flying School. It opened in June 1941, as a training facility for those flying fighters and bombers in both Europe and the Pacific. By 1945, there were 2,300 enlisted men, 300 officers, and an average of 250 pilot cadets per flying class on base. Hundreds of local civilian jobs were connected to the place, from food service to janitors to clerks.

The flying school was familiar to Joe. During his time working at the bus station, he became interested in becoming a pilot but he knew as a poor, uneducated black teenager the odds were stacked against him. Regardless, in the summer of 1943, he went up to the school and took a pilot's exam. He was out of place from the start.

"After I finished, I knew I had no chance to pass. However, a white officer—a Captain—took the time to sit with me and explain the kind of education I would need to become a pilot. To that point, I only had a ninth grade education but he encouraged me to stay in school and try again to become a pilot. I was truly impressed with the gentleness he showed me. He was the kindest man and I can still remember his face. Still, I was very disappointed."

Shortly after that, Joe decided to enlist in the Navy.

As for the flying school, the same year Joe arrived home, the War Department deactivated the base. The war was over.

IN EARLY FEBRUARY 1946, AFTER 25 DAYS OF PASSING THE time, Joe made his way to the Columbus bus station headed for western Tennessee. He was dressed in his Navy uniform as he boarded the bus en route north about 190 miles to Millington and Naval Air Station, Memphis. On base, he found his way to the Bureau of Naval Personnel and entered an office complex for his discharge. He walked in, told them why he was there, they processed the necessary paperwork and moments later, Joseph C. LaNier was officially out of the United States Navy.

"It didn't take long. At 1:30 p.m. I gave my last salute."

His official discharge came February 1, 1946—processed at the Personnel Separation Center in Memphis, Tennessee. (Millington was the actual location and Memphis was listed as the official place.) Joe received $100 in "initial mustering out pay" which was distributed by Lieutenant G.E. Morgan. The official "notice of separation from U.S. Naval service" was signed by V.E. Dudley for Lieutenant Commander Nathaniel T. Williams Jr.

In *section 40* of the notice, when asked "preference for additional training" Joe's form read: *finish high school.*

Joe was now out of the Navy.

He was a civilian again.

J OE'S DISCHARGE PAPERS CAPTURE AN INTEGRAL PART OF HIS life and a glimpse into the country's racial mood in the mid-forties:

Enlisted in the U.S. (Branch of Service): *USNR, V-6*

Date Enlisted: *29 Jan 1944*

Place of Birth: *Lowndes Co., Miss.*

Date of Birth: *25 Mar 1926*

Occupation: (blank)

Sex: *Male*

Race: *Negroid*

Color hair: (blank)

Color eyes: (blank)

Height: *5' 10½"*

Weight: *138 lbs.*

Served on active duty: *from 8 Feb 1944 to 1 Feb 1946*

Authority for discharge: *BuPers Manual Art. D-9104 (EED) ALNAV 6-46*

Like most United States Navy men of his era, he was honorably discharged.

For his service to the country, Joe received citations:

THE SECRETARY OF THE NAVY

WASHINGTON

The Secretary of the Navy takes pleasure in commending the

SUPPORT UNITS OF THE FIFTH AMPHIBIOUS CORPS UNITED STATES FLEET MARINE FORCE

for service as follows:

"For outstanding heroism in support of Military Operation during the seizure on enemy Japanese-held Iwo Jima, Volcano Islands February 19 to 28, 1945. Landing against resistance which rapidly increased in fury as the Japanese pounded the beaches with artillery, rocket and mortar fire, the Support Units of the FIFTH Amphibious Corps surmounted the obstacles of chaotic disorganization, loss of equipment, supplies and key personnel to develop and maintain a continuous link between thousands of assault troops and supply ships. Resourceful and daring whether in fighting in the front line of combat, or serving in rear areas or on the wreck-obstructed beaches, they were responsible for the administration of operations and personnel; they rendered effective fire support where Japanese pressure was greatest; they constructed roads and facilities and maintained communications under the most difficult and discouraging conditions of weather and rugged terrain; they salvaged vital supplies from craft lying crippled in the surf or broached on the beaches; and they ministered to the wounded under fire and provided prompt evacuations to hospital ships. By their individual initiative and heroism and their ingenious teamwork, they provided the unfailing support vital to the conquest of Iwo Jima, a powerful defense of the Japanese Empire."

THE SECRETARY OF THE NAVY
WASHINGTON

All personnel attached to and serving with the following Support Units of the FIFTH Amphibious Corps, United States Fleet Marine Force, during the Iwo Jima Operation from February 19 to 28, 1945, are authorized to wear the NAVY UNIT COMMENDA-TION Ribbon.

(Listed among the units recognized)

Detachment 23rd Naval Construction Battalion (Special)

John L. Sullivan

Secretary of the Navy

More than 80 support groups connected with the Fifth Amphibious Corps serving on Iwo Jima received commendation ribbon honors from the U.S. Navy. The 5th Marine Division was officially disbanded November 26, 1969—a little more than nine months after I was born.

Joe never had any sort of reunion with the boys from Great Lakes. There were no lifelong friends to stay in contact with and when he departed Oregon, they all faded into memory. He ran into one of his fellow Seabees just one time following WWII, on the South Side of Chicago on a summer afternoon in 1954.

Joe was walking to see friends after his part-time job near 47th and South Parkway when he spotted "Jackson" coming out of a pool hall. As black men polished the tips of their cues with chalk squares inside, Joe and Jackson reminisced about their war stories on the sidewalk. They laughed about Jackson's gambling habits throughout the Pacific—Hawaii, Iwo Jima, and Okinawa—and how their friend "Hester" from New York used to sing while they all played cards.

They approached each other and it clicked. Joe had last seen his comrade in the Portland warehouse eight years earlier. They talked a good 30 minutes and then said their goodbyes; it was the last and only time Joe would see anyone from the 23rd Seabees. There was never a reunion and Joe wasn't concerned about losing contact. It was just another part of his life.

H E LEFT THE MILLINGTON DISCHARGE OFFICE, HOPPED on another train south, and headed back to Columbus with his life, as uncertain as it was, ahead of him. Joe knew if he didn't immediately enter school and complete high school, then enter college, he would face a lifetime of manual labor or "digging ditches." For a few weeks, he got a taste of manual labor at a cinder block company, where the blocks were heavy and tore through even the toughest gloves. To try to combat the problem, Joe cut inner tubes in hopes the rubber would protect his hands. It didn't work. He decided during that job that he would go back and get his high school diploma.

Unfortunately, his timing was off. The new semester had already started in Columbus, so it was impossible to start a new school year until summer was over. It was February.

One day during his downtime, Joe was in downtown Columbus at Allen's Drug Store, a black-owned business on Catfish Alley. According to city folklore, the name came from the aroma of cooked catfish that filled the air in this particular section of the city. Its stores sold both freshly caught catfish and fried pieces, ready-to-eat. Many locals, including Joe, had heard the street actually took its name from the George Gershwin opera "Porgy and Bess" and its fictitious Catfish Row in South Carolina.

Regardless, this particular area of Columbus was known as the *black section,* a place where blacks did business with other blacks. It was where laborers and those in the community could gather, do commerce, and socialize. The block was an oasis, surrounded by a society often full of flagrant injustice.

Joe, the loner, met an influential man by simply hanging out in the only part of Columbus he felt truly at ease. He spent time inside Dr. James Allen's street-level drugstore on the south end of Catfish Alley, where he started to work as a volunteer. Upstairs in another office, Dr. Charles Hunter practiced as the town's black physician. Hunter was a handsome, tall, slender man and an excellent public speaker. The black dentist, Dr. James Williams, filled cavities and did oral exams in another office on the ground floor next door to the pharmacy.

North of the drugstore was one of two Greek restaurants in Columbus but because Joe was black, he couldn't eat there. Across from Allen's was another café, where blacks were welcomed. They served traditional breakfasts of ham, bacon and eggs, hamburgers for supper, and offered soul food for dinner. Above the café, Billy Herndon ran a pool hall for blacks; Joe was comfortable there and played pool throughout his childhood.

Allen, who really wasn't a doctor, eventually paid Joe a bit of side money and let him use his car to make nearby deliveries. Joe dealt primarily with people he knew, all usually within a ten-mile radius of Catfish Alley. He used Allen's Ford Mercury to deliver mostly cold medicine and simple remedies—"charts"—wrapped in light wax paper.

Joe received his driver's license in 1941, surprisingly, a relatively easy process despite the segregated society. Joe went downtown to a small transportation office next to the courthouse and simply filled out the necessary paperwork—no driving test or identification needed. It cost a quarter. After he paid the fee, he was officially a licensed driver in the state of Mississippi. There was a small but important obstacle, though. No one in his family owned a car.

ALLEN'S PHARMACY AREA WAS TYPICAL FOR THE TIME. Most prescriptions came in from Dr. Hunter upstairs and from the customers who brought them up to the main counter. Allen had beakers and rows of pills and powders; vats of Caladryl lotion sat on the ground and gallons of liquids, elixirs, suspensions, and cough medicines were stored in a small filling area. Countertops were crowded with tiny bottles, scales, and a typewriter to type out prescriptions. Individual orders were placed in small boxes and then into brown paper bags with typed instructions stapled to the outside, along with the patient's name and address.

It was Allen who pointed Joe in the right direction.

Joe's only true role models were the men in the medical complex. He still knew, in the back of his mind, he would take advantage of the G.I. Bill and he still had thoughts of Colorado. But, first things first. He knew he was almost 20 and hadn't completed the second semester of the ninth grade. He was at a huge disadvantage.

In his downtime, Joe and a friend sat in Hunter's upstairs office and practiced their signatures. They would put "M.D." behind them. They daydreamed.

Joseph C. LaNier II, M.D.

He loved how it looked and decided after his brief time in Catfish Alley he wanted to become a doctor.

"I wanted to be more than I could be in that environment. But there was no way in hell I could be a doctor. I was not an athlete; I was not one of those guys with a brain that is so full of information that I could get an academic scholarship. There was no money, so how was I going to go to medical school? Dr. Allen was instrumental in me deciding the road I needed to travel. He was my first mentor."

Allen told Joe to finish high school somewhere other than Columbus, especially if he wanted to try to enter medical school. The poor state of education in his hometown would put him at a distinct disadvantage. Money was the huge obstacle and Joe was advised to use the money connected with the G.I. Bill to study pharmacy, which could potentially catapult him into the medical school of his choice.

Utilizing what he knew about schools in the area, Joe decided to go away to a school in Holly Springs—population 2,650—about 100 miles away. Dr. Allen encouraged him to look at Mississippi Industrial College, a non-accredited institution run by familiar folks, the Colored Methodist Episcopal Church. It was a college but a high school was attached. This was exactly what Joe needed and it had the potential to work just as Dr. Allen suggested: he could dip into his G.I. Bill benefits to pay for room and board. It would be almost certainly a wise decision, in that in Columbus, some of the teachers hadn't finished high school, yet were leading classrooms. Leaving his hometown was essential for Joe to begin his life post-war.

He never stopped thinking: *I'm 19-years-old and only in the ninth grade.*

CHAPTER TWELVE

AN EDUCATION

JOE ARRIVED IN HOLLY SPRINGS, MISSISSIPPI, BY BUS IN LATE March 1946. He had just turned 20-years-old and immediately took a placement exam to determine where he would resume his high school education. He'd left in the ninth grade but his score boosted him to begin at grade ten. At 20, he was a Navy veteran—and just starting the tenth grade. It truly was the beginning of the second half of his young life.

Joe enrolled in the year-round program as planned at the seven-building, Mississippi Industrial College—or as they called it, MI. He became a part of the 600-student population and roomed on the second floor of a brick dormitory with a guy named Lawhorne, a nice kid about his age. Joe took two consecutive 12-week summer school sessions and finished the equivalent of high school in a year and ten months. The G.I. Bill had worked like a charm but it didn't cover the cost of food. Sometimes breakfast at Holly Springs consisted of molasses and a hot dog, so in the spring, students would tend to nearby crops to grow their own food, just like back home: corn, beans, potatoes. Times were so tough and there often wasn't enough coal for the dorm furnace. Students kept warm by bundling up in their overcoats, even while they slept.

His education included the basics and it was as normal a high school experience as he could get, considering his older age and the fact college students were among the overall student body. At MI, Joe began to come out of his shy shell. He sang in the choir and went out for football—simply because they needed bodies on the squad—and played through an entire season. He wasn't good but in an effort to impress the girls, he did the best he could in his first organized sport. He didn't own a pair of cleats and instead, played in big, broken-in shoes. They battled black schools, like

Grambling, but Joe rode the bench as a part of the practice squad. Finally, he got sick of being treated like a tackling dummy and told his head coach he'd had enough.

Mrs. Slaughter led the MI choir and Joe was a happy baritone. It was a lot less taxing than football. He enjoyed the ladies who surrounded him and he fell for a fellow choir student, Mildred Topp. They became a couple and went on the road to various locations around the state singing together and sustaining a relationship. They fell in love and on a whim and just prior to Christmas 1947, the two decided to get married. One day, another MI student, Reverend Morrow, married Joe and Mildred in the hallway without ceremony or witnesses. Morrow told the couple they didn't need a witness and he could do it right there. They kept their marriage a secret.

ONE OF THE BENEFITS OF SINGING IN THE CHOIR WAS JOE could spend quality time with Mildred, whom he viewed as his new wife. They took part in concerts around the area, including one summer singing engagement at a church fundraiser, southwest of Holly Springs in Batesville, Mississippi. They sat next to each other on a bus one evening on their way back to campus on State Route 278, the woods barely visible in the darkness outside. In the rear of the old bus, the dozen choir members, a minister, and several others were settled in, as comfortable as they could be in the 1935 Ford. Joe was seated in the back row with Mildred in complete darkness when they heard a loud crash.

In a split-second after the noise, the bus began to flip up and onto its right side, sending students, music books, and bags flying. The bus continued to slide several hundred feet on the asphalt before finally coming to a stop. A car had broadsided them at a small highway intersection.

Joe was shaken up and had a cut on his forehead. It was bleeding. Mildred was shaken but otherwise fine and everyone escaped serious injury. The students were terrified but assessed everything and began to crawl out of the wreckage. No one was seriously hurt but they found themselves in the middle of nowhere.

"There was a gas station on the corner and our minister, who was a Mason, got out to go get help. He looked white, so it wasn't a big deal for him to go talk with the white gas-station owner. As it turned out, the owner was also a Mason," Joe told me.

"We all gathered around the station entrance to see what was going to happen next. No one called for an ambulance. The owner had on overalls, a typical farm-looking guy. I remember he was talking on the phone to the police and apparently, they asked him if anyone was hurt. He said to the person on the other end of the phone, 'Well, they say they are but you know them niggers. They lie.' I will never forget that."

"No one said anything?" I asked.

"No! You know where we were? We were in Mississippi and you don't make any waves."

HOLLY SPRINGS, MISSISSIPPI, THOUGH IN THE DEEP SOUTH, was as full of Americana as if it were in the heart of Iowa. A drugstore, a soda fountain, and a hardware store surrounded the two-story Marshall County courthouse.

One fall morning before a homecoming football game, Joe did something that for him was monumental. He got up early, had breakfast, then changed into his Navy blues and walked outside MI to gather for a planned homecoming parade into downtown. He was the only person to march in a military uniform. Later that afternoon he was set to address students and act as the public address announcer at the homecoming football game. Though he had quit the team, his former head coach wanted him to remain connected with his teammates and the student body.

Joe marched, smiled, waved, and when the parade was over, he found himself alone with time to spare before kickoff. The parade route ended in the historic town square, and he looked up and stared at the courthouse. He didn't know it at the time but the building had seen its share of Mississippi history. Originally built a year after Holly Springs was founded in 1836, it witnessed intense Civil War fighting. On December 20, 1862, Confederate General Earl Van Dorn attacked Union General Ulysses S. Grant's supply depot in Holly Springs and forced a temporary halt to Union action in Mississippi. Union soldiers eventually chased Van Dorn and his cavalry brigades out of town but serious damage had been inflicted to supply lines. (The husband of a woman with whom he was having an affair murdered Van Dorn just five months later.) In 1864, Union soldiers held prisoner by their own officers set fire to the courthouse bell tower, which ignited the entire building. It stood in ruins and wasn't completely rebuilt until 1878, and then remodeled in 1920.

As Joe looked at the building, he decided to do something so out of the ordinary that it sticks with him, even today. It wasn't planned. In fact, in relaying the story, he was adamant it was a completely spur-of-the-moment decision.

"I didn't give any thought to the danger in what I did. It could have been catastrophic but I didn't think of that and I don't know why I decided to do it. It really wasn't that I was trying to make a statement or testing the system. I just decided to do it."

He decided to register to vote.

Joe walked down the concrete sidewalk and up a few stairs to a big door with a wooden frame and large glass window. It faced the town square. He opened the door and immediately went to the registrar's office counter, where a white woman was behind a desk, just a few feet in front of him.

It was November 1947, and the office area was quiet. Stacks of papers were on top of a few desks in the area but the white secretary was the only person Joe could see. He smiled at her, trying to break the tension he felt inside.

"She asked me what I wanted and I told her I wanted to vote."

There was a slight pause as the middle-aged woman looked at him from about ten feet away and then said words Joe can still hear today.

"Niggers don't vote here."

Joe didn't respond.

There was no "Thank you, Ma'am" or "Yes, Ma'am."

Joe turned around and walked away.

"She wasn't like, 'Gee, I shouldn't have said that.' It was just normal and you had no choice but to accept it. That's just what they did, all throughout the South when I was growing up."

It never dawned on him as to what may have happened. It could have been ugly. She could have hit him with accusations or she could have summoned other people in to listen to his request. Had the clerk been a man, he could have taken the request as an insult and a confrontation could have ensued.

"I could have been lynched. That was not out of the realm of possibility. I knew better and I should have thought more about it. I should have remembered my father's wisdom that under a segregated system, individual confrontation, no matter how benign, can get you killed."

Joe walked back out of the courthouse and closed the wooden door behind him. He never looked back, walked back to MI a mile or so up the road, and got ready for the afternoon football game and his emcee duties.

He didn't vote for nearly a decade.

Subconsciously, Joe thought trying to register to vote was a long shot. But it took years for him to admit that to himself.

Later that crisp fall afternoon, he got up on a podium and called the game. He cracked a few jokes and was all smiles and affable to the crowd. No one knew what had happened earlier in the day.

★

H E FINISHED HIS HIGH SCHOOL EDUCATION IN JANUARY 1948, without fanfare or ceremony. College was always on Joe's life agenda and with his high school diploma now in hand, he applied to Howard University's Pharmacy School. He mailed off his application and he eagerly awaited a mailed response from Washington, D.C.

His response came.

The pharmacy school had been discontinued.

There was no plan "B."

One afternoon he was in the MI library and grabbed a pamphlet by Dr. W.E.B. Du Bois, the Civil Rights leader from the 1920s. On it he saw *Xavier University Pharmacy School* and on another whim, he wrote them. Xavier later responded and told him what steps he would need to take in order to apply. After what seemed an eternity, Joe was accepted into the School of Pharmacy at the all-black college. Due to the Jim Crow laws of the time, he was unable to go to his in-state choice, the University of Mississippi, or Ole Miss.

"When I came to Xavier, they gave me something like $200.00 a month and that was supposed to compensate me, as a citizen of Mississippi, for not being able to go to the University of Mississippi at Oxford. All of it was based on race. *All* of it on race."

After Joe graduated from MI, he went back to St. Louis by bus to pass time before college and spend time with his brother. There was no rent and he didn't have to worry about food, thanks to Mary's delectable cooking. Joe's "wife" went to teach school in Booneville, Mississippi.

Within a month of returning to Missouri, he found a job at Scullins Steel Foundry, where he helped make frames for rail boxcars. His boss was a fellow from Columbus and the work was hot, steamy, and potentially dangerous. For fun, he played numbers— the equivalent of today's daily lotto drawing—with Clarence. He won $90.00 one time and figured that was about all the luck he had. He never played again.

Joe was just weeks from finally going away to college. He had no concept of where the road ahead would take him.

PRESIDENT HARRY TRUMAN SIGNED EXECUTIVE ORDER 9981 on July 26, 1948, and with his signature, the United States military was desegregated:

EXECUTIVE ORDER 9981

Establishing the President's Committee on Equality of Treatment and Opportunity In the Armed Forces.

WHEREAS it is essential that there be maintained in the armed services of the United States the highest standards of democracy, with equality of treatment and opportunity for all those who serve in our country's defense:

NOW THEREFORE, by virtue of the authority vested in me as President of the United States, by the Constitution and the statutes of the United States, and as Commander in Chief of the armed services, it is hereby ordered as follows:

1. It is hereby declared to be the policy of the President that there shall be equality of treatment and opportunity for all persons in the armed services without regard to race, color, religion or national origin. This policy shall be put into effect as rapidly as possible, having due regard to the time required to effectuate any necessary changes without impairing efficiency or morale.

2. There shall be created in the National Military Establishment an advisory committee to be known as the President's Committee on Equality of Treatment and Opportunity in the Armed Services, which shall be composed of seven members to be designated by the President.

3. The Committee is authorized on behalf of the President to examine into the rules, procedures and practices of the Armed

Services in order to determine in what respect such rules, procedures and practices may be altered or improved with a view to carrying out the policy of this order. The Committee shall confer and advise the Secretary of Defense, the Secretary of the Army, the Secretary of the Navy, and the Secretary of the Air Force, and shall make such recommendations to the President and to said Secretaries as in the judgment of the Committee will effectuate the policy hereof.

4. All executive departments and agencies of the Federal Government are authorized and directed to cooperate with the Committee in its work, and to furnish the Committee such information or the services of such persons as the Committee may require in the performance of its duties.

5. When requested by the Committee to do so, persons in the armed services or in any of the executive departments and agencies of the Federal Government shall testify before the Committee and shall make available for use of the Committee such documents and other information as the Committee may require.

6. The Committee shall continue to exist until such time as the President shall terminate its existence by Executive order.

Harry Truman
The White House
July 26, 1948

The headline in the July 31, 1948, weekly *Chicago Defender,* an influential black newspaper, following the executive order read:

"PRESIDENT TRUMAN WIPES OUT
SEGREGATION IN ARMED FORCES"

Joe was impressed and can recall Walter Cronkite's interview with the President. When he was asked why the order was signed, Truman answered simply, "Because it was the right thing to do."

CHAPTER THIRTEEN

TESTED

And den I do to Orleans and feel so full of fight,
Dey put me in de Calaboose and keep me dare all night.
Weel about and turn about and do jis so,
Eb'ry time I weel about and jump Jim Crow.

—LYRICS FROM "JIM CROW"
UNKNOWN AUTHOR, 1828

B Y SEPTEMBER 1948, JOE HAD SAVED ENOUGH MONEY IN Missouri to, again, go back to St. Louis Union Station, where he boarded the *City of New Orleans* for a trip to a new location. He'd never heard of New Orleans or seen any pictures of the place. He had no concept of the history surrounding the *Big Easy,* its attitudes toward blacks, the culture, or how the land became part of the U.S.—it was yet another adventure. He knew he was going to live on the Xavier campus but other than that, he knew little detail. The train rumbled south as Joe sat in another window seat, dressed in a button-down shirt and dress slacks. They rolled into Louisiana, past vegetation and new landscapes. The tracks cut across Lake Pontchartrain and again, water fascinated the young man. He hadn't been around that much water since his journey back across the Pacific from Okinawa.

"New Orleans is next!"

With the porter's announcement, folks bustled with activity collecting their belongings as the train pulled into downtown New Orleans at Rampart and Canal Streets. Armed with his new two-piece, brown-leather luggage set he purchased in St. Louis, Joe got off the train. He took a streetcar—seated in the 'colored' section—to just north of downtown and stepped on the campus for the first time. (Joe traveled lightly because he didn't have a lot of belongings. His prior luggage, post-military, had consisted of two flat sides of a cardboard box, clothes in the middle, and tied with string.)

Joe was immediately fascinated by some of the blacks he met in New Orleans with their pale skin and fair complexions; some even had red hair. In Mississippi, most were dark blacks like Papa and some, like Mama, had coffee-toned skin. But in this new city, his kind didn't look like his kind. They were so white, in certain cases, they could get by as such. Some blacks even took advantage of their light skin tone by testing the segregated system and would pass themselves as members of the white community. Joe also noticed that blacks from New Orleans stayed in their hometown and didn't migrate to other areas of the country like blacks did in his home state.

At Xavier, Joe went into the unknown, once again, but this time in an all-black, all-Catholic setting. He had never seen the campus and didn't know where to go other than a physical address; there were no friends to greet him or reunite with among the student body of around 1,000 students. By any stretch, he took, at a minimum, an enormous risk and the odds were stacked against him. Fail here and it could be a blow to his ego so severe that he would succumb to the likelihood he would follow in Papa's footsteps and work in the Mississippi fields the rest of his life.

He went to the registrar and then to the office of the Dean of Men. He received the necessary paperwork and room assignment, then went to settle in his new home. Living on campus proved to be the cheapest way for Joe to go and the men's dormitories were in military-style, Quonset huts, with female dorms situated nearby. Each hall on campus was named after doctors of the church and Joe proudly lived in Aquinas Hall. His roommate, Benjamin Clark, was from Ft. Lauderdale, Florida, and while they got along well, they were not close friends.

The dorms shared a common bathroom and shower area, and a cafeteria sat across the campus. It was an organized setting, much like the military, in that there was structure. Classes began in fairly short order after Joe arrived in New Orleans. At 22, he took an entrance exam and, to his surprise, passed the math portion with ease but he failed the English exam, which meant a remedial English course at night and in his freshman year; it automatically put him behind and in conflict with his curriculum outline. Joe remains proud of the fact his professors—while knowing much of the student base came from poor, uneducated areas of the South—did not lower standards for their students.

Because the student body was relatively small, most everyone was known by their first names as they walked from class to class on campus. Sisters Mary William and Veronica took Joe under their wings and even decades later, remembered him when he stopped in for brief visits. While the student body was all black, the faculty was mixed and all the nuns were white.

The high testing standards meant Joe eventually had to make up 27 credit hours in his senior year to graduate, higher than the 21 hours that pharmacy students usually took in an average semester. Other majors averaged just 15 units. Suddenly, the poor boy from Columbus, who was forced to repeat the third grade, was enrolled in organic chemistry, biology, physics, and trigonometry. His success was amazing considering his background and no one before him, on either side of the family, had taken even one college course. Financially, he had to apply for a student loan since the money from his G.I. Bill was used primarily on his high school education and his first year-and-a-half at Xavier. He told me he was stunned to have made it that far.

Teachers treated Joe and the other blacks like real people, like adults. Joe entered labs for the first time and saw considerably more advanced equipment than back at Dr. Allen's drugstore in Columbus. Even with the extra attention and long hours, he was often behind, and chemistry labs and lectures always gave him fits. Saturdays were spent in the lab making up for lost time during the week but Joe remained focused and was not afraid to ask for help or extra tutoring. He was skeptical and wondered if he could make it.

New Orleans and its cosmopolitan feel grew on Joe yet it was still a completely segregated society. There were colored entrances, signs mandating black seating on busses, and white racists who walked Canal Street. The Mississippi River, the bayou and its bustling economy, the food in the French Quarter, the all-black jazz clubs at night: they all seemed to overshadow the injustice, especially while Joe walked the Xavier campus. Because of his major, Pharmacy, he was not able to participate in any collegiate sports due to the heavy school workload. In all honesty, Joe wasn't remotely gifted as an athlete and athletics played no role during his time at the university.

Though he abided by Xavier's rules, he did stray into the unspoken, forbidden zone of Gert Town on occasion, a place unfit for any young man at a Catholic school. It was a crime-ridden, yet popular African-American rough-and-tumble area of New Orleans, full of seedy characters who led risqué lifestyles—the antithesis of Joe's campus life.

The 1948 holiday season was spent in New Orleans, not by any other choice than a financial one. Joe was used to holidays away from home and had become friends with fellow student Gloria Williams, from his English class his freshman year—a happy, bubbly girl "with the prettiest legs he'd ever seen."

His course load settled but Joe began to feel ill during the latter part of his first semester and was later diagnosed with appendicitis. Eventually, he had surgery and Mildred—his "wife"—came to New Orleans for a visit. Joe recovered and when he could, he traveled to see her. Their "marriage," however, was soon on the rocks and ended in heartbreak. Another man was involved and all Joe's trust evaporated. A "divorce" of sorts followed on October 5, 1949. When he later converted to Catholicism, Mildred helped by meeting with the priest and confirming their so-called ceremony was actually nothing more than two kids in a hallway. Even so, the relationship had a devastating effect on Joe's self-esteem.

He recovered, this time emotionally, and took part in his first Mardi Gras in February 1949, with friends Solis and Gloria and their loved ones. He felt a part of the family. Bourbon and Canal Streets were filled with floats, trinkets, and women and the alcohol flowed freely. It was like Christmas with a kick—in February, no less—something completely foreign to Joe. The party ended at Gloria's house with a gigantic pot of red beans and rice.

The study periods were also social times and penny poker games were common as the young black students crammed to memorize periodic tables and the origins and makeup of certain drugs. Joe was fitting in, finally.

"I tell you, if New Orleans hadn't been segregated, I would have never met you," he related to me in one of our sessions.

"I loved New Orleans. I would have stayed there the rest of my life."

HIS FIRST YEAR AT XAVIER CAME TO AN END IN THE SUMMER of 1949. With three more years ahead of him at 23-years-old, and with his background, it made no sense to go back to Columbus. His new college friend, Carl Carter, told Joe he was going back to his hometown of Coraopolis, Pennsylvania, 25 miles north of Pittsburgh, and urged Joe to join him for summer work. Carter was a month younger than Joe, which earned him the nickname, "Junior."

"Sonny" and "Junior" soon began work at the Standard Steel Spring Works Company making braces that held bumpers onto cars. As one 1949 advertisement in *The Pittsburgh Press* boasted, the company proudly manufactured automobile springs, open steel floor grating, universal joints, and coil springs of all types "under the industry's most rigid standards." In WWII, Standard Steel modified its commercial operations to include artillery shells and howitzer forgings. Similar divisions produced gun barrels, tank castings, and other military items. During the peak years of war, the company churned out 160,000 tons of steel.

The two young men boarded a train in New Orleans and headed north to Pennsylvania for the summer, where Joe rented a room from Junior's friends, the Dickerson family. Joe actually found the job, because while he was looking for work, Junior was going to speech therapy for a stuttering problem. Joe simply walked in, told them he was a student looking for work, and they hired him on the spot. Joe said he had a buddy who needed work too, and they told him to stop by as well.

Both Xavier students made $1.18 per hour handling steel and placing it into the furnace. It was hot and brainless but it was good money. Joe would place the steel on a conveyor belt device just so and it would feed into the white-hot furnace, then go on to its next step. He did that eight hours a day for the entire summer. One day, Joe worked a 24-hour shift—$28.32 for 24 hours of work. Joe was just happy to get away from coursework and drug combinations, plus he was able to save most of the money he earned until returning to New Orleans for school. The Dickerson family joked with Joe at suppertime that all he needed to survive was a patch of corn and a cow, since all he ever wanted to eat was cornbread and buttermilk.

Joe and Junior ended up going back to Standard Steel in the summer of 1950, and were just as successful. The bosses remembered Joe and how he worked hard for his wages. In the summer of 1951, they went back again but this time, the factory was closed and workers were on strike. Joe was forced to find other work and he was fortunate to land at a nearby Lutheran church that was under construction. They needed a construction "gopher," something Joe had experienced during his time in WWII. He was the only black on the job.

There were few blacks in this area of Pennsylvania, yet Joe easily made friends with his white co-workers. One day after work, they all went to a country bar on the outskirts of Coraopolis and walked in for a drink. Instantly, the Mississippi native stuck out to the small, white crowd. At the bar, they ordered a beer, to which the bartender responded that he could serve everyone but Joe. He knew some of the world saw him as only a *Negro*, or worse, a nigger.

For the first time in his life up to that point, Joe received support and solidarity from members of another race.

"You don't serve him, you don't serve us," his white friends said.

They all left.

Financially, even with the summer jobs, the new student was just scraping by. At Xavier, he was hired by Sister Mary William to clean lab animal cages for 50 cents an hour but it was not easy for Joe to come to grips with the pay, not to mention the 4:00 a.m. start to his shift. The Sister dubbed him "Rabbit Boy" out of affection and she instructed him to use that money to make small payments on his student loans, because it just "looked good."

Joe later took a more capitalistic approach to his downtime in Louisiana. He opted for a leave of absence from the cage cleanup to take a job delivering postal packages during Christmas break. He made about $200.00 over a two-week span but angered Sister Mary William in the process. She wanted him to realize his work on campus was preparing him for his future, whereas the postal work was purely temporary. He never forgot those words of wisdom.

He did, however, forget to study all that much. Before his last summer away from school in Pennsylvania, Sister Mary William called Joe into the administrative building for a meeting. She told him he was going to receive a letter over the summer and when he got it, he was to send it to back her, at the school, during his time away. Joe had no idea what the letter could be about but he agreed, and then went on up north to work. A short time later, he received the letter from Xavier informing him not to come back because of his poor marks. Without panicking, Joe sent the letter back to Louisiana and Sister Mary William but he had no clue if, in fact, this was the end of his time in college. He waited for weeks and then a letter came from the dean, informing him he was being placed on academic probation during his senior year. Sister Mary William saved him and her faith in the young man changed the course of his life.

Joe failed physics and was behind in other courses. It was a crossroad. He could continue his fun-loving lifestyle and take his chances, or he could buckle down and be the student people were expecting. His brother, Clarence, tried to help by sending small amounts of money whenever he could but it was only a dent in expenses.

The poor grades proved to be the wake-up Joe needed. It also turned out, though he didn't know it, Sister Mary William was a part of the Xavier hierarchy with tremendous influence.

Joe ended up making better grades in those 27 hours his senior year than he did in any of the previous three. He took night classes, cut out extraneous parties and walks to Gert Town, and approached graduation.

CHAPTER FOURTEEN

SOUTH, NORTH…THEN WEST

"GRADUATION WAS A HIGH THAT I CAN'T DESCRIBE BUT nothing compared to when I saw my father in the audience."

Early the morning of June 6, 1952—exactly eight years after the Normandy invasion—Papa climbed on a bus with his grandson, Ira Jr., and they traveled south to New Orleans. Their luggage consisted of cardboard and string; the greasy chicken they wrapped for snacks along the way was their only source of food. Their Mississippi bus ran late and as Joe dressed that morning in his cap and gown, he had no indication any of his relatives would be there to see him. It was a monumental day in the LaNier family—never before in the history of all the relatives from across the South and within the family tree that stretched all the way to Africa—had someone actually graduated from college. Joe was proud, on the verge of getting a Bachelor of Science in Pharmacy, and Papa was determined to see his son graduate in person.

The Xavier gymnasium was packed and the Archbishop was in attendance. Students went up on stage, kissed his ring, and then turned to the audience as they moved their tassel from left to right. Then they took a bow to the crowd. Joe's diploma was actually a blank piece of paper because he still owed Xavier $625.00. No one in the audience knew but he had been given a year to start paying them $25.00 a month. The debt lasted two years but it was eventually paid off and they mailed him his diploma—which is still proudly framed today.

The gym was warm inside, full of hundreds of proud parents and siblings. Joe LaNier II had the typical butterflies of a graduating senior. Then it was his time. His name was called and he walked up the stairs and onto the stage. After he kissed the ring and turned to the audience, Joe looked into the crowd and directly into Papa's eyes.

"It was the most uncanny thing in my life. I don't know why I looked in that direction, because I could have looked anywhere. But I looked that way and there he was, with a smile on his face. His expression told me there could never be a father more proud of his son. I've often wondered if it was providence that guided my eyes straight to him, or if I was just lucky. I can still see it today," Joe said as he cried, tears down his cheeks. "He was so proud."

Papa had only a sixth-grade education.

"It was his dream. He knew our only possible way out of poverty was an education. He saw his son get a degree. He was dressed in a suit and I could just see the pride in his eyes. I know he never thought he would see it. I couldn't wait until the ceremony was over so I could go to him, put my arms around him, and let him know I was proud he was my father."

In addition to cramming 27 hours of courses into his final semester, Joe completed a one-year, unpaid internship in a local pharmacy. The university set up the evening program, which was a requirement in order to take the state board exam. He filled his first orders from prescriptions written in Latin, the universal language in pharmacy at the time. He made his own liquids and powders; pills were made with a dough-like material and a mortar and pestle. Needless to say, there was an enormous sense of relief when graduation day came and the ceremony was completed.

Papa and his grandson stayed for a few days after graduation but Joe was determined to not to return to Columbus with them. He decided to take his chances in New Orleans. He needed a place to stay and his friend, Marguerite Gaudin, told him there was a spare room available in her house in the suburbs. She told Joe she would ask her mother and within two days the answer came. Joe could rent the room but he would have to meet the family—specifically Mrs. Gaudin—before a final decision. As it turned out, Mrs. Gaudin liked Joe and he got the room. While he was extremely attracted to Marguerite, he kept his distance and they became like brother and sister.

I was convinced Joe still had a crush on her and when we all met for dinner in New Orleans in the fall of 2011, it was still evident. It was completely innocent, of course, but evident nonetheless.

Marguerite was a beautiful blonde but she was also black. To her benefit, her complexion was extremely light and could pass for a young white woman. Because of her appearance, they often played a game—"white for a night"—in downtown New Orleans. Major theaters were segregated but when a movie came out that they wanted to see, several of Joe's lighter black friends would "play white." They always got in without a problem. To Joe, it showed the ridiculous nature of race relations at the time.

Joe left the Xavier dorms and moved in with the Gaudin family at 1859 Law Street, in the outskirts of the city. His only expense was the small amount of rent every month.

At 26—after he had graduated—he converted to Catholicism. Joe had made up his mind to convert months before but delayed his decision to avoid being accused of trying to impress the nuns in hopes of receiving better grades.

During that time, Joe stayed up late on Law Street and crammed for the state boards. He took the all-day test at the Board of Pharmacy in downtown New Orleans but the waiting was the hardest part. He was a nervous wreck and checked the mailbox every day for nearly three weeks. Finally, when his letter came, he ripped it open.

He passed the test.

Needless to say, it was a tremendous relief. The career he had wanted for so long was about to take shape.

JOE ALSO HAD PART-TIME EMPLOYMENT AT A LOCAL RADIO station, a job he secured in the second semester of his senior year. The job came with perseverance and a little luck, as Joe remembered what an officer at Great Lakes had told him back in 1944: he had a clear, distinct voice.

During his study time, Joe listened to rhythm and blues, jazz, and soul on WMRY-FM and its host of black disc jockeys. As he listened, he was convinced he could announce as well or better than the current hosts.

"One guy used such dumb language, like 'feets' for feet. So, I just went down to the station one day and applied. I'd never been in a radio station in my life. I just went in and told the white owner, a guy named Silverman, I could do this and could be an asset to his station. And he listened! He had me come back on a Sunday and I observed, and he ended up hiring me for the Sunday shift. They even gave me a title: station librarian!"

Joe's job was like any newbie beginning their career in radio: he had a less-than-desirable shift, in this case, Sunday mornings. He was responsible for patching through various church broadcasts, an important job in New Orleans in the early 1950s. Management eventually let him on the air and he debuted with a short newscast in the summer of 1952. It happened to correspond with the Summer Olympic Games in Helsinki, Finland.

"I kept calling it Hell-*linski!*" he laughed. One of the disc jockeys, Robert "Ducky" Decoy immediately told Joe the proper pronunciation. Despite the gaffe, he earned a spot on the station lineup, surely an accomplishment for his age, race, and experience level.

Joe dubbed himself "The Spider" on WMRY, a pseudonym into which he proudly morphed. He also proudly wore a gold cap on one of his front teeth, a symbol of being hip during his time in New Orleans. His picture appeared in the paper, with the caption: *"Joseph (Spider) LaNier, senior in pharmacy Xavier University, New Orleans, the newest addition to the staff of Radio Station WMRY. Recently appointed librarian for WMRY, LaNier is heard in his disc show thrice on Sunday afternoons."*

Recalling the story still elicits a belly laugh, even today.

"I used to say just as sultry as I could, *'Come into the Spider's web!'* I tried to lure the ladies in!"

Joe had emerged from his shell. College life agreed with him and he had become much more outgoing. While with the radio station, he was even given an offer to do an on-camera commercial for Regal Beer and its *"Enjoy Yourself with that Friendly Regal Flavor"* slogan. The New Orleans-based American Brewing Company did advertising on WMRY and also put its messages before movies in black neighborhood theaters. It was his first time ever in front of a camera.

Here was the shy boy from Mississippi, on his way down to a studio to make a commercial about beer. He didn't even drink beer but it was a great opportunity. He stood before the camera—under the lights and in front of a small studio crew—and pitched suds. As the camera rolled, Joe smiled right on cue, picked up the bottle of Regal Beer, and looked right into the camera lens. Later, he went to the movies specifically to see himself on the big screen. Even with the appearance, he wasn't asked to come back for a second commercial shoot.

Post graduation, Joe was still trying to get a job in pharmacy. One day in the early fall, he saw an ad in the *Times-Picayune* for a pharmacist position. He hadn't worked this hard and struggled so many years to bypass his pharmaceutical degree for a few hours a week on the radio. The job was inside a neighborhood pharmacy not too far from the Xavier campus.

"I called the lead pharmacist and he said excitedly, 'How soon can you get here? Can you be here within the hour?' And I said, 'Yessir!'"

Excitement built for the first time since he saw his father in the audience inside the gym. This was a real interview, inside a real pharmacy. Joe quickly got cleaned up, put on a suit, and caught a nearby streetcar for the quick ride to his future place of employment. He arrived plenty ahead of his scheduled interview and once inside, informed the clerk he was there to interview for the position advertised in the paper. The woman, nonplussed, called the pharmacist in the back, and within a few minutes he came out from the back of the store.

What happened next took its toll.

In a white lab coat, the white pharmacist looked at Joe and the first thing out of his mouth was like a punch to the gut.

"If I had known you were a Negro, I could've saved you the trip," the man said.

It cut Joe deep.

He said "thank you," turned around, and walked out of the drugstore.

"You see, my name doesn't sound black and my speech is relatively normal and he didn't have a clue until I got there. Apparently, I didn't sound like a *Negro* on the telephone. It was just the way it was."

THE RADIO FUN ENDED IN JANUARY 1953 WHEN SILVERman's secretary came into the studio before a shift and handed Joe a letter. It informed him his services were no longer needed.

"I just left. She squashed *The Spider.*"

Joe then applied at the American Drug Store off Canal Street; its pharmacy was upstairs and the regular drugstore was downstairs at street level. Joe arrived for his job interview.

"The lead pharmacist told me, 'You know, we might be able to use you. But I need to let you know, you'll have to stay upstairs. You cannot work down here and wait on people.' I would have taken the job despite the regulations but he didn't hire me. He was also white."

Before he left New Orleans, Joe went down to a local photo studio at the corner of Rampart and Canal Streets to get his picture taken in his Xavier cap and gown. He also brought with him the only photo he had of his mother. In the picture, Savilla was 27, a beautiful woman with a mysterious—if not semi-somber—look on her face. The photographer was able to colorize the precious memento. For Joe, it was a memorable day and the photograph still hangs framed in his dining room to this day.

WITH NO PHARMACY JOB PROSPECTS IN NEW ORLEANS, Joe decided to act on a whim. He decided to again look to the military, this time a potential career in the United States Air Force. Visions of that day he had spent almost a decade earlier at the Columbus Flying School came back to him and he applied. He was rejected.

In February 1953, Joe packed up his few belongings, loaded his brown-leather suitcases and a footlocker full of pharmacy books, and headed back to St. Louis by train. Once again, his destination was Page Boulevard and the home of Clarence and Mary. He settled into his temporary living arrangement and finally landed his first pharmacy job just down the street at a small drugstore near the corner of Taylor and Jefferson Streets. There was a soda fountain, drugstore, and pharmacy all under one roof; the position paid $55.00 per week.

Joe felt he was a competent pharmacist and simply wanted a chance to begin but in his mind Missouri wasn't where he felt he belonged. He constantly reflected on his trip to Denver in January of 1946. Fittingly, that first pharmacy job and his final stint in St. Louis lasted all of seven months.

His heart told him to leave when he found out his girlfriend, Inez Sullivan, was moving closer to her mother in Chicago. Joe was eight years her senior; she was still in high school when they made eye contact at a dance back on the Xavier campus. Inez was there with her college boyfriend and when Joe met her, he was "fascinated" by her voice. The dance ended, folks left, and Joe couldn't stop thinking of this young teenager. Over the course of the next several days, he did a bit of detective work through a friend and tracked her down. They dated Joe's final two years in college and continued their relationship as he went north to St. Louis. Inez never went to college after high school graduation.

When Joe left New Orleans, long-distance communication with the young girl proved costly. In one month alone, the phone bill between Missouri and Louisiana totaled $55.00, the equivalent of one week's salary. Joe paid Clarence his share and never made that mistake again. The easiest way to cut costs was to move back to Chicago and see his girlfriend in person, so Joe packed up his personal items and took a train there, without a clue of where he would live. When he arrived, he literally knocked on the apartment where two of his Xavier classmates lived and told them he needed a place to stay until he found a job. They reluctantly agreed.

Joe worked briefly for a small pharmacy on Chicago's South Side but there just wasn't enough work to keep him employed. That's when he heard about an opening as a chemist to mix solutions at the University of Chicago's Pharmacology Department. Dr. Eugene M.K. Geiling, a highly decorated pharmacist, who, in 1936, became the first professor and chairman of the Department of Pharmacology, headed the program. His groundbreaking, independent investigations looked at the physiological impacts of insulin. Other research focused on the relationship of hormones in the pancreas and the pituitary glands. Joe found himself in the presence of an innovative leader in his field.

From there, he applied for and received a pharmacist position in the pharmacy on campus under the direction of Chief Pharmacist Paul Parker, who himself had a long and storied career. Joe found mentors in Geiling and Parker in much the same manner he did from the doctors on Catfish Alley in Columbus. Parker urged him to join the Chicago Pharmaceutical Association, his first professional organization. Here was a white man who encouraged a new pharmacist from out of state to join pharmacy's equivalent of a fraternity. Just before Joe signed up, Parker took him out to dinner at a fancy downtown-Chicago restaurant where they dined on swordfish steak, a first for the kid from Mississippi. Parker later went on to become President of the American Pharmaceutical Association, an extremely important national position.

All the while, Joe's disdain for Chicago winters grew, especially in 1954. Temperatures dipped to 15 below and it seemingly never warmed up. He promised himself it would be his last Chicago winter.

After a successful year at the campus pharmacy, Joe went back to retail and landed at Black's Prescription Lab at 47 S. Park on the South Side. The business was operated by Mr. J.W. Black and supported by Dr. T.K. Lawless, a world-renowned skin specialist and a man some people in the area considered a miracle worker. He specialized in curing baldness.

Weeks later, Joe decided to go back to New Orleans for a visit with friends and Mr. Black—who was also from the bayou—had Joe take a letter to his parents.

"I went down, met those people, delivered the letter and told them what a great guy he was. When I came home to my apartment in Chicago, I had a registered letter waiting for me that said Black's Pharmacy no longer needed my services!" Joe laughed.

It was now 1955. He had no job. He had just saved enough to put a down payment on a brand new, $3,800.00 chartreuse '55 Pontiac Bonneville. The first week he owned the car, someone stole his spare tire. Life in Chicago was going nowhere. He had proven to himself he could work in a pharmacy but he needed more stability in a better environment. He didn't like the big city and to top it off, his relationship with Inez ended when he found out she was seeing another man. With his self-esteem at an all-time low, he needed a change. He needed out.

Joe began to think about Colorado again. When he enlisted in the Navy, his best friend from Columbus, Charles Lewis, was drafted and had served in the Marine Corps. He later graduated from Howard University in Washington, D.C., and by 1953 had moved to Denver. Joe took what money he had left over from the car down payment and bought a plane ticket to see Charles and, most importantly, to look for a job. He compiled a resume and went on a job hunt.

Skittish about flying for the first time, Joe boarded the airplane at Chicago's O'Hare Airport and tried to get to sleep as fast as he could. Three hours later, the plane landed at Stapleton Airport in Denver and his pursuit of a new life at altitude began.

THE STREET SWEEPER.

The ice cream cone.

The usher.

It all came back, though it had really never left his mind. Denver. It called to him. He was euphoric about coming back but had no guarantee he would find a job.

While in Colorado, Joe met an acquaintance in the pharmacy field and eventually, it was his guidance that directed him to National Jewish Hospital. The lead pharmacist there was older and decided to retire. After an interview with administrator Sol Abraham and others, they hired Joe. He promptly flew back to Chicago, loaded up his car, and never looked back. He was on his way to Denver, as he had always hoped.

Joe arrived in the Mile High City September 5, 1955.

It would turn out to be one of the best decisions in his life.

CHAPTER FIFTEEN

SECRECY

*All marriages between negroes or mulattoes of either sex
and white persons are declared to be absolutely void.*
— COLORADO'S "MISCEGENATION" STATUTE, 1864

JOE LANIER NEVER THOUGHT NINE YEARS WOULD PASS BEFORE
he came back to the city that had made such an impression in
early 1946. He was about to become the first African-American
Director of Pharmacy in the long history of National Jewish Hospital, a tubercular institution known worldwide as a leader in research
and treatment. It began treating patients in 1899.

"From 1952 through the time I came to National Jewish, Jews
were the only group of people who let me utilize my talents. I
ended up learning a lot about Judaism. I think our views, African-
Americans and Jews, are similar in terms of how society treated us
and what we all had to go through in order to get where we were.
They understood what I had gone through. It was big for me to be
in my position, because while there were a few black nurses, the
rest were in housekeeping and no one of color was in charge of a
department but me."

His starting salary was $75.00 per week, while most white
retail pharmacists were making $125.00 per week.

Joe and Charles shared a basement apartment at 2900 Race
Street in Denver, and by gentleman's agreement, Charles did the
cooking while Joe handled the cleaning. It worked for about three
months, until Joe saved enough to get his own place.

His first morning commute, from Race Street to the corner of
Colfax Avenue and Colorado Boulevard, made for an inauspicious

start to his new position. He ran a red light and received a ticket near Denver's East High School. *What a start,* he thought.

J OE IMMEDIATELY ADJUSTED TO HIS NEW POSITION BUT THE restlessness he had felt so many times back in Mississippi during his childhood crept back into his mind from time to time. Perhaps it was the fact he had just turned 30-years-old; maybe, it was because he was 30, not with the right woman, and had no children. In May 1956—eight months after accepting the Colorado job—he decided to once again apply for a position in the military. This time, it was the United States Air Force Reserves, which would allow him to continue at National Jewish in the event of a call-up. He applied specifically for the Air Force Medical Service Corps.

On May 10, 1956, Joe drove to Lowry Air Force Base, just a few miles from downtown Denver, and was examined by Captain Stuart Schneck, an Air Force physician. According to medical records, the doctor found an "Apical systolic murmur Grade I, untransmitted" after listening to Joe's heart and diagnosed it as a "functional murmur." This was the most thorough exam he had been through since Great Lakes in early 1944: height, weight, blood pressure, temperature, vision, ears, nose, throat, medical history, and all of the normal probing, prodding, and looking from head to toe. When all was tallied and reviewed, Joe was deemed qualified— medically—for a commission to the Air Force Reserves. Less than a week later—May 16, 1956—he filled out the official application for employment and then waited.

Joe had informed the Air Force he would enter at no less than a Second Lieutenant MSC, considering his prior experience in the Navy, his educational background, and his age. To him it was logical. But on June 21, a rejection letter arrived in the mailbox. "The Air Force does not have current or foreseeable vacancies for officers with your qualifications. In view of your age…your application is not favorably considered."

It was the last attempt for Joe to serve his country again. His future was in pharmacy—deep down, he knew it all along.

NATIONAL JEWISH HAS ALWAYS RELIED HEAVILY ON GRANTS and private donations to fund its operations, thus its official motto: "None may enter who can pay—none can pay who enter." As part of fundraising opportunities in 1957, brochures were routinely put together and mailed out across the world to potential donors. Though Joe had a highly-respected position, they felt if his picture appeared in those brochures, it may cut down on the number of contributions—especially in the South.

"Had you been white?" I asked.

"It wouldn't have happened, no. I would have been on the brochure. They told me and were honest about it. Sol told me matter-of-factly, 'You know, we're not proud of this but this is why your picture is not included. The reality is we have to raise money and your picture, in the South, would not have gone over well.' But those were the times and I understood. Still, I didn't feel good about it."

No one said anything to Joe in advance of the brochure distribution. He simply saw it one day and decided to ask why he was excluded and at first, it was a bitter pill.

Besides the "reality" of the fundraising, National Jewish was fully integrated. The few blacks mixed with relative ease with the whites and Joe felt comfortable eating all his meals at the hospital cafeteria. He met and became friends with most of the top hospital administrators and the shy loner began to engage both personally and professionally. Joe joined state pharmacy organizations, wrote articles for *The Rocky Mountain Pharmacist* and *The American Hospital Pharmacist Association,* and became just the second (and first black) president of the Colorado Hospital Pharmacists Association. He immersed himself in his work, something that would prove to be a challenge over the course of the next three decades. At night and on weekends, Joe also worked a part-time job at Larry's Pharmacy, on the corner of 22nd and Humboldt, to make extra cash.

"When I was able to leave work, I thought a lot about the mountains. I had never been in mountains, save for the train trip through. So every weekend early on, I would drive up alone up to Echo Lake. Charles and I would also go to Five Points and spend a lot of time at the Voter's Club and the Rossonian Hotel and Lounge. It was *the* place, man!"

The Rossonian—built in 1912, at 26th and Welton, near downtown Denver—hosted a number of jazz greats including Louis Armstrong, Nat King Cole, and Count Basie. The black musicians often staged separate shows at the Five Points hotel because while they played at other Denver locations, they were often refused a hotel room at the very place they were paid to entertain.

JOE KEPT IN TOUCH WITH THOSE WHO HELPED HIM ALONG HIS career path. There was no outside family member who had more influence on his life than Dr. James Allen, the pharmacist back in Columbus who took the time to explain to Joe how to go about getting his high school diploma and eventually his college degree. As luck would have it, Dr. Allen's wife Pauline—a teacher—came to the University of Denver to work on her master's degree over the course of several summers. She drove out from Mississippi in her maroon, four-door Buick and spent the next few months working on her degree. In late summer of 1956, Mrs. Allen asked Joe if he would mind driving her back home. He gladly agreed and began preparing for their multi-state road trip.

They avoided any racial issues and made it through several states without incident. Just after sundown a few days into their journey, they pulled into downtown Memphis. Joe saw the flashing lights and pulled over, figuring he was a target due to his out-of-state license plates. The street was clogged with cars, so Joe knew it wasn't about speeding.

He pulled the Buick over to the side of the road and didn't say much to Mrs. Allen as the officer got out of his patrol car. The white man cautiously approached from the left rear of the vehicle and Joe rolled down his window. Before anything was said, the officer got on his knees and briefly shined a flashlight underneath the car. He then stood up and told Joe to get out of the vehicle.

The officer began a search, likely instigated because of the color of Joe's skin. Though nothing was found, the officer asked, "You got any beer in here anywhere?" After Joe told him no and asked if he had done anything wrong, the officer said, "Well, you were driving too close to the white line. Get back in your car and follow me!"

Joe climbed back into the driver's seat and explained the situation to Mrs. Allen. They knew they had no choice but to do as they were told and follow the officer. The patrol car pulled out from behind them and Joe began to follow the black-and-white car through Memphis. He gripped the steering wheel a bit tighter and told his passenger everything was going to be just fine. They drove to the outskirts of Memphis and then turned down a country road.

"I was concerned. That's when I turned to Mrs. Allen and told her words I had never said before. 'I'm *not* going to take a beating. If he does that, he's going to have to kill me.' I was dead serious."

Mrs. Allen kept quiet.

It was a turning point for Joe.

Never before, even in his mind, was he so convinced he could go against the norms of society. Having had the taste of living in a desegregated society in Colorado, he was not about to conform at this stage in his life to the racism in the South. *No more.*

As he drove down the dirt road in darkness, he could taste the dust being kicked up from the patrol car in front of him. His headlights illuminated the road and he kept a safe distance and though he vowed he would fight back and would rather die than take a beating, Joe never thought of turning the Buick around and racing from the scene. If they were caught, there would be hell to pay.

Joe was certain a physical assault was just minutes away.

They continued down the dirt road and a few minutes later, in the middle of the dark Tennessee countryside, they saw tiny lights from a house ahead. Both cars stopped at the residence. It was quiet. They had no idea where they were. Besides the sound of car doors opening and then closing, crickets off in the fields made the only sounds.

The officer motioned for them to get out of the car and get inside the nearby house.

"This was not a municipal building or any kind of official police location! We walked several feet over the front yard up to the front door and the officer knocked on the door. The porch light came on a few seconds later and a man opened the door as he adjusted his robe. That's when we all walked inside."

Joe assumed the man in the robe was some sort of judge. The officer talked just briefly with the judge and then sized up Joe and Pauline, who now stood in this man's house. They were being held for a crime that Joe didn't understand or agree with and he wondered when the beating would begin.

The two blacks and two whites walked over into the living room and sat down.

The judge proceeded to ask Mrs. Allen if she had any money. When she said no, he then asked her how much her watch was worth. It wasn't valuable enough for the judge and as he contemplated what to do next, Mrs. Allen asked if she could call her husband in Columbus—she would ask him to wire money.

It was a complete scam and the "lawmen" got their money.

Still mentally jarred, Joe and Mrs. Allen got back in their car and the officer led them out of the countryside and back onto the highway. They were now clear to continue their drive back to Columbus.

Pauline Allen got to keep her watch.

"Inside that living room, it was a court of injustice."

WHILE THERE WERE EVENTS THAT REMINDED JOE OF his past, there were myriad reasons for him to realize the times were slowly changing and his future was bright. He was in the top pharmacy position, at a respected hospital, in a city he loved. He made more and more friends, both within and outside National Jewish.

The pharmacy was relocated to the main hospital building across Colorado Boulevard and was placed just down the hall from the main dining area. That's when it happened. It was January 1957.

"I saw this young lady that was coming over to have lunch. She had a ponytail and her jeans rolled up at the bottom, penny loafers and white socks. It was the sexiest thing I had ever seen. I had no idea how to approach her. There were three problems: one, she was a patient and National Jewish had a strict regulation that employees and patients could not have personal relationships. Two, she was from Oklahoma and I was from Mississippi. The third, and most important, I was black and this beautiful woman was white. Interracial couples were certainly not accepted in early 1957."

Her name was Eula Inez Long.

COLORADO'S BAN ON INTERRACIAL MARRIAGE — THE STATE'S miscegenation law—officially went into effect in 1864 and declared any marriage between Negroes (and mulattoes) and white persons "absolutely void" with a fine of between $50.00 and $500.00, or imprisonment between three months to two years, or both, depending on sentence. Sympathizers did not fare well, either. Anyone caught performing an interracial marriage ceremony faced the same penalties. The fines were one issue but the social stigma was another ugly issue altogether. In 1942, with the country at war with both Germany and Japan, the Colorado Supreme Court reaffirmed the ban in *Jackson vs. Denver* and ruled the statute constitutional in that "it applied equally to Negroes and white persons."

In a twist of irony, in 1957—the year Joe met Eula—Colorado's anti-miscegenation statute was repealed in the Colorado State House 63-0 and Senate 35-0. It wasn't until a 1967 ruling, in *Loving vs. Virginia,* by the U.S. Supreme Court that interracial marriage was deemed constitutional under the 14th Amendment. At the time of the ruling, 15 states in the South still had anti-miscegenation laws in effect.

EULA LONG WAS BORN APRIL 30, 1934, AND WAS A STUDENT nurse at the University of Oklahoma when she was diagnosed with tuberculosis (TB). She spent most of 1956 in isolation at a hospital in eastern Oklahoma and University Hospital in Oklahoma City. While she was there, a doctor—who had done his residency at National Jewish—told her of the TB rehabilitation program in Denver. She was placed on a waiting list four months and arrived in Colorado, December of 1956, where they promptly prescribed medications. Eula remained a patient at National Jewish for all of 1957 and much of 1958.

"The first time I remember seeing him, he was standing in the lounge near the entrance to the patient's library. He had on a white, short-sleeve pharmacist's jacket and he stood with his feet apart. His toes were pointed outward," Eula laughed as she recounted their first encounter to me. Joe sat next to her at their dining room table, a smile on his face as he giggled.

"I remember the first time he remembers seeing me. I really wasn't interested in him, because I had a boyfriend. Bob was another TB patient who I met in Denver and he was also from

Oklahoma. He only had one lung and after several surgeries they decided maybe the lower altitude of Oklahoma would help him," Eula said.

Bob went back to Oklahoma, where he later died.

Joe remained interested in her but was cautious. In Mississippi, if he even gave the impression he was going to approach a white woman, Joe knew it could mean punishment, including death.

Despite wanting to meet Eula, he knew he could also lose his job.

Days passed but their routines kept them in close proximity to one another. Finally, Joe made his move.

"The first time he spoke to me, I was sitting on the floor with my back to the wall, waiting in line for the cafeteria to open, and he asked me where I was from and said something about me looking sad and could I give him a smile," Eula told me. "It was a short conversation."

Joe took a more serious tone.

"I never thought of her as a white woman. It was *someone* I was attracted to, not someone's color."

Then Eula lightened things up again as we all talked.

"At first, he was just kind of annoying."

In July 1957, Eula went back to Oklahoma but not before Joe helped her with a prescription. He filled the doctor's orders and when she got back home, she looked at the typed label on the bottle.

"I noticed he spelled my name 'Y-U-L-A' so I sent him a picture postcard from Oklahoma and told him he had misspelled my name."

I told Eula that could most certainly be considered flirting and she smiled ear to ear. In addition to the prescription, Joe did secure some information. He got her address in Sulphur, Oklahoma, so he could contact her while she was home. Shortly after, Joe left on vacation to Columbus to visit Papa. While he was there, he wrote a letter letting Eula know how he felt—and he apologized for his spelling error. He told her he wanted to apologize in person when she came back to Denver.

Joe continued to send postcards and letters that summer; Eula has kept all of them to this day. There were long-distance phone calls as well but despite Joe requesting dates, for the most part, she ignored him through the fall of 1957. In January 1958, Eula's father had a stroke and her mother was ill, and she again made travel plans back to Oklahoma. She had called a cab but it never arrived near the pharmacy entrance. Destiny.

"I was about to miss my train, so I went to the pharmacy. It was almost closing time and he said, 'Oh, I'll take you!' So he drives me to the train, he carries my suitcase, and he puts it in the overhead rack for me and everything," Eula recounted.

There was a thank you but no hug goodbye.

When she came back, Eula continued her studies as an X-ray technician and they continued to build their secret relationship. They'd talk in the hallways and Joe even helped her with physics problems on occasion, at his desk in the pharmacy. Joe vowed to help her just as long as she needed assistance.

"He was eight years older than me and I really didn't know what his intentions were but he never gave me any real reason to dismiss him. One Saturday, in the latter part of January 1958, I got off work at 2:30 in the afternoon and I met him on the corner of 18th and Gilpin Streets. He was so persistent on the phone and in letters, so I just wanted to tell him in person, face-to-face, 'Hey, get lost!'"

Joe had traded in his Pontiac Bonneville for a new, 1956, blue-and-white one, which he was in at the rendezvous point.

"He greeted me with a broad smile and a, 'Hello, there!' and I noticed how his eyebrows went up in an unusual way when he smiled," she said as they laughed together at the memory.

"He was wearing a tan-colored, French-beret cap, and a golf shirt. I'd only seen him in a pharmacy jacket at the hospital. So he took me for a drive out east of Denver to Bennett, a rural place with a lot of silos around. We never parked—just drove."

IN REALITY, THE FIRST DATE WAS IN THE RURAL LOCATION BY choice. They couldn't risk being spotted by anyone connected with National Jewish. The late afternoon was full of small talk and pointless conversation but they were connecting. They drove back to Joe's basement apartment, where he introduced her to the landlords who lived upstairs. Pizza was ordered and Joe put on Nat King Cole records for the soundtrack.

Neither one of them had ever heard of pizza before coming to Colorado.

At 7:30 p.m. that Saturday night, Joe dropped Eula off at her dorm. The date went well enough to where she agreed to meet Joe the next week. Like clockwork, he picked her up at their designated spot, drove out through Golden, and up Lookout Mountain, which offers a spectacular view of Denver out onto the eastern plains of Colorado. They stopped at Buffalo Bill's grave, then continued down into Red Rocks near Morrison, and then back into the city through Cherry Creek and Washington Park. It was a sweet and relaxing Sunday.

The following week, they did basically the same route but this time Joe brought a Sunday newspaper along and they read it as they watched the ducks on the small lake at Washington Park. Their journey ended at Cheesman Park, near National Jewish.

"On the way back, he stopped under a tree and kissed me," she blushed.

It was the end to their third date.

"I didn't give her a chance to reject. I just did it. And she responded."

"The tree is still there," she smiled.

They still go there on occasion to reminisce.

THEY WERE BOTH CAREFUL. WHEN THEY CONNECTED, THEY met at their designated offsite pickup spot. They avoided anything that could remotely be considered public displays of affection and, in fact, did their best to avoid each other in the hospital setting. Eula continued her pursuit of becoming an X-ray technician at nearby Presbyterian Hospital while Joe continued his duties as director of pharmacy. Joe also continued part-time, evening work at a local pharmacy, a way to get extra cash and more experience.

They avoided holding hands or cuddling in public; the times simply didn't allow that type of interracial behavior. Both Joe and Eula were keenly aware of a local story where a mixed-race couple went into a movie theater and were shot in a racially motivated hate crime.

Eula had never dated a black man before.

"I didn't think about his color. I had always been friendly with everyone. It was just a normal thing. But because of the way society viewed us, it led to arguments between us. I told him it just wouldn't work because of our differences," Eula mused.

Yet Joe's persistence continued.

ON VALENTINE'S DAY 1958, JOE GAVE EULA A HEART-shaped box of chocolates with artificial yellow roses placed on top. She gladly took it back to her room and placed it on the top of her desk. She still has the box.

The couple trusted Joe's friends more than Eula's. Joe felt the women in Eula's circle would be more likely to relay their personal information to administrators at National Jewish; therefore, they spent most of their outside time with Charles and Joe's other friends. They both knew Joe could lose his job if everyone knew the truth but he says he never gave it much thought. Eula did. She proved it to me, thumbing through her 1958 diary.

"I just knew that was the rule and it wasn't a good idea. I had a chat with my roommate on the second of March and she gave me a long lecture on how I needed to stop seeing him. Turns out on March 6, 1958, Joe was called into the director's office."

Their secret was out. The meeting with Sol Abraham wasn't confrontational but it was an official warning that Joe could, in fact, lose his job if their relationship continued.

ULA LaNier HAS KEPT IMPECCABLE DOCUMENTATION, scrapbooks, photo albums, and mementos over their decades together. She often looked through her diary as we spoke at their dining room table; she told me how even though she wrote down her daily activities and thoughts, she often did so in code. After all, her diary sat on top of her desk, and was easily accessible to curious eyes, specifically her roommate. As such, she wrote in code quite often. Joe was simply referred to as "J" in her notes.

By March 1958, Joe and Eula had a perfectly executed system down. After her classes ended about 10:00 p.m., Joe picked her up in a dark parking lot at Presbyterian. She sometimes met him at his apartment. Yet because of the fear of social mores at the time, there was always the specter of keeping things on the down-low. Eula was falling in love but she reluctantly moved forward. Joe was ready. That month, Joe told Eula he loved her. He knew they were destined to marry.

"He told me one time, 'I wish we were already married.' It was the first time I had heard that. That's when he told me he loved me. I think I loved him but I didn't want to admit it," she said. "In fact, I said, 'Don't make me say it.' But he sat there and cried. It was in his basement apartment, on a green couch. You had on a red golf shirt, which I still have," Eula told Joe. "Sometime shortly after that, I finally admitted I did love you."

With love in the air, it was just a matter of weeks before he asked her to marry. There was no going to the knee and there was no ring.

"We had talked on the phone and then I met him on Colfax Avenue. I went to the drugstore and got a double-dip of ice cream; then Joe picked me up on the corner. I hopped in the car and we stopped in the parking lot at University and Alameda—in a church parking lot. That's when he asked me to marry him. He said, 'Let's get married.'"

Eula said yes.

"At that point, I didn't know if it was legal in Colorado. I had heard about a couple at the hospital that had to go to New Mexico to get married. Even when we were married a few months later, I wasn't sure if it was legal. I never checked. In those days, information wasn't easy to come by."

Joe was at least familiar with the risk.

"Years earlier in St. Louis, I met an interracial couple that just happened to be from Denver. I told them that I wanted to live there. I hadn't met Eula and I don't know how it came up in conversation but they told me that the picture of Denver in my head wasn't as pretty as I had thought. They told me they had to go down to Raton, New Mexico, to get married. I remembered that years later but that didn't bother me. I wasn't concerned at all. If they had told me that I couldn't get married here, we would have just gone down to Raton to get married!"

After the parking lot proposal, Eula prepped for a train trip back home to Oklahoma for a couple weeks. While there, Eula kept her marriage plans quiet. It was a secret. She did stop in Oklahoma City to visit her best friend, Rosalee, who heard all about Joe and her plans to marry, but that was the extent of spreading the news. Rosalee's mother was there and indicated it wasn't a good idea.

Then Eula showed the woman a picture of Joe and she changed her mind to, "Well, maybe."

"I didn't know what to tell my family," she said reluctantly. "I felt if they met him, they would like him. But if I told them I was marrying a black man, they would visualize something else, somehow."

She bowed her head and looked at the table in front of her.

"I told him I was willing to give up my family for him."

The weeks to their wedding day flew by and the first item on the agenda was to secure a marriage license. It cost $3.00, a debt that is still up for debate even today.

"He borrowed the $3.00 from me and he's yet to pay it back!"

Joe had to be strategic in his thinking. He knew if he went to get the license in downtown Denver, the couple took a risk of the news being published in *The Rocky Mountain News* or *The Denver Post,* so he drove 30 minutes north to Boulder and filled out the necessary paperwork. Their fear was clearly that someone at the hospital would see the notice and their ruse would be exposed. They were both certain the news "would spread like wildfire." They also submitted to a blood test.

They had no money for a traditional wedding but the date was set: June 1, 1958. Joe's friend, Charles Lewis, suggested his Baptist minister, Reverend Liggins, should both host and preside over the ceremony. They reserved a time and showed up at his Denver home and, matter-of-factly, the event began. It was held between the living room and dining room in a small, open space. Their official witness was Reverend Liggins' wife.

Eula added, "She also put on a record for our wedding music and the needle got stuck on the record player!"

Eula used her class ring, turned around on her left ring finger, as a makeshift wedding band. Joe didn't have one.

"We were poor as church mice, let me tell you."

There in front of the Reverend, his wife, and Charles Lewis (Rosalee couldn't make it up from Oklahoma), Joe and Eula became Mr. and Mrs. Joseph C. LaNier.

Joe gave Eula her wedding ring two-and-a-half years later, at Christmas in 1960. In January of 1961, the couple went ring shopping for Joe.

Though they were married the first of June, they lived apart until the afternoon of the twentieth of October, when Eula took three different cab trips from her dorm to Joe's apartment, each time with more and more of her belongings. "I never even spent the night there until late October," she told me. "Well, we spent nights together, just not *all* night," she blushed.

The relatives in Oklahoma found out in the fall that Eula had married a man named Joe but she never told them he was black. In a strange discovery, decades later, when Eula went to apply for Social Security, she needed a copy of her marriage license. On it, she saw something that caught her eye.

"I saw it in writing. They assumed in Boulder that because Joe was black, I wasn't white."

Under the blank section designated for a person's race, the clerk, in 1958, had written Eula was actually black.

JOE AND EULA RENEWED THEIR WEDDING VOWS ON THEIR 18th wedding anniversary, June 1, 1976, in front of family and friends at Risen Christ Church on Monaco Street in Denver. Longtime Denver-area Father Joseph M. O'Malley presided.

CHAPTER SIXTEEN

CAUTION

JOE DIDN'T MEET EULA'S MOTHER UNTIL 1963. THEY PICKED her up at Union Station in downtown Denver and Joe stayed in the car while Eula went inside to greet her mother and help with luggage. The first time he saw his mother-in-law in person, it was one of those awkward moments because he was in the car and she got in the back. Joe was made to feel completely at ease, though Eula admits she was nervous.

They drove home and when they parked, Joe got out and hugged her. Eula let out a silent sigh of relief. They liked each other.

Joe never felt like he was being hidden from his in-laws but also, didn't really care one way or another. It didn't matter to him. He was with the woman he loved and they had started their life in the city where he felt comfortable.

"I didn't know how her family would accept me. I had never met them. I left that up to Eula as to how and when she wanted to tell her mother and brother. I had already told Papa when we decided to get married. I wrote him and told him she was white, and that if he had a problem with it, to let me know, but it would not be a determining factor relative to how he decided to react. I told him if he had a problem, we just wouldn't come around him. He wrote me a few weeks later. He said whatever choice I made in a wife was ours and he supported what we were doing 100 percent. My race never came up with Eula's mother or her brother, Charlie. (He was 14 years her senior and also served in WWII but health issues kept him stateside as an MP, then a mechanic.) Never once did Eula's mother seem to wonder what my ethnicity was until the day she died. Charlie and his children visited us and race never came up with him. I never met Eula's father, who died when he was 83," said Joe.

Eula was unable to attend her father's funeral due to a massive snowstorm that blanketed much of southeastern Colorado and the Oklahoma Panhandle.

Overall, Joe felt so uncomfortable for his own safety he didn't accompany Eula on any of her trips back home to Oklahoma for years. The stakes were too high, in his mind, to risk getting into a critical situation based on his skin color. The racial difference was simply not an issue with his in-laws but that wasn't the case within his own family. Joe's youngest sister, Gladys, never approved of her brother marrying a white woman and she took that disapproval to her grave. Gladys was civil at best and made it clear to her brother she felt it wasn't right.

Joe didn't feel safe enough to travel to see Eula's hometown of Sulphur—90 miles south of Oklahoma City—until 1972, a full 14 years after they were married inside a Colorado minister's living room. They stopped as part of their road trip back to New Orleans for Joe's twentieth college reunion. Even into the seventies, Joe would have Eula stay in the car with the kids and get the hotel rooms on his own. On their first trip to Oklahoma, their route took them through the northern tip of Texas, where Joe felt uncomfortable. When he stopped to buy gas, he told me he was nervous. They had devised a plan to follow if anyone ever questioned why they were together.

"Joe told me to tell anyone who questioned us that he was my chauffeur. Lucky for Joe, with his hat on he could pass for a Native American," she said.

It was a sad state of affairs that the couple had to have an exit strategy in case of trouble.

During this particular interview session with me at their dining room table, the couple thumbed through scrapbooks and the pages of their lives. They were taken back to their past, which was documented right there in front of them. Their old memories came to life. Eula recalled that due to Joe's complexion, she often hinted with her friends and relatives back in Oklahoma that her new husband was at least partially Native American. This eased the pressure somewhat but Joe, to this day, is not completely convinced they bought it.

"They knew. They *had* to know."

IN THE EARLY FALL OF 1958, EULA CONTINUED HER COURSE-work and her full-time, on-the-job training as a student X-ray technician, until she found out she was pregnant.

It wasn't planned.

"I guess I was a little disappointed because it interfered with my schooling. But a couple of other radiology students were married and expecting and I thought, 'Well, it's the thing to do, I guess.' The people before me continued working but the radiologists made it clear that the next person to get pregnant couldn't work. I was, though, allowed to continue evening classroom studies."

Joe was a typical expectant father. He was excited and would often bring home cotton balls, Q-tips, baby shoes, and other baby items as they readied the nursery. They prepared to have a baby the following spring. But to his detriment, Joe had discovered the game of golf. A salesman with the Winthrop Drug Company introduced him to the sport and he loved it.

"First time I ever had a club in my hand, I took a swing and it went straight. I thought, 'This is easy!' and I was hooked. Then Eula became a golf widow. I was lucky I had a good woman," he laughed.

"He was a workaholic," Eula said.

Golf quickly became a Sunday morning ritual and every now and then, there were rounds on Saturdays, too, at the Willis Case Golf Course. Joe had poker games on Friday nights with co-workers and Charles Lewis came over for dinner every Sunday.

Eula had reason to say something but she stayed the course and remained positive.

They still lived apart when Eula called Joe on a Saturday night and asked if he would give up his golf game the next morning. She needed to talk with him.

"The phone rang. I had no clue. She was never very demanding of me, so when she asked, I knew it was important. I took it well. I wanted children, so I was happy she was pregnant. The hardest part was waiting the nine months for the baby to come."

Joe started to act like a doting, anxious father.

"I was proud! I was going to be a daddy and I was convinced we were going to have a boy and I was going to name him after his daddy! And then nine months later, we had a girl."

An instructor allowed Eula to continue working but made it clear she would have to stop—out of concern for radiation exposure—when Eula began to show. Her last day in the lab was the fourteenth of November.

The date was an important one.

That night in Denver, the LaNiers received a phone call from Ruth, Joe's sister: Papa was extremely sick and needed treatment for an abdominal hernia. The original plan was to send him from Columbus to Meridian, Mississippi, and the state hospital there. Joe felt the care would be poor, so he consulted with his brothers and sisters, and they determined it would be best to hire an ambulance and get Papa to a hospital in St. Louis, where Clarence lived.

With a heavy heart out of concern for Papa, Joe and Eula loaded their car about 6:00 p.m. and headed east. It was a trip that had its own trials and tribulations, with no interstate and the racial divide that existed in the country. Here was a black man driving a new vehicle with his passenger, a much younger white woman. It looked peculiar, if not suspicious.

Once again, they were concerned driving through small towns. In Colorado, they were fine but other states proved to be the great unknown. They even packed bologna sandwiches so they wouldn't have to stop to eat; they simply had no idea whether they could enter an out-of-state restaurant together. They never chanced it.

"Eula didn't drive, so I would have to pull over and sleep for a while. I'd driven all night and just before sunrise near Lawrence, Kansas, I pulled over on the shoulder to get some sleep."

Within a few minutes, Joe was asleep in the front seat, his head in Eula's lap. It was cold outside and she covered him in a blanket. That's when she noticed the headlights.

A Kansas State Trooper pulled up behind them and got out of his car.

"He came up with a flashlight to the passenger-side window and I rolled down the window. He asked if I was in trouble and I told him no, my husband just got tired and we pulled over. As I talked with the officer, I pulled the blanket over Joe's face to hide him. It was still relatively dark, so I'm not sure he would have recognized he was black or not, but I just kept thinking about what could happen," Eula articulated.

She paused.

"Later on, I found out a nurse friend of mine had a terrible story about brutality in Kansas. She was white and her black husband's uncle was burned alive at a stake, not too many years earlier. He was killed because of his race."

The trooper wished her well, turned out the flashlight, and walked back to his patrol car. Bits of dust kicked up as he pulled off the shoulder and back onto the asphalt, while Eula sat there, motionless. Her heart beat a bit faster. She watched the tiny red taillights disappear down the road and out of sight.

Joe slept through it all.

He had no idea the trooper had paid them a visit.

T HEY FINALLY ARRIVED IN MISSOURI THE NEXT AFTERNOON. Papa was in the hospital and didn't look well; there was deep concern within the family. As luck would have it, two of the doctors who took care of Papa were Joe's Xavier classmates. It was a godsend.

Papa was extremely sick and full of infection, so doctors treated him with antibiotics for several days before surgery. After the procedure, he stayed with his daughter, Gladys, who also lived in St. Louis, as he recovered. Their scare and fear they might lose Papa had been averted, and Joe and Eula retraced the route back through the Midwest and came back home to Colorado.

I N MARCH 1959, JUST WEEKS FROM BECOMING PARENTS, THE LaNiers moved into their own apartment. Eula went into labor on the first day of May, and because Joe was at work, she called herself a cab.

"Lisa came two weeks early. I thought I was having false labor pains and decided I'd better call the doctor. I did and he told me to go ahead and get to the hospital. It was a quick cab ride," Eula said.

It was also a quick labor. Eula went in about 9:30 a.m. and Lisa was born a short time later, at 11:12 a.m. There was no time to call anyone else and even if Joe had been present, he would have been kept far away from the maternity ward. Expectant fathers, in the late 1950s, were not able to witness childbirth like in so many hospitals today.

When the hospital called Joe, the nurse informed him he had a new baby daughter and as he held the receiver, a swarm of emotions filled the 33-year-old. He was a new father. Joe hung up the phone, grabbed his car keys, and drove like a bat out of hell the few blocks over to Mercy Hospital to see his wife and new baby.

Their big day had arrived.

"What a joyful day it was. She was the prettiest baby in the world. I was actually at work when I got a call from Mercy telling me I had a baby daughter. Eula had called that cab to take her to the hospital, imagine that. I wanted a boy but when that girl was born, it didn't matter. It just didn't matter," said Joe.

The couple didn't even have a name picked out and chose one from a baby book at the hospital *after* the little girl took her first cries and feedings. The middle name was easy; she would be loosely named after Joe's mother.

Lisa Seville LaNier was born May 1, 1959—it was 14 years to the day since Joe had arrived at Camp Shoemaker, California.

Eula had taken her final exam the night before Lisa was born but still had three months of training to complete before she could take her state board exam. She never did complete her degree, something she regrets to this day. Instead, she spent the better part of two decades being the best mother she could and finally went back, as a volunteer, at Rose Medical Center in Denver in 1980. The move led to a full-time position in the mailroom but her X-ray career goals were never fulfilled. (In a bit of irony, Eula's boss within her department, in the eighties, actually reported directly to Joe.)

While she was pregnant in both 1958 and 1959, Eula worried from time-to-time about bringing mixed-race children into the world.

"I thought about that. I remember one day leaving the X-ray department; I was walking across a pathway that led to the street and there was a little boy about six-years-old coming toward me. He was a mixed-race child and real cute. He smiled at me and I thought, you know, this is going to be okay."

Joe knew there would be people who wouldn't agree and that his children would face potential problems. But his philosophy was that as long as there was love in their home, they would unite against the world if need be. The family unit, he preached, was in a safe environment with a solid foundation.

L ATER THAT SAME YEAR, THE COUPLE BECAME HOMEOWNERS for the first time. They loved this small, Tudor-style, three-bedroom home at 2940 Elm Street in Park Hill, and purchased it for $14,500.00. Joe decided to act on the advertisement he saw in the newspaper and never thought twice about asking Eula what she thought. His mindset was framed by what he remembered as a child growing up in Mississippi. He never saw Mama and Papa have a lengthy conversation, let alone about finances. It was what Joe knew. Men took care of these types of things without consultation, he thought. Joe quickly borrowed $500.00 for the down payment and they closed on their new home.

The LaNiers went on to become the first black family, anywhere in the neighborhood, to move east of Colorado Boulevard in the city's Park Hill section. In Denver, Colorado Boulevard had long been the line of demarcation separating white and black neighborhoods. To that point, no black family dare cross Colorado Boulevard and realtors stopped selling to blacks east of York Avenue. It was understood. Slowly, the color barrier was broken and block-by-block, black families moved east.

Within a week of the LaNiers moving in, several homes on the very same block—homes owned by white families—went up for sale on Elm Street. Signs began to pop up, including next door. One neighbor came and knocked on their door and actually told them they were not the reason he was moving.

To the LaNiers, it was extremely obvious.

Eula wasn't happy about the home purchase especially because Joe went into a contract without her approval. They had to take out both a first and second mortgage and ended up with a house payment of $149.00 per month. Joe made just under $500.00 per month and was under financial pressure, so he took on other pharmacy work and balanced three jobs at a time to make ends meet. He burned the candle at both ends throughout much of his career.

"I was always deathly afraid of leaving Eula and the kids with nothing. I took out multiple life insurance policies to make sure if something happened to me, they would be financially secure. I didn't want her to have to marry someone so she and the kids could eat. I took out an enormous amount of insurance on my life. In fact, I was insurance-poor but I did that because I constantly worried about what would happen to Eula and the kids if anything were to happen to me. I knew she probably wouldn't get married again if I died but if she did decide to marry again, I wanted her to do that because she wanted to, not because she needed a means to survive."

ULA WAS BUSY AT HOME AND JOE REMAINED BUSY AT WORK.

Eula's father became ill, once again in Oklahoma, and she decided to take baby Lisa on the train back home. There was a sense of urgency to see him, because her father was 83 and had experienced a series of small strokes. Soon after she came back from the trip, Eula found out she was pregnant, again.

"I cried. I came out of the doctor's office and I cried. They were not tears of joy. Joe didn't understand and he was upset with me but I had just found someone who could take care of Lisa, so I could go back and finish school. So, I had to call my instructor and tell her I couldn't come back."

Thirteen months and six days after Lisa was born, Joseph Conklin LaNier III was born at Mercy Hospital on June 5, 1960. Joe was extremely proud to have a son named after himself and his father—proud there would be another male to continue the family name.

"When I look back, it really wasn't fair to Eula. She was left with the children, all alone, most of the time. I can remember I'd come home from my full-time job and she would have Joe in her arms with a bottle in his mouth; Lisa would be at her knees with a bottle in hers. I'd walk in and want to know what was for supper. It's fair to say she wasn't happy during that time and it was thoughtless on my part. I didn't mean it that way and in fact, I saw it as taking care of my family."

Eula had wanted twins. They were common in her family but with two children so close together, Lisa and Joe may as well have been. The work, meals, and cleanup were a constant. For a time, the dirty chore of washing diapers was done in the bathtub because they couldn't afford a washing machine.

Joe followed a pattern throughout his first decade in Colorado: he worked those multiple jobs. He had at least two and oftentimes three at a time, to pay the bills. National Jewish was his full-time job and the part-time positions were held at various local pharmacies. His salary at all these locations was sub-par to his white counterparts but he needed the money and one particular pharmacy job offered a unique work environment. T.K. Pharmacy in downtown Denver, at 27th and Larimer Streets, was owned by a Japanese man and three Japanese pharmacists worked behind the counter.

This was the late 1950s and not 15 years earlier, Joe was on both Iwo Jima and Okinawa fearing Japanese who wanted him and others like him dead. The irony was not lost on the men inside the pharmacy and they all talked about it a few times over the years Joe was employed there. But they were *Nisei*, or American-born Japanese, and they didn't connect themselves to their parents' homeland. Another irony was that not too far away from the pharmacy, Japanese-Americans had been put into Colorado internment camps, not 20 years earlier. Joe knew the men he worked with were descendants of the very people the U.S. fought in WWII.

IN A SPEECH TO THE STUDENT BRANCH OF THE AMERICAN Pharmacists Association the evening of November 11, 1959, Joe told the Colorado audience about "opportunity" in his field. As the students listened, they had no idea what he had been through in life, both in the military and in the segregated society in which he grew up. This was not part of the speech. Instead, he talked of opportunity and optimism within his chosen field.

"I believe it is very evident that the opportunity is there, more than you have realized," he told them.

"Make no mistake about it, the opportunities in Colorado are almost unlimited. To take advantage of them is going to take a tremendous amount of work, but a good, honest day's work never hurt anybody. You must never forget that taking advantage of an opportunity is a two-way street—in other words, if you expect something from hospital pharmacy, you're going to have to give something to it," his speech concluded.

JOE CONTINUED FILLING PRESCRIPTIONS, RUNNING THE department, and climbing up the pharmaceutical ladder in Colorado and the region until 1964. He had spent nine years at National Jewish when he decided to get some experience and new challenges in a general hospital setting. Nearby Mercy Hospital, where the children were born, had an opening for Director of Pharmacy; Joe applied for and was chosen for the position. He lasted just eight months before certain inventory issues caused a rift and Joe was asked to leave. There was also a racial incident.

"At Mercy, three pharmacists were under me. I was the only black man there and one of the pharmacists didn't want to work for me. I wasn't aware of it in the beginning but there became many issues with trust, due to race. Even the secretary was disrespectful, like she was in cahoots with the one pharmacist. In my mind, it was all a racial thing and I've never thrown that around lightly."

It all made him question whether he should have ever left his comfortable position at National Jewish.

IN THE EARLY 1960S, A NEW SUBDIVISION CALLED "APPLEWOOD" was being built and the LaNiers went to look at the model home. When they arrived, the salesman on-site acted strangely and then disappeared. The man went and called the owner of the development and within a few minutes, the owner was on-site and asked the LaNiers to leave. He told them to 'Get out. Right now.' They did. Later, Joe's friend told him to see a lawyer acquaintance, who suggested they go to the Fair Housing Department. The developer eventually apologized.

Prickly race relations were one thing to come to grips with as adults but another issue altogether with Lisa and Joe III. In both the sixties and seventies, the LaNiers were sure to convey to their children that if people didn't agree with their racial makeup at home, it was strictly *their* problem.

Joe was a founding member of the Colorado Society of Hospital Pharmacists—the only black man in the organization—and would later become the group's second president. During this time, the once-shy boy from Mississippi met for an hour with the governor of Colorado, Stephen McNichols, brother of the longtime mayor of Denver, Bill McNichols.

"My whole focus was learning. When you're the only African-American in a group, you need to know how to do things. In my gut, because of my race, I knew I could not fail. Plus, this was my profession."

Joe made his appointment, secured a place on the docket, and made his first-ever trip to Colorado's state capitol building. He wasn't intimidated and made it clear he represented a board of hospital pharmacists who felt they needed to be a part of the Board of Pharmacy, right alongside retail pharmacists.

In 1964, Joe applied to become the executive director of the state Board of Pharmacy. He and colleague Sam Cohen took the required civil service exam and did extremely well. They came in first and second but Cohen quickly decided he didn't want the position. This left Joe as the natural—and logical—choice to fill the void. Sadly, race prevented that from happening. He learned that some board members had held a special "meeting" in the mountains and one member told the group, "No nigger is going to be the secretary of the Board of Pharmacy here in Colorado." Joe had every reason to believe it was true and that race had everything to do with it. He was never appointed.

JOE LANIER STILL ADMITS HE WORKED TOO MUCH WHEN THE kids were young. He played too much golf. He could have paid more attention to his wife. But overall, they were happy.

"A world opened up to me that I had never imagined. When I was growing up, in all probability, I was going to live in that society the rest of my life. And then, all of a sudden, I go to the Navy and things begin to open up for me that I could have never imagined. I just became..." he said as his voice trailed off.

"I just became involved in living my life, regardless of racial strife all around me. I saw what I did as a necessity."

CHAPTER SEVENTEEN

RIGHTS

*I run to seek new policies—policies to end the bloodshed
in Vietnam...to close the gaps that now exist between black
and white, between rich and poor, between young and old....*
—ROBERT KENNEDY, 1968

LIKE MOST AMERICANS, JOE AND EULA WATCHED THE 1960S and the Civil Rights movement unfold on television, on the radio, and in the newspaper. Joe followed Dr. Martin Luther King but told me he would have never been so bold and proactive.

"How willing were you to stand up for yourself?" I asked him.

"Very much so, as an individual, but I was not willing to get beat for somebody to say I did a great thing. I'm not a martyr. At the end of the day, I believe Civil Rights is going to be solved 'one on one.' I have directed my whole life in trying to make sure that I can communicate across the color line. At the same time, if it had not been for Dr. King...the Civil Rights movement? We wouldn't be there yet. It took that kind of pressure. It took people dying. When you saw them turn hoses on people and kids, and they went flying around like paper because the water was so strong, the people then decided that wasn't right."

IN 1957, A YOUNG TEENAGER BECAME A PART OF CIVIL RIGHTS history and later, a part of Joe's family.

Carlotta Walls LaNier, who became Joe's niece by her marriage to Ira Jr. several years later, became a part of a national tragedy in Little Rock, Arkansas. She would forever be a member of the Little

Rock Nine. At just 14, she joined eight other students enrolled at Little Rock Central High School and tried to make her way to class on the first day of school September 4, 1957. Hundreds formed an angry mob, which later had the protection and encouragement of the Arkansas National Guard. Strangers screamed racial epithets and spat on the children; later in the month, by orders from President Eisenhower, members of the Army's 101st Airborne Division escorted the nine students onto school grounds. It would become one of the biggest events in the Civil Rights movement and a terribly ugly moment in U.S. history.

The NAACP enrolled the nine black students, chosen based on grades and attendance. The decision, despite compliance by the Little Rock School Board, appalled then-Arkansas governor Orval Faubus, who openly defied orders from the President and the historic 1954 United States Supreme Court ruling in *Brown vs. Board of Education,* which declared segregation in schools unconstitutional and ordered schools desegregated.

In 1960, Carlotta became the first African-American female to graduate from Central High School and in 1999, President Bill Clinton—the former Arkansas governor—awarded the Little Rock Nine the Congressional Gold Medal.

JOE DIDN'T REGISTER TO VOTE UNTIL HE MOVED TO COLORADO. The "niggers don't vote here" phrase from back in Holly Springs, Mississippi, still resonated in his mind. He began to cherish his right to cast his own ballot and to have a voice in the political process. This was about the time John F. Kennedy came on Joe's radar. He remains, to this day, fascinated how such a wealthy family cared so much about the plights of the poor and African-Americans in general. He followed Kennedy's national rise and watched the Kennedy-Nixon debate on their new, black-and-white television. Seventy million Americans tuned in for the first of the four debates, held September 26, 1960.

"Kennedy was able to win African-Americans over but we lost a lot of respect initially when he picked Lyndon Johnson as his running mate. We all thought Johnson was a racist but he changed. Eula and I both can remember walking into the voting booths at Steadman Elementary School in Park Hill, just three blocks from our house. We took turns watching the kids while the other went to vote."

On November 22, 1963, just after lunch, Joe was standing near the switchboard at National Jewish and in mid-conversation with Maude, the operator. Like tens of millions of Americans, he can pinpoint exactly the moment he heard the news. It devastated him.

Eula was home at the sink, washing Lisa's hair, when the television broke in with a special report. She immediately went to the phone to call Joe. He already knew. President John F. Kennedy had been assassinated.

Joe had never heard of Vietnam when it became a part of the national lexicon. That said, he was adamantly against the Vietnam War. He felt the country had no business being a part of a political war and his feelings intensified as the years dragged on into the seventies.

When Martin Luther King was assassinated April 4, 1968, Joe wasn't surprised.

"I had mixed-race kids. I saw all those people kicked and brutalized, both blacks and whites. So people who can do that, you don't have to go very far to think they would do anything to a person."

Joe didn't agree with Malcolm X; he felt his approach was simply hate. Joe didn't support the Black Panther movement.

As the sixties came to an end, there was yet another murder. Joe watched Bobby Kennedy's speech, from the Ambassador Hotel in Los Angeles, the night of the California primary and the subsequent chaos that broke out on the television. It was another shock in a tumultuous decade. Kennedy's speech was just past midnight the early morning of June 5, 1968—ironically, Joe III's eighth birthday. Robert Kennedy died of his wounds the following day, June 6, in a Los Angeles hospital—the 24th anniversary of D-Day in Normandy.

What is the world coming to, Joe thought.

"I had just seen Bobby at Lisa and Joe's elementary school, not too long before. He flew into Denver and was on the campaign trail. He was shaking hands with the kids and I was so close, I could have reached out and touched him," Eula remembered.

T HE 1960S ALSO REPRESENTED A DECADE OF UNCERTAINTY for the LaNiers. Joe left a job of nearly a decade, worked those multiple part-time pharmacy jobs, and finally decided to go into business for himself. He bought a drugstore from a pharmacist at 16th and York Streets but was never able to get the necessary daily prescriptions to keep the store open. He had to shut its doors. It was still a monumental leap for the man who, just two decades earlier, had come back from WWII having only completed half of the ninth grade.

Two blocks from his home in Park Hill, Joe fell in love with a corner location at 28th and Fairfax. It was already a drugstore and he fixed it up and turned it into "LaNier's Pharmacy," with a *Know Your Pharmacist* slogan printed on every prescription label. It was 1967, and Joe thought he had reached the pinnacle of his career.

After new carpet, fresh paint, a remodel of the pharmacy area, and dealings with the Small Business Administration and Colorado State Bank, Joe celebrated a spring grand opening. Local politicians were there and his store even gained press coverage in *The Denver Post* and a preview piece in *The Park Hill News* on September 14, 1966; ",,,The remodeling now in progress at LaNier's Pharmacy includes a complete new prescription department, carpeted floor, and stereo-taped music."

But soon the problems surfaced. The neighborhood was changing from white to black, and income levels and subsequent choices within those two different groups were quite different. Joe quickly began to lose money. Besides his own long hours, he had three clerks on staff, along with a part-time pharmacist. He told me he never made more than $600.00 per month.

Shoplifting was also a problem. Joe caught thieves all the time. One acquaintance even told Joe his store was just too nice and he avoided coming in because he didn't want to get the new carpet dirty. Other blacks in the neighborhood were also afraid to come in because they felt it was too nice for them. Another problem was his competition: grocery store chains had started to open pharmacies at various locations. They offered cheaper prices and eliminated the need for a separate stop at the local pharmacy.

Joe also had a medical scare with high blood pressure and the nearly seven-days-a-week schedule had taken its toll. To make matters worse, the Denver gang problem had started. As a result, he contacted the police department to acquire a gun permit—though he hadn't held a weapon since WWII. The officer told him they weren't issuing permits but that Joe should go buy a gun and keep it in the store. The same officer then told him if he had to use it and if he shot the guy outside, bring him inside before the police were called. It would be considered self-defense that way.

Joe asked the officer about weapons training. He was told to point "the business end" at the target and pull the trigger. Joe bought two guns: a .45 he kept underneath the counter and he wore a .38 on his waist; often he went to the shooting range to keep comfortable with the weapons.

"It was scary and when he would come home at night, I'd make him take the bullets out of the gun and put them in the drawer so the kids couldn't get at it. It was scary," Eula said, regret in her voice. The two had many discussions where Eula tried to discourage him from having weapons at the store and in the house.

One spring day in 1968, Joe was in the back filling a prescription. "LaNier's" had barely been open a year when he heard the tiny chimes of the front door and looked up. He couldn't believe what he saw. A man entered with a gun and pointed it at Joe as he approached. With every step, the barrel of the gun got closer and closer.

As luck would have it, another customer had come in the front door about the same time. In a matter of seconds, that guy clocked the would-be robber in the face and knocked him out cold. It turned out the man who came in happened to be an ex-fighter. The fact was, Joe stood there and was wearing his small .38 in his waistband. It could have played out to be a tragedy.

Besides the drama, the receipts just never added up and finally, in 1969, Joe told the bank he just couldn't make it. "LaNier's Pharmacy" was turned back over in a foreclosure. The drug companies worked with him to take back inventory and suppliers knew Joe was an honest man who made a risky business decision. All of his creditors were understanding and never pursued any legal action.

J OE WOULD BE THE FIRST TO ADMIT—EVEN IN THE TUMULTU-ous 1960s—he was not an activist. But the evening of May 26, 1969, he did deliver a speech, *Black Power—Riots* to the Toastmasters Club in Denver.

"I say to the power structure—to white America—you have given enough lip-service to the problem. Now do something. Start *now* to change some of your attitudes. Hire people on the basis of their ability and forget the quota system. When you come in contact with black people, train your mind to see a *man* who happens to be black and not a black who *might* be a man," he told a crowd.

"I say to black America, let us take a look at what we suggest white America should do and use it as a guide for what we ought to do. We must use every *lawful* means available to obtain all we are entitled to under the Constitution of the country. We should be proud that all men are *not* created equal but rather all men are equally responsible to the law."

THROUGH HIS CONNECTIONS, DESPITE A FAILED PHARMACY, Joe landed on his feet at Spaulding Rehabilitation Hospital in Denver where he once again became the first black pharmacist. He also gained his first experience in purchasing, which paved the way for parts of the next two decades of work.

The pay was low. Once again, Joe pursued part-time work but this time he harkened back to something he loved from his days in New Orleans: he again turned to radio. He bought broadcasting lessons from a traveling salesman out of California—$550.00 for a kit from the Columbia School of Broadcasting. It was a decent way to potentially supplement his income. As a part of his broadcast practice, he set up an ironing board in the bedroom and practiced into a reel-to-reel recorder, pretending to do newscasts.

He sent in the tapes like clockwork. They'd critique them and send them back with pointers. One day, Eula had had enough and told her husband he had wasted a lot of money. The next day Joe went to the phone book and called Denver radio station KDEN.

Just as he had done at WMRY back in college, he called a radio station cold—out of the blue. He talked with the program director, Dick Brehm, and as luck would have it, they were looking for a part-time person to fill weekends. He went to the station on Jewell Avenue in the Ruby Hill neighborhood in southwest Denver, met with the station manager, John Wolfe, and was hired. The Spider was back but he was wise enough to simply go by his real name this time around.

(In another parallel between Joe and me, in early 1993, on my own job hunt through Colorado, I interviewed at the same radio station facility. However, unlike Joe, I wasn't offered a job and eventually moved to Fresno.)

As a disc jockey, Joe played jazz Friday and Saturday nights until midnight on KDEN-AM. His theme that opened each shift was *Harlem Nocturne* by Willis Jackson, a sultry saxophone-driven piece with big horns. When the jazz shift ended, Joe powered-down the AM side, then went across the hall to KDEN-FM and played classical music overnights. Sometimes he fell asleep during his long shifts.

Joe had an active listening audience and sometimes it was unforgiving. In fact, on more than one occasion, the director of the Colorado Symphony called him in the studio to correct him on his pronunciation of certain performers and composers.

"One night I was introducing Spanish composer Manuel de Falla. I called him 'de-FELL-uh' instead of 'de-FYE-uh' and the symphony director, Dr. Bricoe, called me up and chewed me out. During one call, she said simply, 'Man, you are *so* bad!'" Joe laughed.

Joe had no clue about classical music. But he did the job. He learned. He also did newscasts as a part of his shifts at the top of every hour. He became fascinated by news and read the copy provided by the Associated Press newswire machine at the station. He also became friends with his counterparts at KOA, my current employer. At the time, KOA radio and KOA-TV were connected and Joe became friends with the legendary Denver Broncos play-by-play man, Bob Martin.

There he was, alone in a studio, in charge of a station's sound. During our interview session, we laughed at the irony that in my college days at Cal Poly, I did much the same shift at KWWV-FM, though at "K-WAVE" I spun adult contemporary hits from a small business park in Morro Bay. As my college friends partied on weekends, I worked to gain on-air experience.

EULA LISTENED TO HER HUSBAND ON AIR. SOMETIMES SHE heard him more on the air than at home because he was gone so much. When kids came over to see Lisa and Joe III, their friends would be instantly impressed that their dad was on the radio. He gave them shout-outs on the radio consistently over the two years of part-time work.

In 1972, Joe left Spaulding after an opportunity came up at General Rose Hospital in Denver. Rose, like National Jewish, had a large contingent of Jewish doctors—many of whom, early in their careers, went through prejudice and demeaning situations based solely on their ethnicity and religious beliefs.

Through various channels, Joe found out about a position as director of purchasing at Rose and went for a meeting with the CFO. Joe considered a job offer a long shot at best but he got one. (More irony: of course unbeknownst to me at the time, when at Rose, Joe had worked just two blocks away from where, in 1995, I bought my first home on Cherry Street in Denver.)

Joe returned his application and became a nervous wreck. There was no other black person in Denver who held such a position, if anywhere in the region. If he got the job, he would be in charge of purchasing for a 300-bed hospital instead of Spaulding's 80. At Rose, there were operating rooms, a trauma center, and other departments a rehab facility simply didn't have. Getting the job at Rose meant Joe would close the book on his pharmaceutical career, yet it was something he was ready to do. He remains adamant he never did miss being in a pharmacy by any stretch.

In a final interview with the top Rose administrators, the topic of salary was put on the table. Joe told them his salary at both Spaulding and his part-time radio job, and a bit later in the interview process, they offered him the position. They told him they would pay the combined salary of both, with the caveat he leave his radio career behind. He was fine with that arrangement.

Joe agreed to the annual starting salary of $14,500.00 and began the second half of his career in a position that challenged, frustrated, and rewarded him. He found himself in a position of authority. People looked to him for leadership and opportunities, things he could have never dreamed about in his first few jobs as a kid in Mississippi. He started to learn how to manage people, including his secretary, Sharon Lambert—a white woman. It was not lost on Joe that his first social contact with a white woman was during that troop train stop in Omaha and that his first interaction with a white woman, in Colorado in 1946, made such an impact he eventually moved there. Now, Joe was in the position of interviewing women to hire as his own personal secretary.

The times had changed.

Joe spent a total of 17 years at Rose—10 as Vice President of Support Services. A push for more diversity within the department helped Joe elevate to a bigger position and a $75.00-per-month raise, something he is not ashamed to admit. He told me on numerous occasions during our chats that there were times, in the seventies and eighties, where his race actually opened doors that normally would have been sealed shut.

The new CEO wanted to promote from within and also wanted an African-American among his vice presidents. Joe fit the desire perfectly. At one point, eight different department heads reported to him and he was responsible for as many 250 employees. Several years later, however, Rose was sold for nearly $180 million to Hospital Corporation of America, a huge medical conglomerate. With the sale, in came a new CEO and Joe's work life became miserable. Despite being responsible for nearly $27 million a year within his hospital division, he felt the new boss simply wanted someone else in his position.

Joe was told to increase revenue, and it was his idea for Rose to design and build a $2 million hospital laundry facility that could handle up to 30 million pounds a year. It was the laundry facility that led to Joe's decline and eventual departure.

LISA AND JOE III ENTERED THEIR TEENAGE YEARS AND excelled in music and sports, respectively. Joe became a track star and for a time, was the second-fastest half-miler in the state of Colorado. He was quiet, private, and dedicated to becoming as good as he could be at sports and because of his skin color, no one seemed to be able to pinpoint young Joe's racial background. In fact, in college at Colorado State University in the late 1970s, he ran into trouble during the United States conflict with Iran. Many thought he was Iranian.

While Joe III was quiet and focused on sports, his sister was focused in a different way.

"Lisa, she was another matter. She was independent beyond belief. I wanted people to see her and say, 'There goes Joe LaNier's daughter.' It didn't work out that way. She was strong-willed and wanted to be treated as an adult. Compromise wasn't good enough and not being able to relate to her the way she wanted me to was the most serious problem."

Lisa left the house the day after she turned 18, barely making it out of high school. Joe could not be more proud of her today and they have a warm, loving affection for one another. Both Joe and Eula knew they were providing a better life for their kids than their own and that made them proud.

"He was good but he was absent a lot because of work. I did it alone quite a bit," Eula said.

I N 1988, JOE'S 17 YEARS AT ROSE CAME TO AN ABRUPT END. AT 62, he was just three years shy of his target retirement date; he'd never missed a budget and had learned to successfully manage people and departments. But he made a mistake when he ordered a piece of equipment without the approval of the finance committee. He called the president to apologize and was assured there wouldn't be an issue. A month later, a scathing letter came—and shortly after, the new CEO levied a scathing allegation in a face-to-face meeting.

"I thought I was going in to give him a briefing. When I finished, he told me he wanted me to leave Rose and he wanted it done 'right now.' He told me he had knowledge that I had received a red Cadillac from a company we did business with, which he did not name. I fought for my job. I figured I had a right to save my position. It turned out he just wanted me gone."

There was never a red Cadillac. It was a fabricated story.

"I knew you couldn't accept a car! That would be dumb. It didn't happen," Joe told me. Eula weighed in.

"It was supposed to be a red Cadillac. That's what blacks were supposed to drive, just like they eat watermelon. There were racial undertones," she said.

Joe was fired over a red car that didn't exist.

Fred Davine, his friend and one-time chairman of the board, insisted Joe be allowed to resign instead of a straight termination.

In perhaps the biggest mistake of the second half of his life, Joe did resign. He had every reason to file a lawsuit but instead he stepped down. Even one of the members of the Rose board of directors later told the CEO—a man Joe still describes as "an unprincipled man with no conscience"—he was lucky the hospital didn't get sued.

"Do you regret that?" I asked.

"No. I had had a good life. I had reached a time and reached a salary of roughly $60,000.00 a year and I had been there 17 years. I knew I could have sued them but I thought about my past. I had done what very few black men in this profession had accomplished. Why ruin it by having a lawsuit? It's not going to get my position back. I just feel I didn't need to do that. So no, I don't regret it."

As I drove home from our interview session, I couldn't get the red Cadillac story out of my mind. For the first time, in the more than 80 hours of talking with Joe, I disagreed wholeheartedly with him.

He should have sued.

CHAPTER EIGHTEEN

HISTORY

This is the land of opportunity. What's great about our country is our enduring belief that anyone can make it— and everyone should try.

—President Barack Obama
September 27, 2011
Denver

Air Force One touched down at Buckley Air Force Base in Aurora, Colorado, about 1:25 p.m. Tuesday afternoon, September 27, 2011. President Barack Obama was on the final leg of a west coast fundraising trip and delivered a 22-minute outdoor speech at Abraham Lincoln High School in southwest Denver. Here, he touted his American Jobs Act. It was a quick Colorado stop (less than three hours from wheels down to wheels up) at the end of a three-day, three-state tour.

President Obama had spent the previous two days raising funds for his re-election and the 2012 campaign. He began his trip in Seattle with stops at the home of the Microsoft COO and another private fundraiser that included a photo opportunity with the Commander-in-Chief for $7,500.00 per picture. The President headed next to San Jose and a reception at the home of Silicon-Valley-based Symantec's chairman, then on to the home of Facebook's COO for dinner.

After an overnight in the Bay Area and a Monday morning town hall meeting at social media giant LinkedIn, it was on to Marine Corps Air Station San Diego and another private fundraiser, this one in La Jolla, where I spent summers snorkeling as a kid. Less than three hours later, Air Force One was on its way to Los Angeles, where entertainment-industry executives later greeted the President at two evening events. After an overnight at the famous Beverly Wilshire Hotel, he departed southern California for Colorado.

While the President spoke in front of thousands of cheering students, residents, and local politicians at Lincoln High, Joe and I sat in our familiar positions at his dining room table, about 15 miles to the south. Since the President was in town, I figured it would be as good a time as any to get Joe's views on what Mr. Obama represented. From what he had told me previously, I knew his feelings. But it was nonetheless important to capture, on-the-record, Joe's unique perspective on the President and the state of race relations, early in the 21st century.

"I never expected to see a black President, certainly not in my lifetime. Never. When he decided to run and made his announcement official, I thought he was nothing more than another sacrificial lamb in the party. I thought there was no way he could win in the atmosphere of today. I was delighted that he did but I never thought I'd see it. I thought it would happen, but not now."

Fittingly, a line in Mr. Obama's Denver speech that warm fall afternoon resonated with the Joe LaNier story: "We have a lot to do to make sure everyone in this country gets a fair shake, a fair shot, and a chance to get ahead…. We are tougher than the times we live in…. We are a people who write our own destiny."

It was as if the President of the United States was speaking directly about my friend.

DENVER WAS THE HISTORIC SITE OF THE DEMOCRATIC National Convention in 2008, and Invesco Field at Mile High hosted a crowd of tens of thousands as Barack Obama made his acceptance speech and accepted the party's nomination. Tens of millions more watched on television and listened on radio. I covered the convention and co-hosted our coverage that historic summer evening from downtown to our audience across the Rocky Mountain region on 850 KOA. Regardless of politics, it was one of the most invigorating, inspiring, well-delivered speeches I have seen in my lifetime. Joe watched it unfold on television, from the comfort of his living room about 20 miles south.

"We are not an old country. Slavery ended in 1865. What I lived through is hard to convey to people who didn't go through it—for example, the Civil Rights movement. It is hard for people, after that generation, to understand what life was like in our country. Certainly people today can't really comprehend *total segregation.* They can imagine what it was like, say, for two water fountains: one white and one black. But it's hard to really *understand* it. You think about me? Think about my father, who was born in 1891. Or think about my mother's father, who was a slave. When I think about the things I have personally seen—physical violence to another human being—and how, in a sense, I had to walk on eggshells in order to have some sort of life—that's what I'm comparing when I look at how far we've come," Joe stated.

During this particular interview session, he was very determined and methodical in the way he addressed my questions. It wasn't as if this was more important than anything else we had talked about but it seemed he took things to heart and much more personally than when he talked about certain stories in his life.

"When I was growing up, I would sometimes have to get off the sidewalk when a white person was coming toward me. They didn't ask me to do that but I knew that if I touched them in a way they didn't like, that could be dangerous for me. If you were in line at a store, and a white person came in to be waited on, the salesperson would stop everything and go wait on the white person. Blacks couldn't return clothing. If we bought it and it didn't fit, no one would take the items back."

He contemplated a bit.

"There were stores I went in where I couldn't sit down next to a white person, when I tried on shoes, for example. That's what I mean by how far we have moved but it doesn't mean that we've moved so far that we don't have to look back at that and say we have to learn from that, in order to continue forward progress."

Joe then reflected on his grandfather—his mother's father—Watt Barnett. According to later U.S. Census documents, he was born in Charleston, South Carolina, in 1852—or nine years before the start of the Civil War.

Joe saw him once, in St. Louis when Joe was just 23.

"He was visiting my Uncle Robert, his son; and I re-routed myself from my college job in the steel factory outside Pittsburgh, back through Missouri, so I could meet him in the latter part of August 1949. I was there less than a day and didn't see him very long because I had to catch my train back to college in New Orleans. No one in the family *ever* discussed his slavery past. It wasn't until I started researching my family tree at the Federal Center in Lakewood, Colorado, that I learned he was a slave."

Watt Barnett's grandmother was likely from Africa. He was 97 when Joe met him for the first and only time. Thin, with short salt-and-pepper hair, his grandfather was sharp, coherent, and clean-shaven. Though Joe looked hard, he couldn't tell any family resemblance.

"I really wanted to meet him. One of the reasons why it was important was that years back, my mother and sisters went to meet him when I was about 13. I had to stay home due to money concerns and I was very upset. So when I learned he was going to visit Uncle Robert, I just routed myself from the Pittsburgh train station down to St. Louis."

The family that owned Watt Barnett operated a Civil War-era plantation in South Carolina and several years later, moved the slaves and the family to a plantation in Alabama. After the Emancipation Proclamation, Barnett moved west to Columbus, Mississippi, where he met his eventual wife, Louisa.

"When I met him, he had on a T-shirt and a pair of pants, and was sitting on the bed when I walked upstairs and into the small room. I told him who I was and he said he was happy to see me and then, immediately, he starts telling me how my grandmother had treated him! I said to myself, 'It's been 50 years and he's *still* mad?'" Joe laughed.

During their two-hour conversation, Joe sat in a chair next to the bed where his grandfather held court. The walls were bare.

Joe memorized his grandfather. The man looked white but appeared as if he had a dark suntan. His chiseled features indicated to Joe that he wasn't completely black.

"I bet he worked at what they called 'the big house' and was not a field slave because clearly his father was white. That corroborated what my father told me he had heard when I was a little kid."

The time went quickly. There was never any discussion of the war and when they agreed it was time to go, there was no hug goodbye—no physical contact. Joe had to catch a train later that evening back to New Orleans. Still, Joe was extremely happy to have met the man he considered a missing link in his life—a connection to his past.

As he recapped the meeting, Joe paused.

"One of my greatest regrets was that I didn't have the where-withal to ask him what it was like being a slave. Today, I read all that stuff and can visualize it but I just missed the opportunity. I was 23 and that just wasn't where my mind was."

Joe would have been unable to pick out his grandfather from a lineup. He had never seen a picture of the man and never saw him again. In his later years, Joe has thought about that meeting in St. Louis a thousand times: the things he *could* have asked, *should* have asked, and *wanted* to ask. The meeting proved to him that slavery was not something strictly from the history books. This was Joe's connection—proof there was still a link to an ugly past.

"There's no way I can understand what he went through. You don't have to have a broken leg to know it hurts if you break it. But I can know that when I saw him, he wasn't a slave anymore. So that tells me something about what my country is doing. There's no such thing as a perfect Union. That's why we always say we are trying to make it a *more* perfect Union, because each generation is going to have something they need to fix that the previous generation didn't do."

I N THE MID-1990S, EULA FINALLY CONVINCED JOE TO BECOME equally fascinated with researching her family tree. (Over the decades she was able to trace her relatives to England, Ireland, Holland, and to Chickasaw Indian tribes in North America. Her research traced back to 1790.) At first Joe dismissed the idea, and then he too became obsessed with researching her roots. By 2005, the couple had put in hundreds of hours and quite a bit of money in pursuit of filling in their ancestral blanks. On one trip back to Mississippi, Joe was in pursuit to find someone who could assist him in finding some needed answers. To his good fortune, he met a helpful white woman, Mrs. Sparrow, at the Columbus library. A few weeks later, she sent him a letter with six names of people who could potentially assist. Joe picked a name at random.

It was a lucky choice.

He picked Libba Johnson, who was actually a descendant on the female side of the "white" Laniers. Joe sent her a copy of his autobiography he had written for his children and they had dinner with her on their next trip to Columbus.

Joe also used this time to search the Internet and he connected with a man, Wayne Lanier, who was also a descendant of the "white" Laniers—original slave owners in Brunswick County, Virginia, in the south-central part of the state, on the North Carolina border. They owned Joe's distant relatives beginning around 1818. Joe's great-grandfather on his mother's side was born in that very county.

Wayne Lanier—no capital "N" in the way he spelled it—lived in Charleston, South Carolina. Joe wrote Wayne a letter and it turned out both had an extreme interest in their family history. It was a dream match-up for both men. Wayne loved reading about Joe's life, and Joe loved getting bits and pieces of his past from Wayne's knowledge. Both were tracing their roots in different directions and they intersected. It was an incredible link.

The two men developed a long-distance friendship and among other things, discussed slavery and their common distant relatives. They were, in essence, still total strangers but in 2004, the LaNiers invited the Laniers to spend a week in Colorado. They flew into Denver, Joe and Eula picked them up, and it was as if they'd known each other their entire lives.

By pure chance, just hours before one of our interview sessions, Joe had talked by phone with Wayne Lanier. Here was my friend, Joe—grandson of a slave—talking with his friend, Wayne, whose family not only owned Joe's relatives, but also shared a branch on the family tree. You may have to read those last two sentences again to let it fully sink in. I was dumbfounded then—and now. What were the odds?

"At one point, I pushed Eula so hard during the research of our family tree she said she was going to divorce me!" Joe laughed. Eula smiled but didn't deny it.

We all looked at each other and laughed.

CHAPTER NINETEEN

REMEMBER

As my summer of 2011 continued with Joe, several things began to develop. They would not only become key events that would help shape this project but events that would offer him the ability to look back at his amazing life from a perspective he never thought possible. It became clear to me early on in my friendship with this incredible man, that in order to get an accurate understanding of where he grew up and how his physical surroundings made him the man he is today, we would have to travel together back to Mississippi. He would also have to get back to Iwo Jima. One journey was certainly more feasible than the other, though Joe had come about as close as he could get to Iwo just months earlier.

After endless planning, eight WWII veterans were set to travel back to Iwo Jima in March 2011. This trip was the original reason Joe came up on my radar. That particular The Greatest Generations Foundation (TGGF) program started March 10, 2011, in Denver, then went on to Los Angeles, Honolulu, and finally the men arrived in Guam on March 11. At the Hilton Guam, weary veterans quickly made their way to their rooms to get some needed rest but what they didn't know was that very day they touched down, the largest earthquake in the history of Japan had hit the Iwate Prefecture and caused massive structural damage. The odds of this happening at the time of their planned return to Iwo Jima had to be ten-billion-to-one. Sadly, the 9.0-magnitude quake would go down as one of the planet's five biggest earthquakes in recorded history.

As Joe unpacked his suitcase that day and adjusted to the humidity on Guam, the most devastating tsunami in Japan's storied history sped toward hundreds of unsuspecting villages and cities. More than 10,000 people were killed. In the Iwate Prefecture alone, nearly 10,000 fishing vessels were destroyed and 108 of its 111 ports were decimated. The damage from the quake, tsunami, and the incredibly dangerous threat of a nuclear meltdown forced the Japanese to come together like at no other time since the latter stages of WWII. Rescuers and civilians rushed to the aid of their homeland and their countrymen. They came from all parts of the Japanese islands and as the U.S. Navy and Marines rushed to the aid of our critical ally, they too rushed in a small, select number of personnel to the north coast of Japan from Iwo Jima.

The commemoration ceremony and veteran opportunity to return to Iwo was officially canceled.

Alicia Harms, a dedicated, caring, recent College of the Ozarks graduate, and lead TGGF staff member on the program, learned of the disaster. It soon fell squarely on her shoulders to inform the veterans on her watch that their lifelong goal, dream, apparition, and challenge of going back to hell on earth was no longer a possibility. Joe said after Alicia informed the group at lunch, she broke down and cried.

"It was disbelief. We came all this way and we're not able to go? Quickly, I realized there was nothing we could do about that. It was an act of God."

Individually, the veterans stayed strong and they spent the next few days touring the battlefields on Guam. Deep down, they thought they would never return. It became my goal to get Joe back on the next TGGF Iwo Jima opportunity the following spring.

As we continued our interview sessions over that summer, Joe and I learned we would both travel to Pearl Harbor, Hawaii, as a part of another TGGF program. We would be there with other WWII veterans to commemorate the 65th anniversary of the Japanese surrender aboard the USS Missouri. It was, as I expected, an incredibly emotional journey for Joe and his fellow veterans.

Memories and different emotions crackled and zinged in his mind as he returned to places like Ford Island, Hickam Field, Kaneohe Naval Air Station, Schofield Barracks, and Waikiki. Joe hadn't been back to Hawaii since he left Iroquois Point in early 1945. Sixty-six years later, he experienced the same temperatures, tropical air, and island smells. The morning after the veterans checked into the Hilton Hawaiian Village, Joe walked out past the manicured hedges and clean pools to the sandy beach and off to his left, hotels stretched several miles down the sand. Diamond Head stood proudly, keeping the same stoic watch over Honolulu as it had for centuries. In front of Joe were the waters where he first touched the ocean, rented that swimsuit, and climbed aboard a wooden surfboard. The memories were all still there.

For the fourth time in as many years, I had the honor of accompanying these WWII vets back to Pearl Harbor. Our program culminated with a special ceremony on the teak deck of the Missouri, site of the official Japanese surrender in Tokyo Bay, September 2, 1945. Like Joe, she served her country in the battles of Iwo Jima and Okinawa. On a beautiful Hawaiian morning, our group sat on white folding chairs among the veterans and dignitaries under her 16-inch guns, each capable of firing a one-ton shell up to 25 miles. Joe and his fellow veterans were treated with great respect, like the honored guests they were. It was a fantastic sight.

D URING PREPARATION FOR THAT HAWAII PROGRAM IN August 2011, I had already started planning our journey back to Mississippi. Joe LaNier's life, I decided, was not only good enough for a book but would make an incredible documentary as well, so I called on a former colleague of mine from my days at WNYW-TV in New York and re-connected with my friend and videographer, Andre Greller. He was onboard from the moment I explained my desire to document Joe's life. We then began our countdown to the October departure.

My goal was to capture Joe's story, through honest and heartfelt discussion. I told him from the first day he would not be out one penny in costs related to travel, publishing, editing, or anything else connected with the project. He and Eula live on a fixed income, so I went into my savings account to ensure the only thing he had to worry about was remembering and relaying his incredible past.

In our final interview session, two days before leaving Colorado for New Orleans, I asked him to give me some of his thoughts and feelings on the upcoming trip.

"It's an incredible feeling to do this because it never crossed my mind I would be going back for this reason. Never. I never thought that anyone would be interested in my life as you are. I'm not uncomfortable with it, it's just..." he struggled for the right words and cleared his throat.

"Maybe it's a feeling that I don't know if I've accomplished enough to have all of this kind of attention. Having lived long enough to have had some small part of participating in changing the way things are today, maybe what we are doing will benefit someone else way down the road. I'm not a senator, not a governor—just an ordinary person able to accomplish a lot of things under sometimes very difficult circumstances."

THE MORNING OF THURSDAY, OCTOBER 13, 2011, I WOKE AT my usual 3:00 a.m. with bags packed for our journey to the South. I thought, as I pulled out of my driveway in the Denver suburb of Highlands Ranch, the next few days would hold an incredible amount of emotion. For me, I knew it would be emotional to finally see with my own eyes all the places I had only conjured up in my mind but for Joe, of course, it would be a great deal more emotional. He was going home in a way he had never gone back before—to face not only pleasant memories but the demons of his past as well.

I signed off the air on KOA, scrambled quickly to my car, and out to the airport. Joe III took his father because of time constraints and when I arrived at Denver International about 10:00 a.m., Joe was waiting in front of the United Airlines ticket counter as we had planned. We hugged, laughed, and smiled and both knew we had a lot of work ahead in a relatively short amount of time. Three states, thousands of travel miles, multiple interview sessions, and hundreds of questions loomed.

With bags checked, we made it through security without any problems. I felt like I was escorting a celebrity, yet no one knew his story. *If they only knew,* I've thought during the multiple times I've been out with Joe in public. *If they only knew* his story and the trials and tribulations he's gone through—the places he's been and the oath he took to defend all enemies, foreign and domestic. *If they only knew* at times, his greatest enemies were in his own backyard.

After boarding, we took our seats and waited for takeoff. Joe and I both had aisle seats and every now and then, I reached over and patted him on the arm and smiled. It was my way of thanking him for agreeing to go back to his roots. He was dressed in slacks, collared shirt, and sweater and his ensemble was completed with his trademark Stetson. I was proud to sit next to him as we rolled down the runway toward the Rocky Mountains and jolted skyward, en route to Louisiana.

W E LANDED AT LOUIS ARMSTRONG INTERNATIONAL Airport—the first time for Joe—and headed to baggage claim. Andre had arrived an hour earlier and was waiting at another carousel. We hugged and it was great for me to see him, six years after I left WNYW-TV, Fox 5 in New York. The two of us walked back down so I could introduce Joe to Andre and from the very first moment, the two of them hit it off with laughter and stories. Andre immediately respected Joe and his story when I pitched him on the idea via email and on the phone, so to see it in person was something special. I will forever be grateful to Andre for believing in my idea and for showing Joe the proper respect he deserves.

Baggage in hand, we secured our rental car, a 2011 Toyota Camry, for the drive into New Orleans. Andre climbed in the back, Joe in the passenger seat, and me behind the wheel and as I put the keys into the ignition, I took an extra deep breath and smiled to myself. My vision of seeing Joe, happy, back in his region of the country, had come true. I patted him on his leg as he clicked-in his seat belt.

"Let's do this," I said to both men.

It was time to get to work.

THE HEAT OF MID-OCTOBER IN LOUISIANA SURPRISED ME. We drove immediately from the airport to a convenience store to load up on a case of water and then drove east a few miles to our first destination: Xavier University.

As we walked on campus, Joe immediately reminded us of where things were and what used to be where. The campus was fairly small and showed its age in certain spots, but it was refreshing to see a mix of students who walked past us every now and then. What had been an all-black school when Joe attended, was now integrated.

Our first interview on-camera took place on the backside of the school's administration building, inside a grassy area surrounded on three sides by multi-story structures. We stood in the presence of the Virgin Mary, her statue watching over us as we wired Joe with a wireless microphone. With Andre behind the lens and me standing out of frame and to Joe's left, it was time.

Rolling.

"How does it feel to be back? What's going through your mind?" I asked Joe.

"I had no clue what would happen to me after the service," he said.

The answers that followed were rich, honest, and poignant. This campus changed the course and direction of his life. As he had told me many times: failure was not an option and failure here certainly meant he was destined for some sort of manual labor the rest of his life back in Mississippi.

We wrapped the first video interview and immediately went to our first appointment of the trip. In advance of our Denver departure, Joe had set up a meeting with his old college friend, Norman Francis. I had no idea he was such an iconic New Orleans educational leader.

Andre stayed outside to film. Joe and I went through a heavy, old, wooden door and up two flights of stairs to Xavier's administrative offices. We were greeted by a secretary and waited a few minutes before the two friends were united once again. Outside the doorway of his cluttered office, Dr. Norman Francis welcomed Joe just as he was: an old, longtime friend. We were led inside, introductions were made, and we took seats at a table. I was instantly mesmerized by their conversation and recollections.

As I would learn that afternoon in New Orleans, Francis had an amazing story of his own. Born in Lafayette, Louisiana, to poor and uneducated parents, he went on to receive a scholarship to Xavier, where he met Joe. In 1952, Francis was selected to integrate Loyola University's School of Law in New Orleans, where he became not only the first black accepted there, but the university's first black law school graduate in 1955. Almost exactly six years Joe's junior, Francis served but missed the war and instead was a part of the "peacetime" Army in Frankfurt, Germany in '56 and '57.

At Xavier, the two became close friends and for a time, Joe acted as Francis' campaign manager as he ran for class president. As the two men talked, I grew more intrigued and at one point, asked Francis about Joe's demeanor on campus, just a few years removed from Iwo Jima. Not surprisingly, Joe didn't bring his war stories with him to college.

"Most of the guys didn't talk about it a lot. Here's Joe, a guy coming out of the service, served his country, got his butt shot at, and he comes back to the United States. He has to ride in the back of the bus, can't go into the front door of a theater, and has to sit in the balcony—can't vote. He's a second-class citizen. I come back in '57 and I'm a lawyer, an officer of the court. I can't go in the front door of a restaurant, all the same things. When we look back at that, it's amazing that we kept our sanity. In particular, guys like Joe. They were in the war. I was peacetime," Francis told me.

"One of our classmates was a Tuskegee Airman. You figure they fought for their country, taking their lives into their own hands, and they come back to their *own* country and they're second-class citizens. It's hard to imagine. Joe came back, got a degree, became a pharmacist, and made a life for himself. He always knew who he was. Other folks, they didn't."

Francis was named Xavier President in 1968, a position he still holds today. As we visited, he had just started his 43rd year, almost unprecedented in today's university setting. He remains close friends with Bill Cosby and Gladys Knight, knows every major politician in the Gulf Coast region, and has met popes and presidents. In one of the highlights of his life and distinguished career, he received the Presidential Medal of Freedom from President George W. Bush in December 2006.

As the two old friends sat and reminisced, I mostly looked at them in silence. I had so many questions but wanted to be more of a fly on the wall and allow them to naturally progress from topic to topic. I wondered if Joe wished he had been born at a different time, like his friend, yet deep down I knew the answer would have been a resounding "no."

Meantime, Andre continued getting us video images outside on the Xavier campus. The sun started to set over the bayou and the natural lighting inside Francis' office began to fade.

"What does it mean to you to see Joe now?" I asked.

"Joe hasn't changed! He looks the same! These guys were always well dressed, shoes shined; and that was a real message to those of us younger guys. It set the tone for those of us who came after them. And when Friday rolled around, they left campus and came back about 10:00 Sunday night! But here's the message in that: they knew when it was time to play and knew when it was time to study."

Our time at Xavier came to an end and I asked Francis if, when the book was published, we could get an audience on campus.

"Sure! We throw a parade down here whenever we hear a horn, so of course you're welcome back!" he laughed. "We gotta get you back here."

WE WRAPPED UP OUR LONG DAY WITH DINNER IN THE French Quarter at one of my favorite spots, The Gumbo Shop on Saint Peter Street. Joe, Andre, and I were running late from our time at Xavier and when we arrived, she was standing there waiting. It was Marguerite, Joe's longtime friend and confidante. They greeted each other warmly, with hugs and laughs. As I watched them interact, I could tell she was as Joe had told me: incredibly attractive back in her day, based on her beauty into her eighties. We all talked over jambalaya, seafood gumbo, and beers and had a delightful late evening.

The next morning, Andre and I captured more of New Orleans on video and then took Joe to historic Jackson Square for more interviews, where we talked about the racism he saw in this part of the country in the late 1940s and why he thinks the way he does today.

"If you allow yourself to be bitter when there were times you were not allowed to be equal under the law, what it does is it takes away from the brainpower that you have to move forward with what is given to you. If I allow myself to hate, then they win."

From our position in the square, we walked to an overlook of the Mississippi River on a gorgeous, crystal-clear Friday morning. After we watched the mighty barges float silently past us and on to the Gulf of Mexico, we all moved northeast half a block to another one of my favorite New Orleans locations, a place where Joe was refused service during his time here. Café du Monde originally opened its coffee stand in 1862 and has served their incredible chicory coffee, Café Au Laits, and beignets—fried in cottonseed oil and dusted with powdered sugar—ever since. To share a coffee and beignet with Andre and Joe, in a place where not that long ago our friend's color would have prevented him from enjoying what we did on this day, was truly a satisfying and gratifying moment in my life.

Bourbon Street bustled with delivery activity as Joe reminisced about his first Mardi Gras and how as a black man, he was unable to enter nearly every music club in the French Quarter.

"Blacks could entertain the whites in clubs but we couldn't come in and watch as a member of the audience. We were good enough to perform for them but not good enough to be considered an equal-paying customer. It was racism. I could walk the streets and go into a store to buy something but if I wanted anything to do with social activities—a movie theater, a club—that's where segregation began."

Our tour of New Orleans continued with a stop outside a jewelry store off Canal Street. This was the location of the American Pharmacy, where Joe was told if he got the pharmacist's job, he would have to stay upstairs to fill his prescriptions and out of view of the white customers on the first level.

"You know you're qualified. You know they need you, yet because of your color, you're not allowed. I knew when I walked in I was as qualified as anyone else looking for a position. My color was what caused them not to hire me."

As we put a wrap on the New Orleans leg of the trip, we walked down a block to where an old photography studio had been—the one where Joe had his graduation picture taken and Mama's only photo touched up. It was now a restaurant with metal bars covering its main entrance and every street-level window. Joe took pride as he recapped what a special day that had been for him back in the 1950s, and save for the modern-day cars on Canal, the place likely looked almost identical to the way it did when he lived there. He smiled as we got back into the rental car.

Our final stop was at 1859 Law Street and the small home where Joe had rented a room after he graduated from Xavier. He sat on the front steps and recounted the kindness of the Gaudin family that took him in and how they treated him like a son—and how he stayed in New Orleans because segregation was so severe in Columbus, he didn't want to go back.

The New Orleans portion of the project was complete.

O N FRIDAY AFTERNOON, OCTOBER 14, JOE, ANDRE, AND I drove out of New Orleans on Interstate 10, having just completed an amazing 24-hour period. We headed northeast, past the Bayou Sauvage National Wildlife Refuge and over Lake Pontchartrain, for a lunch of southern food and iced tea at the Cracker Barrel restaurant in Slidell, Louisiana.

An interesting thing happened as we walked out of the restaurant. As we stood on the front stoop area of the Cracker Barrel, Joe struck up a conversation with a large white man who limped and walked with a cane; a stereotypical bayou man, complete with overalls. Within a minute, the two men knew of each other's military service and had shared quick stories. In a thick southern accent, the man informed us he was just 68-years-old and had "dead feet" from Agent Orange during his Army days in Vietnam. He was on the frontlines as a communications man, which explained why his hearing was poor. If I had to make a guess at how old he was, I would have said closer to 80. War—and life—had been hard on him. As we said goodbye in the parking lot, I truly wished things could have turned out differently for this complete stranger.

Crossing the state line, we all stopped at the Mississippi visitor's center, stretched our legs, and walked close to the welcome sign. A white man came up almost out of nowhere and offered to take our picture. Times have changed, I thought. We smiled, posed, and thanked him and then got back in the car.

We needed to drive nearly the entire length of the state on Interstate 59 and kept up a good pace as we headed north for Columbus. Our plan called for two nights in Joe's hometown, then stops in Holly Springs and Tupelo before an overnight in Memphis that Sunday.

Joe, Steffan, and cameraman, Andre Greller, just inside Mississippi, October 2011.
(Steffan Tubbs)

I drove through places I had never heard of, this being my first trip to Mississippi. I recall being surprised at just how lush and dense the state was as we rolled through Poplarville, Lumberton, West Hattiesburg, and Laurel. In-between our conversations in the rental car, I tried to imagine what it was like in these very towns back when segregation was the norm. It was a difficult proposition.

Just south of the town of Moselle, we needed gas. Joe had hinted since we arrived in New Orleans that he wanted to drive and help split the long road trip; I knew it was important to him, so I obliged. I think the trip finally sunk in with Joe as he climbed behind the wheel and began to drive us north in his home state.

"When I talk about *home*, I still think of Mississippi," he said.

"As difficult a life I had, it's still home. Of all of the things I remember, you would think I wouldn't want to remember it. But it's home."

WHAT HAPPENED IN THE NEXT HOUR PROVED TO BE ONE of the funniest moments of our trip to the South. The 85-year-old drove, well, like an 85-year-old. I say this with all the love in the world but I quickly found out my good friend has quite the lead foot. We pulled out of the Moselle gas station, back onto I-59, and Joe must have averaged 90 miles an hour, much faster than I was going. (He did hit 95 at one point to pass a big rig.) I was in the front passenger seat and at one point, caught Andre's eye in the back seat; our eyes bugged out at each other. We shared a laugh. Joe, bless his heart, was oblivious. We kept going and I assumed because this was Joe's territory, he knew our destination with pinpoint accuracy. That is until I saw the "Welcome to Alabama" sign in front of us. Before we knew what happened, we were idling near an off-ramp in Cuba, Alabama. Joe had missed the turn to State Route 45, north.

"Who knew we were also going to Alabama on this trip!" I joked with Joe.

We all laughed and soon were headed back in the right direction.

Off the interstate, we took Lauderdale Toomsuba Road and headed north to connect with SR45. It was along this stretch of rural pavement, as the sun began to set, Joe started talking about the real-life Mississippi Burning case. Not knowing much more than what I could remember from seeing parts of the 1988 movie of the same title, Joe and Andre went back and forth recounting the story of three Civil Rights workers who were murdered in Neshoba County, one county to our northwest, about 20 miles away.

ON JUNE 21, 1964, THREE YOUNG CIVIL RIGHTS WORKERS, James Chaney—a 21-year-old black man from Meridian; Andrew Goodman—a white 20-year-old student from New York; and Michael Schwerner—a white 24-year-old also from New York, were shot to death near Philadelphia, Mississippi. Both the sheriff and deputy sheriff were members of the White Knights of the Ku Klux Klan and the trio was arrested for a speeding violation that afternoon. While they sat in jail, local Klansmen plotted to kill them.

The Klan set up an ambush on the route back to Meridian and the men were released on orders to vacate the area. As they left the county, they were pulled over again and held until Klansmen arrived. The men were then taken to a rural area where they were beaten and shot to death. The bodies were then buried in an earthen dam, where they remained undiscovered for 44 days. In the time the three men were missing, the Civil Rights Act of 1964 was passed in Washington.

Federal prosecutors—after an extensive FBI investigation— indicted 18 people, including the sheriff and deputy sheriff. Seven were sentenced; and after lengthy appeals, no one found guilty in the triple murder served more than six years in prison. The sheriff was acquitted.

Joe continued to drive as the story continued. We drove past extremely rural homes and trailers that looked as if they were stuck in a time warp, right out of the fifties and sixties. As ridiculous as it may sound, I honestly had a moment where I thought to myself—as the sky grew darker and we tried to follow our small map—'What if we broke down here?' Here we were in rural Mississippi: an old black man driving, lily-white me in the passenger seat, and a Latino cameraman in the back. Perhaps it was simply because of the context of our conversation (like convincing yourself you're scared because you've chosen to watch a scary movie) but the feeling was very real at the time.

We arrived in Columbus under a full harvest moon and drove Joe to the outskirts of town, where he stayed with his great niece. Andre and I checked in at our cheap motel back in town and I went to bed thinking about Mississippi Burning, wondering what the next two days had in store for us all.

ON SATURDAY MORNING, OCTOBER 15, ANDRE AND I WERE up early, verbalized a game plan, and then went across town to get Joe. His great-niece, Sheila, his brother Charlie's granddaughter, welcomed us inside, where we met three different generations of LaNier women. Before we left with Joe, he posed for pictures and they wished us all luck in finding that for which we were looking. They were most hospitable and friendly.

Within the hour, the three of us ate breakfast at a local buffet restaurant and while I was present at the table, my mind was already racing with places I wanted to go, questions I wanted to ask, and shots I wanted captured for the documentary. Andre and I finished our coffee (water for Joe, as he doesn't do coffee) and soon we were off driving south through Columbus to the rural farmland where Joe entered the world in 1926.

Our morning road trip took us through Memphis Town for the first time and out to Mr. Russell's store where Joe used to buy tobacco for Mama and Louisa. What was back then a dirt road was now the paved, two-lane Highway 50. Beautiful sunshine permeated the morning; perfect weather, I thought. We stopped at the now-abandoned store and Joe got out and walked around the perimeter. He talked of seeing horses and mules tied to hitching posts decades back and how just down Tabernacle Road, the members of the community had those great potluck feasts on Sundays under large, shady oaks and magnolias at Cross Road Church.

About 10:30 a.m., we headed back no more than a quarter-mile on Highway 50 and made a right turn on Eulie Drive East and down the country road. Off to our right, in the backyard of a home, was the spot.

"There it is," Joe said.

There was nothing there but a few shrubs and open space.

A small, flowering bush was the only indicator of the home where Savilla gave birth to Joe in the spring of 1926. It stood about three-feet-tall, in the backyard of a home that was rebuilt after a tornado roared through in 2001. One of the magnolia trees Joe looked at while growing up—and where Mama made lye soap— was destroyed as well. A somber mood fell over us as we got out of our rental car.

We noticed a man outside in the back of the home off to our right. As Andre and I got our equipment out of the trunk, Joe went over to talk with a man in a Mississippi State Bulldogs T-shirt and struck up a conversation. The owner's name was Mr. Ray, and after Joe explained why we were there, Ray offered a brief history of how his family was connected with the property. Ray developed the property that his father, Paw Paw, owned in previous decades. He told us the story of what happened on February 16, 2001, and how he hid under his living room table as a tornado roared through; another would destroy the home less than two years later.

Joe told Ray about the two bricks he still has from his childhood home, bricks made in the 1920s. Joe remembered Papa working corn and cotton patches nearby and how Papa once shot a cow in the rear in hopes of teaching the corn-eating bovine a lesson.

"This brings back a lot of memories," Joe said to Mr. Ray. "A lot of memories."

Andre set up the camera and light and we placed Joe in a folding chair on loan from his niece. We began our interview as Ray walked away to tend to other business. Joe was transformed back to the sights and smells of this place 80 years earlier; he closed his eyes and recalled Mama's cooking and the layout of the small, sparse home where many of her seven children were born.

"I remember the bodark tree, supposedly the hardest wood anywhere. Mama would sit at the base of that tree and make her lye soap. She used the ashes from the fireplace and mixed them with lye and water to make soap to wash our clothes," he told me as his eyes remained closed and a breeze blew across his face. He recalled the barn where Old Prince and Old Pete—family horses—were penned. Papa used them to help till the soil for sweet potatoes, sorghum, and cotton.

Joe seemed overwhelmed by our interview location; at times he had difficulty answering my basic questions. I understood. After a nearly 20-minute interview, we packed up, waved goodbye to Ray, and drove a few hundred yards down Highway 50.

SIRENS BROKE THE NORMAL CALM AND QUIET OF COLUMBUS on Sunday evening, November 10, 2002. The skies swirled and the barometer dropped dramatically as a major storm system hovered over southern Tennessee, northeastern Mississippi, and northwestern Alabama. A series—or swarm—of tornadoes boiled in the skies above and would soon have a devastating impact on Joe's birthplace on Eulie Drive.

As Columbus residents scrambled for shelter and heeded the tornado warnings from WMBC-AM and WCBI-TV, Mother Nature unleashed some of the worst weather in the region's history. The National Weather Service issued an official tornado warning for Columbus proper at 7:01 p.m.—19 minutes before an F3 tornado ripped through Main Street and Catfish Alley. At 7:20 p.m., Lowndes County was at the center of winds between 160 to 200 miles an hour and in a matter of moments, dozens of downtown buildings were leveled.

Churches, home basements, and other designated shelters were packed full of terrified Mississippians and the fact the roaring tornado hit under the stealth of darkness only made things worse and more terrifying. Residents in poverty-stricken Memphis Town wondered if they would be spared. As parts of trees and other debris whipped through the air and on the ground, 60 people inside Bethel Presbyterian Church activities center moved inside to interior hallways; the tornado roared closer. Minutes later, the activities center collapsed. Remarkably, no one was hurt, but Bethel Presbyterian was completely leveled. A granite marker honoring the former church is now in place. The church was never rebuilt.

Columbus was in chaos. The sustained winds ripped homes off their foundations; rooftops were tossed and debris was thrown for miles around. People cried in terror in their bathtubs as the deafening sound of the F3 roared over them. Yes, some thought, it *does* sound like a freight train. The NWS weather forecast office in Jackson, Mississippi, reported ten tornadoes and issued 37 tornado warnings between 3:00 p.m. November 10, and 2:00 a.m. November 11. One person was killed after the mobile trailer he was in was thrown 150 feet. Sixty others were injured in the region. (In February 2001, the NWS reported 114 category-F2 tornadoes in the general area in a two-day span but none were as powerful as this one.)

Off Highway 50—near Tabernacle Road and the old store owned by Mr. Russell in the 1930s—neighborhoods and rural farm homes were demolished. Joe's birthplace had been demolished by new developers years earlier but the home built near the old LaNier place was obliterated in just seconds. The home, which stood on a part of the lot where, back in 1926 Mama had delivered Joe, was gone. It was one of 122 homes destroyed in the Columbus area; 340 homes were damaged at a cost of more than $60 million. The lone magnolia tree left from Joe's childhood, the one that survived one tornado and had once stood proudly off to the side out the kitchen window, was uprooted and deposited down the road. Concrete and brick structures came down like a house of cards. The true extent of damage wouldn't be known for hours.

When the sun came up that Monday morning, the devastation was hard to fathom. Trailer homes were battered and upside down, some relocated to different neighborhoods; cars were thrown like toys and trees; Joe's magnolias that had stood for more than a century were gone. The skeletal remains of other nearby trees jutted like broken matchsticks into the morning air. Red Cross and Salvation Army volunteers offered coffee and hot meals to battered residents at various disaster assistance shelters, assessing the worst damage in at least a century in this portion of the state.

As more people came outside after their sleepless night, they viewed the damage and walked over broken glass and dangerously sharp, jagged shards of metal. FEMA workers spent the early hours interviewing survivors while rescue operations continued across Columbus. Rescuers spray-painted structures with red "OK" notifications, placed on areas they deemed searched and secured. Multi-ton train cars near the old Moss Tie Plant were toppled as FEMA photographers captured the scenes with their digital cameras. Homeowners began to move tons of debris that ended up in local landfills. It took months to clean up and years to fully rebuild. The terrible, life-altering tornadoes in Mississippi, Alabama, and Tennessee would come to be known as the "Veteran's Week" tornadoes, due to their proximity to Veterans Day.

On November 14, President George W. Bush declared Lowndes and five other nearby counties federal disaster areas. FEMA assistance totaled nearly $25 million and a National Oceanic and Atmospheric Administration report later described the tornado swath as "dramatic."

W E CROSSED THE HIGHWAY AND DROVE DOWN A LONG dirt driveway and came to a stop in front of a newer home, likely rebuilt after the tornado. Two children played outside on a swing tied to an old hickory tree. The rope was frayed in spots and the seat was a worn piece of 2x4 lumber. A dog barked off in the distance.

"This was the Weathers' place," Joe announced.

Within a minute he was at the front door talking to a friendly white woman, who explained a few things and pointed at the home 200 yards away. Andre and I stayed back for a bit and then I walked up behind Joe. He explained how he knew one of the women in the house across the field and we headed that way. I could easily imagine this place in the early part of the 20th century and many of the same structures, spared by a tornado's wrath, still stood. Under an old, weathered open barn with a tin roof, I noticed a New Holland 3930 Ford tractor with 914.1 miles on it. Why it even occurred to me to look at a tractor's odometer, I may never know.

While I was busy, Andre took exterior shots of the place—including clothes on a line, blowing in the breeze, and vines growing over old farm equipment. Joe walked to the other home and reunited on the front stoop with Mrs. Weathers. He reminded her of who he was, told her why we were there, and even explained, in detail, how he used to take mules over to the very barn where Andre and I had been standing moments earlier. As Joe talked, Andre and I continued getting images of the old structures. One of them had to be nearly 100-years-old and I peeked inside to see rolled barbed wire and worn tillers. The shed's planks were separated and warped, and moss grew on much of the outside walls. Grapevines curled up toward the rooftop. I tried to soak it all in, in hopes this location would bring me closer to understanding Joe.

From the Weathers' place, it was off to an emotional location: the cemetery where Joe buried his mother in 1940, his brother Ira in 1942, and his father in 1966.

CHAPTER TWENTY

TRUTH AND RESPECT

We owe respect to the living. To the dead we owe only the truth.

— VOLTAIRE

W E DROVE WEST ON HIGHWAY 50 AND LEFT THE memories of Joe's birthplace behind. The magnolia trees may have been gone but the visions of his childhood played in his mind. As I drove down the two-lane highway, I had no idea what to expect of the cemetery. I'd heard Joe talk about where his mother, brother, and father were buried but I was still lacking in my understanding.

"Here," Joe said firmly.

I put on my signal and slowed, making a right turn down Young-blood Road. Of course, my assumption was there would be some kind of entrance, some sort of official delineation, an indicator of the final resting place for so many people over the course of a century-and-a-half. Instead, we drove for about a half-mile before making a turn down a private dirt road. The street sign read *Lazy Acres*.

Joe had given no indication until this very moment that this "cemetery" was one only in theory. The place was on private property, among hundred-year-old oak, hickory, and pine trees, vines, roots, caved-in tombs, and dead leaves that had toppled down on one another for decades.

A yard sale was underway in front of a doublewide trailer, the only structure within hundreds of yards. It stood on the north side of the cemetery. A heavy-set woman looked at trinkets and junk on folding tables. The owner wore an Alabama Crimson Tide T-shirt and spoke to us in a thick southern accent. She was immediately friendly as Joe got out of the rental car, and we learned her property was basically an island, surrounded by 40 acres formerly known as the Lanier Plantation. I was floored to hear that and vowed in my head to do more research on the origin of this meaningful place.

Joe wasted no time in telling her why we were there, and from what she said, we weren't the first to come looking for a long-forgotten grave. She said the last time she had been over there, the headstones were few and far between and the ones she could make out were those of children.

"The condition of the cemetery surprises me, it really does," the lady said, almost embarrassed.

She told us how to cross the weed-covered ditch without too much trouble and wished us luck. After we thanked the stranger, Joe, Andre, and I walked down about a hundred yards to where the ditch was manageable. I was concerned Joe would fall and break a hip or a leg but I stayed close to him as we crossed and then entered a field. To our right, toward the west, was a dense amount of vegetation. I remember thinking there was no way this could be the place.

Joe knew.

What he didn't know was where his loved ones were buried. His last attempt was nine years earlier and on that trip home with Eula, neither could locate that for which they were looking. It was a sad disappointment. They had made several phone calls and both the city of Columbus and the coroner's office had promised there would be a cleanup effort. It never happened.

For our documentary—and purposes of this book—I wanted a shot of Joe walking into this thick Mississippi countryside, approximately three acres in size. In my mind, I visualized how we would capture him going into this wooded abyss and disappearing out of frame. I went ahead to make sure his path was relatively clear and immediately I saw a headstone, perhaps 20 yards ahead. The vegetation and overgrowth almost took my breath away. The trees and wooded areas were so dense, I wondered how they picked this location so long ago.

"It's like these people are forgotten," Joe said, interrupting the sound of crunching leaves that fall afternoon.

We got the shot and Joe continued ahead into the seemingly booby-trapped and certainly potentially dangerous location. Though the skies were crystal-clear blue in the midday sun, it was much darker just a few feet into the woods. Joe, obsessed with finding the graves of his relatives, continued. I dodged large spiderwebs and stopped to look at the first headstone, the only one I had seen. It was placed after the funeral of a 14-year-old girl. She died in 1895.

Andre followed us in and began getting video of this long-forgotten place, about 15 minutes from downtown Columbus. There were broken bottles; a rusted, white campfire coffee pot; and a washbowl. It was trash from yesteryear. Every few yards the earth was indented, indicating a gravesite below our feet. I remarked to Andre that with the soil condition, root activity, and decay, we were likely only a foot or two from coffin and skeletal remains. It was also very unusual for this to be a mixed-race burial site. It was commonplace to have whites-only and blacks-only cemeteries. They didn't mix in this life, so why should they be desegregated in the afterlife? I quickly realized that here, off Lazy Acres, the whites had their section, the blacks another.

Rays of sunshine filtered through as we walked carefully over the forest bed. The crunch of leaves came with every step and birds could be heard chirping in the distance. With the sunlight, particles of dust could be seen floating everywhere. At one point, I caught up with Joe, the back of his sweater covered in spiderwebs. Because of the rolling topography, downed limbs, and fallen trees, Joe was out of breath when I stopped him and asked him a few questions on camera.

He was dressed in red pants—the kind of pants only an 85-year-old man could get away with wearing—but in the typical Joe LaNier-style, he looked fashionable. He wore a black button-down shirt with a Navy-blue, five-button Cardigan sweater, buttoned three down from the top, and on top of his head, his signature 7-3/8", light-tan Stetson hat. Joe's size-13 shoes trudged over the vegetation, as he looked desperately for his loved ones.

He breathed heavily as he searched.

"The reverence is just not here," Joe told me.

"It's like these people are forgotten and their relatives were never in a position to keep their graves clean, to keep their memory alive. Unfortunately, I'm not sure I'm going to be able to find those three graves. It has been 50-60 years and nobody—*nobody* has taken care of this cemetery."

Joe's voice began to crack. For the first time since our trip began and for only the third time since I met him seven months earlier, he cried.

"I don't even know where to start looking anymore," he then paused.

"At least they know I tried. At least they know."

Joe spent the next several minutes walking alone.

Joe had had enough. His search was in vain. As I continued walking around desperately looking for a sign of the LaNier dead, Andre collected video images of our surroundings. We barely spoke due to the intense, emotional moments inside this dilapidated cemetery. It was about this time that Joe shocked the both of us.

He gave up.

Without saying more than a few words of sadness, he headed back south, walked over dead trees, sprawling vines, and a barbed-wire fence and again out into the field. His search was futile. I cannot begin to describe the anguish I felt because I was certain we could locate three graves, side-by-side-by-side. As he walked away, I felt a tremendous sense of lost opportunity. *They are here somewhere. Somewhere,* I thought.

I continued my slow walk through the southwestern portion of this forgotten graveyard when I decided to look at one final headstone.

At 12:50 p.m. my heart stopped. There, in front of me, on a faded slab of old concrete:

IRA C LANIER B 4/1/15

Most of the engraving had faded from years of harsh weather and exposure. But it was *him*, the man who at times had treated my friend so harshly as a child for myriad unknown reasons. My hair stood on end when I exclaimed to Andre in an almost out-of-body experience:

"My God! It's Ira's headstone! It's Ira's grave."

The emotions were overwhelming. Andre walked from his tripod and came over to see it for himself. He was equally shocked. It was then that I asked him if Joe's wireless microphone was still turned on, and if so, to start recording as I called him in from the field with this amazing news.

Rolling.

"Joe!" I said. It took him a few seconds to hear me.

He began to walk back in to the cemetery again, over the barbed wire, stray branches, and limbs and as he came into view I told him.

"Joe, I found Ira's headstone."

He looked at me with a bewildered expression.

"Did you?" he said, out of breath.

I showed him and he walked over slowly and methodically.

He began to cry.

"This is him. Thank God. I know where they are now."

He stood for a time to collect his thoughts.

"Before I die, I'm going to have headstones put here," he said as he looked at his brother's grave marker.

"Okay," he said through tears. "Now you know you're not forgotten."

He then turned to me and repeatedly said thank you, and then we hugged. I began to cry.

"All these years…," he muttered as his voice trailed off.

Joe couldn't understand how he could have missed it, not only during this visit but others in the past. Andre and I let him have his space as he tried to piece together the logical location of both Mama's and Papa's graves. While he did that, the two of us began to clear off the vines, leaves, twigs, and small roots that were strewn everywhere. The earth had pushed up this small, weathered headstone; its concrete base was tilted upward and back at about a 45-degree angle.

"Mama's here, Ira's here, and Papa," Joe said softly as he pointed to the ground below him.

"Papa is here."

It was the will of God, I thought. There was no other way to explain it. No one can convince me otherwise.

With the area cleared of the largest pieces of debris, Andre walked away and returned with two small sticks, one shorter than the other. He found a piece of vine and within two minutes had constructed a cross. It was perfect. We pushed it into the ground and Joe offered a touching, emotional prayer. He vowed again to place proper headstones on this site before he died.

We prayed as I held his right hand with my left.

"In reverence to our Lord, I want to publicly, and in whatever way is appropriate, say thank you to Andre Greller and Steffan Tubbs for helping me find the graves I thought I would never find again. For my mother, my father, and my brother Ira, this cross is a makeshift cross but its symbol is what it needs to be. I make a pledge to God that if He will let me live long enough, I will get a headstone for mother and my father to tell them how much I loved them and that I'm thankful I lived long enough to find them. In the name of the Father, the Son, and the Holy Ghost, amen."

We were all emotionally spent.

Andre packed up his gear while Joe and I began the trek out of the cemetery and into the field on the south side. As we walked, I could again hear the sounds of the dry grass collapsing under our feet. I didn't say a word.

Joe broke the silence.

"You know, I wish I had longer to live—so I could remember you longer," he said to me.

I smiled as tears began to well and a lump grew in my throat.

"That is quite possibly the nicest thing anyone has ever said to me. I wish I had met *you* sooner, Joe."

We got to the ditch and carefully crossed. The yard sale was still going on several feet away from the car when we got back and Joe climbed inside. He was tired but grabbed for his cell phone.

"We found one grave," I said to the lady in the Crimson Tide T-shirt.

I thanked her, then walked away and over to Andre, who was still loading gear in the trunk.

"Can you believe that?"

"I know. Unreal," Andre said.

We climbed in the car and Joe was in the process of leaving a voicemail for Sonny, Ira's son back in Colorado. As he hung up, I backed out down Lazy Acres Road and looked at my watch. It was 1:25 p.m. when Joe picked up his phone again and called Eula. He told her exactly what had happened and I distinctly remember his words:

"I want dignity back to this graveyard," he said to her.

Our day was a success.

I N LATE OCTOBER, ABOUT A WEEK AFTER WE RETURNED FROM our journey, Joe and I met as we always did. This session, though, was different. I wanted to recap and capture some of the emotion he felt in going back to Mississippi.

"Tell me about going back to that cemetery," I said.

With a heavy sigh, he began.

"It was very emotional. I wanted to find the place where my mother, brother, and father were buried but I had no thought that I would be able to find them. We had gone there before, and it just wasn't possible. Nobody has ever kept up that cemetery as far as I know. It's just totally grown over. It is total disrespect for the dead. I was just disgusted with the way it looked. This type of thing happened because most of the family members of the blacks buried there never had the money to keep it up and it just wasn't important to the state or the city. We were told nine years earlier that someone would go out and document the area and clean it up. That never happened. My folks were not able to afford headstones and there were only makeshift markers. They disappeared over the years," he said with a heavy heart.

"I only took you there for purposes of the book, so you could see where my parents and my brother were buried," Joe told me.

The trees that were just small saplings when Mama was laid to rest in 1940 were now huge; many of them were down and rotting. Aggressive kudzu vines had taken over nearly everything.

"When I walked out of the cemetery, it was a type of sadness that I had never felt before, because I knew I would never again try to find where my parents and brother were buried. And then I heard you say, 'Joe, I found Ira's headstone!' and I couldn't believe it. When I went back in and read it, I just absolutely lost it in terms of emotion. I don't ever remember having that kind of feeling before. I had given up."

There was now a new sense of purpose that Joe exuded. He then continued.

"It was an incredible discovery for me and I promised God that before I die, if it is at all possible, I'm going to get a headstone for my mother, my brother, and my father. I will put it there if He lets me live that long. The emotion was just more than I can describe."

It was God's will that we found the graves. It would be His will that we would place proper headstones on our next trip to Mississippi.

★

L ITTLE DID JOE KNOW, BUT IMMEDIATELY UPON MY RETURN to Colorado, I was on a mission. I was determined to get those three headstones even if I had to pay for them myself. After work on Wednesday, October 19, 2011, I decided to call the local headquarters of Horan & McConaty, a Denver-based funeral home with community ties that stretched back to 1890. I recalled they were KOA advertisers, so I picked up the phone. I'm not sure why but it was so important to me that I was nervous as I spoke to a secretary and asked to speak with owner, John Horan. She asked me what it was regarding, I briefly explained, and then I was transferred to his voicemail. I left as brief—but detailed—a message as I could and then hung up the phone. It was my first step in trying to go the extra mile for Joe and ensure his loved ones' gravesites were properly marked. Two hours later, my phone rang.

"Steffan, its John Horan. I just got your voicemail message and it just so happens I'm in Atlanta right now at a mortician conference. It's great timing because I have people who can help, who are sort of held hostage in the same room as me. Now, tell me a little more about the story," he said.

I did.

For the next few weeks, John kept me up-to-date as he worked his connections. I saw firsthand how this company kept to its mission statement: *compassion and professionalism.* They also proudly follow the motto: *Live Well, Leave Well.* I had never met John Horan and though there may have been the possibility he knew my name from the radio, there was nothing in it for him but the feeling of goodwill and helping another Coloradan. Much to my relief and elation, I received an email on Monday, November 28, from Key Blair at Columbus Marble Works in Mississippi.

"I will be happy to help with this request. Please let me know what needs to go on the stones and I will have our CAD operator make a layout for [Joe's] approval," the email read.

Words cannot adequately describe my emotion the moment I read the communication.

ONE HIGHLIGHT DURING OUR MISSISSIPPI JOURNEY happened in less than a 30-minute time frame. Joe, being the avid golfer he is, wanted to make a statement by hitting a golf ball off a tee box at the Columbus Country Club. Since 1923, it had been a place blacks went only to work in the kitchen, serve, do maintenance, or caddy for the wealthy, white Columbus elite. It was the place where white kids were told they would die if they swam with or after black kids.

We pulled into the parking lot off Military Road, just down from Memphis Town, and walked inside and down a flight of stairs to the clubhouse. The walls were covered with old golf photos from yesterday and today, and I noticed few—if any—black golfers.

When we got to the starter's desk, Joe explained why he was there and what he wanted to do. Ira Jr. had called ahead several days earlier to make sure it was okay. The starter was gracious and handed Joe two golf balls, a driver, and a handful of tees. He also informed us we could take one of the golf carts parked outside. Joe and I thanked the young man, went outside, and climbed into the cart.

"I bet you never thought a white guy would be driving you around this course, Joe!" I said.

We laughed.

We picked up Andre at the car, loaded our camera equipment in the back, and then drove over a bridge above Military Road.

We stopped at the number-nine tee box. It was a beautiful day, with blue skies and a slight breeze, and I could feel the excitement grow in Joe's voice. He was giddy to get out on this course; he had something to prove to himself and in my estimation, show that times had changed there. He'd never played the course and only once did he caddy for a white golfer. It was exhilarating for him to be back.

"I never thought that I would be standing here on a tee box hitting a golf ball at the Columbus Country Club. I never thought that would be possible. We've moved forward in a positive sense; sometimes it's slow but it happens. That's why I'm proud to be an American."

Andre set up the tripod well behind Joe as he took the graphite driver and conducted exactly one practice swing. Birds chirped off in the distance as the sun shined down, in my mind, on just one lone golfer that day. Joe reached into his pocket, pulled out a ball and tee, and then set up his shot. He stepped to the right of the ball, smiled, and took his swing. With a nice smack, the ball was headed down the fairway. It would play nicely and he smiled as he watched the ball fly.

I told him to hit one more and he gladly repeated his ritual. This time, on his second swing, the ball sailed down the fairway a good 40 yards farther than his first shot. This was the perfect shot, straight and right down the middle.

"That felt awful good," he said as he smiled ear-to-ear. "And I'm keeping that ball!"

We all laughed at the symbolism of Joe, in 2011 and 85-years-old, hitting a white ball at this previously whites-only golf club.

As we drove back across the small bridge toward the clubhouse, three white men, standing on the practice green to our right, stopped and looked up, almost as if in disgust. Perhaps it was the way I read their expressions but it seemed as though they did not approve of this elderly black man on their course. That feeling continued when we returned to the clubhouse. The starter was just as friendly but other white men inside seemed to act as if we were had intruded on their territory.

"I came here to do something important to me," Joe said as we walked out of the clubhouse.

"Now, let's go."

CHAPTER TWENTY-ONE

LOVE REGARDLESS

My countrymen! Know one another and you will love one another.

—MS Congressman L.Q.C. Lamar
House of Representatives
April 25, 1874

T HE THRILL OF OUR CEMETERY FIND AND THE GOLF COURSE outing the previous day had re-energized Andre and me. On Sunday morning, October 16, we began our day about an hour before sunrise in Columbus. For our two nights here, Joe stayed about ten miles away at his great-niece's house, while Andre and I shared a shabby motel room. We got up and headed southeast to capture video for our documentary; I wanted to shoot the fog and mist, and get beauty shots of the early morning Mississippi countryside. Mother Nature did not disappoint. With coffee in tow, we drove to an open field, with a low, grey fog that hung just above the vegetation. It was an eerie sight as birds began to chirp and crows squawked ahead of dawn. Above, clear skies offered a beautiful glimpse of a full moon.

As the sun peeked above the eastern horizon, Andre captured spectacular shots. We then headed east on Highway 50, down the two-lane road with open pasture on either side, and as we continued, we passed a few homes that sat among a small patch of woods. I drove slowly as Andre pointed his small camera out the window for the standard rolling shots for the documentary. We then made a slight left and I saw what I had expected all along in this part of the country: cotton fields. I came to a sudden stop, flipped the car around, and drove up a small dirt road that offered an expansive view of the rows and rows of cotton. The white bulbs of cotton had a purplish glow as the sun continued its slow rise that Sunday morning. Again, the birds sang in the brisk mid-October air.

As Andre did his job and captured the images, I stood in front of the rows and bent down to touch a wild cotton ball, still in its bowl. I imagined Joe as a little boy, in this very spot, and what it must have looked like as blacks from around the area went row by row, making just 35 cents for every hundred pounds of picked cotton. It was an emotional experience and the land in front of me gave no indication that this scene was not straight out of the 1930s.

With our shoot finished, I just knew we had to get Joe back to this place. I wanted to interview him on camera as he stood in front of these rows of cotton. I only imagined what an experience it would be for him. Two hours later, we were back in the same spot, with Joe, and he acted as if he had been transported back to his childhood. I asked him questions and he gave moving answers. Many of them I had heard before but this was different because he was in his element. I again asked him to close his eyes and tell me what he saw. Joe talked of the children, the cotton-picking adults, and the heat—the ache in his body, and the water bucket and ladle at the ends of the rows. He then began to sing:

> *Go down; go down, Moses*
> *Way down in Egypt's land*
> *Tell ol' Pharoah*
> *To let my people go.*

It was beautiful. His baritone voice cut through the fields of cotton and into my soul. Just the chorus of the song transported me back to when he was a boy. Before we left the field, Joe gathered a few pieces of cotton—kept some for Eula—and gave me a soft clump to take back to my kids in Colorado.

★

Downtown Columbus looked almost the same to Joe as it did back in the 1940s. He led us on a tour of Catfish Alley and most of Main Street, pointing out buildings and memories every few seconds: Dr. Allen's old office, Billy Herndon's pool hall, the Greek restaurant, Sanitary Laundry, the Straight Eight Café. Midway down the block on South Fifth Street, we stopped on the sidewalk. Across the street, we saw a faded sign for the Princess Theater. It was here, in 1938, at the age of 12, Joe saw *Gone with the Wind.* As per the usual, he had to sit upstairs in the crow's nest. He told me the movie's depiction of the Civil War era offended him, because he knew what happened in Atlanta and Tara at that time in our history also happened in his hometown of Columbus during the same period.

"Overall, going to the movies was never a pleasant experience. In this town, you were always less of a person."

As we continued to walk around, more of the memories surfaced.

"I was called a nigger more times than I can name," he said.

"What I felt was not emotional. It was a feeling of degradation. It was a feeling of 'I can't do anything about that.'"

About mid-morning we left Columbus and headed north toward Tupelo. Joe wanted to see an old friend, 82-year-old Joyce McCaleb-Cade, whose father owned the land Papa sharecropped on the outskirts of Columbus in the late 1930s. I was excited to at least drive through Tupelo, known best as the birthplace of Elvis Presley. Like so many of these southern towns, its quaint, historic downtown made it easier to imagine what the place looked like decades back.

I parked the car in front of the house and I could tell Joe was anxious to see her. They had visited a few years earlier but this trip was different, with two strangers who tagged along. Joyce greeted us at the front door and shared hugs with her lifelong friend. Here was a white woman, hugging the black son of a sharecropper who used to work for her daddy.

The small home was filled with tiny trinkets and knickknacks; mementos of forgotten years filled every shelf. Old photos were framed and scattered about, while newer ones covered the fridge. Joyce's house brought back memories of my own childhood as I stood and breathed in that familiar scent of yesteryear—a mix of older furniture, older carpet, and a hint of a musty attic. It reminded me of my grandparents' homes as a child. Joyce wore bright red lipstick, which I found adorable. She showed instant southern hospitality and talked with her thick southern accent. We sat down on her living room couches and I listened to her reminisce with Joe. When the time was appropriate, I asked her what it meant to see him.

"It's wonderful. It makes me want to cry," she said as she sat back in a well-worn, comfy living room chair. "We're such close friends; we keep in touch. I'm close with his wonderful wife. I've got pictures of them and their family."

Joyce was born in New Albany, Mississippi, in 1928, and as a little girl helped out at her family's store near Memphis Town. She recalled Joe as a boy, doing odd jobs around the family's property while Papa handled sharecropper duties on the McCaleb/Lamar land. I watched Joe intently as he described his amazement at the friendship between his Papa and her daddy. There was no color barrier. Joyce told Joe she still has the letters he wrote to her daddy until near his death.

"Why wasn't your family racist?" I asked her.

She looked at me from the across the room on the other couch and instantly responded.

"I really can't answer that. I just know that I had the most wonderful daddy anyone could have. He was a Baptist and a lifetime deacon of the First Baptist Church in Columbus. We were in that church from the moment the doors opened. We were taught to respect everyone."

Joyce was full of southern warmth and charm, two of the qualities she shared with a distant relative with deep political ties. Down her family tree, on her mother's side, was a politician so famous his name still adorns public buildings and counties; even a river in Yellowstone National Park.

Lucius Quintus Cincinnatus (L.Q.C.) Lamar was born September 17, 1825, and went on to a long and distinguished career in politics, through secession, the Civil War, and national recovery. He was also a slave owner. In 1857, Lamar was elected to the United States House of Representatives, where he served in Washington until 1860. On February 21 of that year, Lamar delivered a long and passionate speech titled "The Slavery Question." On the floor of the House of Representatives—the state of the union in perilous flux—Lamar addressed slavery in a blunt, biblically referenced, methodical manner. His stance was abundantly clear:

…the calamity of the times is, that the people of the North do not understand the people of the South; and it is to the interest of a certain class of politicians to perpetuate the misunderstanding…. We maintain that these justifying circumstances do exist in relation to our institution of negro slavery. They consist in the unfitness of the black race for a condition higher than that of slavery. Our proposition is, that when these two races are brought into contact, the supremacy of the white man must be acknowledged, and his right to govern both races with reference to the happiness of both. This is the principle upon which, until recently, the legislation of all your northern States was founded. They all asserted the supremacy of the white man and the subordination of the black man.

Lamar continued on the floor of Congress:

The African, with all its foulness, with all its prosaic vulgarities, domesticated and disciplined, has been by that same wave borne up higher and higher, until now it furnishes inspiration for northern song, heroes and heroines for northern romances, and is invited by northern statesmen into their charmed circle of political and social equality. Not just yet, gentlemen, if you please. He is not your equal; and history proves that even when he has reached this point of civilization, if you take from under him the institution which has borne him up to it, he relapses into his pristine barbarism.... I ask of what has humanity to complain against the institution [slavery]?

Lamar defended slave ownership. He proclaimed while not all southerners owned slaves, they backed the system:

There has never been a race of men more maligned and lied about than that very class of freemen in the South.... The southern planter is not the indolent, aristocratic nabob which he has been represented to be. He is, in general, careful, patient, provident, industrious, forbearing, and yet firm and determined. It is these qualities which have enabled him to take a race of untamed savages, with no habits except such as inspire disgust, with no arts, no information, and out of such a people to make the finest body of fixed laborers that the world has ever seen.

In conclusion, Lamar asked his Northern colleagues to act in good faith and exude common sense for the betterment of the United States:

The sentiment is rapidly approaching to unanimity among them [Southerners] that any attempt to impair...or place over them the party which arrogates to itself the right to do any of these things, will be a fatal blow at the peace and stability of this great country.[2]

The words are chilling to read, even today. Less than 14 months after Lamar's speech in Washington, Civil War broke out between

Union and Confederate troops April 12, 1861, at Fort Sumter, South Carolina.

With his allegiance to the south, Lamar joined the Mississippi Secession Convention and when the Civil War began, he became a Lieutenant Colonel and had the ear of Confederate President Jefferson Davis. He was named Confederate Minister to Russia and traveled to Europe as a special envoy to France and England. After the war, he returned to Mississippi and briefly taught metaphysics at the University of Mississippi before voters elected him once again to Congress in 1873—the first Mississippi Democrat elected since the War. Lamar went on to serve in the U.S. Senate from 1877 to 1885, until President Grover Cleveland appointed him Secretary of the Interior. His term that began in 1885 lasted through 1888 and from there, he was appointed to the Supreme Court. He remains the only Mississippian to serve on the High Court.

In his latter years, Lamar dedicated himself to rebuilding relationships with northern states. He was even featured in John Kennedy's Pulitzer Prize-winning book *Profiles in Courage*—published in 1956—and was portrayed as a man who, despite deep resentment, forged relationships and tried to bring peace among a wounded nation. Lamar's moving, 1874 eulogy to counterpart Charles Sumner, a political rival, on the floor of House of Representatives talked of a commitment to rebuild a nation, literally and figuratively.

Lamar died January 23, 1893, at the age of 67. Three U.S. counties are named after him, as is a 40-mile-long, trout-filled river in northwest Wyoming.

IN MID-JANUARY 1966, JOE WAS AT HOME ON ELM STREET IN Denver when the phone rang. It was his sister Ruth informing him Papa wouldn't eat. It was two weeks before his death.

"He was living alone in the same Memphis Town house he had built with his own hands back in the mid-thirties. It wasn't an emergency phone call and Ruth didn't know how serious a situation it was. I immediately called Dr. Hunter, the same person who helped me shape my education and career choice. Unfortunately, he said Papa probably had the flu but I think he told me what I wanted to hear," Joe said.

Papa had been suffering from diabetes, yet everyone in Colorado thought he had the disease under control through monitoring and medication. Two weeks later, the phone rang again.

On Wednesday February 2, 1966, Papa died.

He was 74.

"It was a shock to me," Joe solemnly told me.

Gone was the most influential person in Joe's life. More than a quarter-century after he lost his mother, both of his parents were now dead.

"After the initial shock, I accepted his death. It wasn't a long grieving process but the memories are *still* there today. None of my memories were negative, even though we didn't have the best relationship when I was a child. That negativity wasn't there after he died. The one memory I had of him was seeing him in that audience as I graduated from college. It was *the* most influential and important moment between us."

He stopped to let his speech catch up with his mind.

Joe went on to recall Papa's last visit to Colorado. The time had come for the son to talk with the father about his mortality and Joe asked if he had a will—and in the event of his death, what his wishes would be. It was a difficult conversation. When Papa returned home to Mississippi, he wrote a will and named Joe the executor.

In that position, Joe had the unenviable task of dealing with the funeral home, settling debts, dealing with the courts, and informing people in his family's circle. From conversations during his father's final years, Joe found that two family members owed money. It was stressful and caused severed relationships for several years.

"In the months after his death, I sometimes looked up in the sky and told him, 'You know, you didn't do me any favor.' I had to deal with it all."

Two days after Papa's death, Joe took a flight out of Denver's Stapleton Airport back to Mississippi. He went alone, while Eula stayed home with the kids. Visions of his childhood were a constant as he traveled east, arrived in Columbus, and eventually, the Sunday funeral service held at Sanders Chapel at Sixth Avenue and Fourteenth Street. Joe had informed the Sykes Funeral Home of his desire to have Papa in a closed casket at the front of the church; he was still haunted by seeing Mama in her coffin back in 1940.

Joe thought of his Navy days and how his service helped Papa every month with an allotment; he recalled how Papa was honest, hardworking, and respectful of others. He also remembered—even when immersed in the direst of circumstances—how Papa did not hate and how that was passed down and manifested in Joe. It shaped him.

By 1960, Papa had fully recovered from his hernia surgery and traveled west, once again, to Denver. His lifelong dream had been to continue west and visit California but had never made it, due to his financial state. As a surprise, Joe and his siblings chipped in and bought Papa a ticket to Los Angeles to visit old family friends he hadn't seen in 40 years.

"He never had any nice clothes. He always wore hand-me-downs, so when he arrived, I took him to Neusteter's department store in downtown Denver and bought him a suit and sport coat, pants, shirts, underwear, and two pairs of shoes. Normally, he would take shoes we didn't wear anymore and fix them with new soles because he didn't have the money to buy them. I wanted him to have things bought specifically for him. When he left to catch the train, he could have been the President of the United States, to quote Eula. When he came back through Denver after that trip, I never saw a man so happy."

Joe arrived in Mississippi with sadness hanging over him but also with a sense of calm that was made possible by the fond memories he carried with him.

"On his final visit to Denver just prior to his death, I had a strange feeling. When I dropped him off at the Greyhound bus station in downtown, I decided to stay. I wantcd to watch him leave but I did so from a distance. He didn't know I was watching him. He was dressed in a suit and when I saw him enter the bus, somehow I knew I would never see him alive again. I just knew it and I didn't know why. I still have that suit he wore hanging in my closet," Joe said with a heavy heart.

T HE MORNING OF SUNDAY, FEBRUARY 6, 1966, JOE ARRIVED at the church and walked inside. It was quiet, save for the hushed conversations in front of him. There was no music. The casket was open.

"I wanted to remember him as the last time I saw him alive, at the bus station in Denver. Unbeknownst to me, my sister, Gladys, had gone to the funeral home and made the decision to have the casket open. We were close to being seated for the service and when I walked inside, I saw it. I saw him from about 25 feet away, inside the casket. Now, I was never going to be able to remember him as I had seen him when he was alive," Joe explained, anger in his voice.

Joe left the church in pain and went outside. His old elementary school principal at Union Academy, Mr. Hunt, noticed he wasn't inside as the service was about to begin and came out to find him. Joe had taken a seat inside one of the cars that would eventually take the casket to the cemetery and had every intention of sitting right there until they closed the casket and went on to the graveyard.

Hunt served as Joe's principal from the time he registered in 1935 until he left for the Navy in early 1944. The educator told Joe he understood his sadness and anger but pleaded with him to come inside, which he eventually did. Joe tried his best to avoid looking up during the simple service.

The ride to the cemetery was a quick one. They arrived in a small caravan of cars and the small group of family members and farming associates stood around freshly turned dirt that Sunday afternoon. Despite Papa's relationship with many white farmers and members of the community, there were no whites present at the burial. After brief words were spoken and tears shed, Joe watched his father's modest casket lowered into the ground near Mama and Ira.

With no money for proper headstones, the preacher placed a metal stick into the ground after the dirt was placed back into the gravesite. On a handwritten piece of paper, Papa's name, date of birth, and date of death were slipped inside a plastic sheath—it was common practice in situations like this where the family had no money. The "marker" was simple and surely wouldn't last in the elements. (Amazingly, I found this piece of LaNier family history on my second trip back to the Mississippi graveyard more than 46 years later. It was weathered but the handwritten information was still readable.)

It was the first time Joe had been back to the cemetery since Ira's funeral in 1942. Joe thanked the individuals for coming to the funeral and watched as people quietly left the cemetery. Soon, he was the only one standing among the trees and gravesites. He stood in silence for a good five minutes, just as he had done at the conclusion of Ira's graveside funeral in 1942.

"It was my way of telling them I cared. It was closure for me. It was my way of telling them that though I'm not with you anymore, I care."

He left and never looked back.

Afffter he settled in at his father's home in Memphis Town, Joe contacted an old friend. He reached out to Mr. McCaleb to inform him of Papa's passing. McCaleb was extremely saddened by the news of losing his friend of more than 30 years.

"I think it was overwhelming to him, looking back at the decent life he had lived among both African-Americans and whites—and how he decided that he was going to treat all people with respect. He didn't have to treat us the way he did."

Joe and Gladys put on their coats and drove across town to the McCaleb home. The two walked up the front yard and rang the doorbell. It marked the first time Joe had entered a McCaleb home without entering through the back door.

"That was just custom—out of habit—back when I was growing up. It was nothing they requested. He was not racist but I do remember hearing him use the word 'nigger' one time, when I was about ten-years-old. He didn't know I was in the area and when our eyes met, I cannot express to you the sadness I saw on his face. I knew he regretted that I had heard that."

Mr. McCaleb came to the front door to greet Joe and Gladys. Joe hadn't seen him in more than 20 years but still had the sense that the McCalebs were part of his extended family. They talked for more than an hour, making up for lost decades.

Mrs. McCaleb soon joined them and at one point, as the four sat and visited, Joe looked Clarence McCaleb in the eyes. He then spoke from the heart.

"I wanted him to know what my feeling was to his family. I wanted him to know that we appreciated the fact that as a family, he treated us fairly, decently, and there was never the name-calling and all of that. He got emotional. He cried. Tears started to roll down his face. I got emotional, as well. I was proud of myself in how I really felt about this family."

Joe and Gladys said their goodbyes and Joe went off to settle the family debts. He left Mississippi two days later to get back to his pharmacy in Colorado.

JOE AND CLARENCE MCCALEB WROTE EACH OTHER LETTERS over the next 20 years until his death. Regrettably, Joe saw his friend just one more time, when he drove to McCaleb's nursing home and picked him up for dinner. They talked and McCaleb brought out a stack of letters he had kept over the years; he told Joe he read them on occasion. Late that afternoon, the two had pork chops for dinner at the restaurant inside the Holiday Inn on Highway 45 in Columbus. When the waitress came to take their order, McCaleb explained with pride that he knew when Joe was born, in a house with two magnolia trees out on the side yard. They had a wonderful time.

"As I was driving him home, he wanted to know how much money I made. I told him about $50,000.00 per year and he laughed and said, 'Hot damn!' Remember blacks were lucky to make $3.00 a day back when I lived there," Joe laughed.

DURING A FOLLOW-UP INTERVIEW SESSION IN THE SPRING of 2012, Joe handed me three letters he and Eula had saved over the years. They were postmarked Columbus, MS, between February 1977 and April 1981. They were from C.L. McCaleb.

Columbus, Miss.
Feb. 25, 1977

...I am afraid we do not deserve all of the wonderful things you said about us, but we do try to live right and treat our fellow man right.... My wife and I are both getting feeble and we cannot write to [sic] well, but we wanted to let you know

*that we are proud of you and if we had any small part in the
direction of your life we are proud of it.*

Your friends,
Mr. & Mrs. C.L. McCaleb

Mrs. McCaleb died November 22, 1979. Clarence McCaleb
died June 11, 1987, in Columbus. He was 90-years-old. Joe got the
news from James McCaleb, the son.

"I was sad. This was a good man. I instantly thought how he
was now in Heaven, getting rewarded for the decency he showed.
He wasn't perfect but he was a good man."

Despite their difference in color, Joe loved the McCaleb family.
But while this was the unusual norm between and McCalebs and
the LaNiers, in the world outside—indeed, within Lowndes and
surrounding Mississippi counties—segregation and racial unrest
were alive and well.

J UST FOUR MONTHS AFTER PAPA'S FUNERAL, WHILE ON A
March Against Fear rally to encourage blacks to register to
vote, black activist, James Meredith, was shot by a sniper at the
University of Mississippi in nearby Oxford. (Less than four years
earlier, Meredith had become the first African-American student
at Ole Miss. With tensions at a boiling point, Attorney General
Robert Kennedy sent hundreds of U.S. Marshals and an Army
combat battalion from nearby Fort Campbell, Kentucky; President
Kennedy ordered MPs and troops from the Mississippi National
Guard to control Oxford. Two people were killed and more than
200 soldiers were wounded in violent clashes. Meredith graduated
with a political science degree August 18, 1963.)

On June 6, 1966, Meredith lay sprawled across a highway
in excruciating pain after being shot in the back. The incident
happened about 100 miles from Joe's birthplace. A 26-year-old

photographer captured the moment. The photo shows Meredith dressed in a short-sleeved plaid shirt, jeans, and heavy-soled shoes; lying on his right side; elbow down on the ground. His mouth is agape, his voice screaming out in unimaginable agony. The James R. Thornell photograph won the Pulitzer Prize in 1967.

THE LATE AFTERNOON SUN HAD SETTLED OUTSIDE AND WE wrapped up our visit with Joyce McCaleb-Cade in her Tupelo home. We spent our final minutes looking at photo albums, some of them 70-years-old. She was so appreciative of our time and I felt bad that when we left, she would be alone in her house— full of memories. She hugged Joe goodbye and watched us as we walked down her driveway and into our car. I wondered how many more times she and Joe would be able to visit.

On the road out of Tupelo, I talked with Joe about the experience with his longtime friend.

"Her family had such a calming effect on my family that it gave us, and me, a feeling of hope that all people don't think of you as sub-human. When I was in their presence, I never had the feeling they were treating me any differently than they would anyone else."

Joe called her "Ms. Joyce" though she was three years his junior. It was standard. James, Joyce's brother, specifically told Joe later in life to stop calling him "Mr. McCaleb." They were equals and James would suffice.

A BIT BEHIND MY SELF-IMPOSED SCHEDULE, WE CONTINUED north on Interstate 22 toward Holly Springs. Here we would see the abandoned Mississippi Industrial College and the infamous county courthouse, scene of where Joe tried to register to vote. It was as quaint as Joe had described, with a vibe that only a southern small town can exude. We went to the abandoned train depot on the outskirts of town and did an interview for several minutes on camera, where I listened intently as Joe reminisced about his high school days in this town southeast of Memphis. From the train station, we headed west a few blocks and stopped in front of a two-story brick structure, surrounded by two-dozen pecan trees.

"This is the building. This is the courthouse where I was told, 'Niggers don't vote here,'" he said.

I parked the car at the southeast corner of the courthouse, near East Van Dorn (named after the Confederate General who disrupted Grant's supply depot) and South Market Street. In 1980, the Holly Springs Courthouse Square Historic District was placed on the National Register of Historic Places. The historic marker near us presented nearly 150 years of its history into three sentences: "Holly Springs. Ante-bellum cotton town and center of social and cultural life. Home of 13 generals of the Confederacy. Grant's southern advance halted here by Van Dorn's great raid, December, 1862."

The town was quaint and pretty but I also learned it held its demons. As we stood there that quiet Sunday afternoon, none of us realized the lawn and town square where we stood had been the site of countless Ku Klux Klan rallies and marches. Holly Springs historian Olga Reed Pruitt wrote of "…silent, white-robed Klansmen [who] sent terror to many a traitor heart on the public square…."[3]

Andre, Joe, and I got out of the car and within a few minutes, I explained to Joe exactly what I wanted him to do next. In my mind for our documentary, I encouraged him to recreate that walk he took up the sidewalk and into this building more than six decades earlier. Andre set up the camera about 50 yards from the entrance as I helped Joe with his microphone. I told Joe to start walking and talking from behind the camera and continue up to the front door of the courthouse. I wanted to avoid anything staged but longed to capture the moment and his true feelings being back in this place.

He was eager to document his emotions.

Rolling.

He started to walk toward the building; the area was empty, save for a family off to our right side, picking pecans off the ground.

He started to speak.

"I was in uniform and walked down this very sidewalk," he began.

Joe continued to move toward the courthouse.

"I had decided on a whim that I would come here and register to vote. I walked up these three stairs and opened the door. To my left, a clerk was inside and asked me what I wanted. Without hesitation, I looked at her and told her I wanted to register to vote. She looked at me and said, 'Niggers don't vote here.' I had just served my country for two years. I remember it as if it were yesterday."

At that moment, Joe put his hand on the doorknob and tried to open it. For dramatic effect, he rattled the wood and glass door. It could not have been scripted any better but it was completely natural. He stood looking inside the window as Andre and I looked at each other in stunned silence. It was brilliant. In one take, he had captured his painful past in this small Mississippi town.

In typical Joe fashion, he turned around, walked back and then looked at the two of us.

"How was that?" he said with a slight smile.

I hugged him for what seemed an eternity. It had to be so difficult to exorcise that demon.

"Joe, it was perfect. Let's go to MI and then I think we're done here," I said.

He looked off into the courtyard in front of him and stared.

"What are you thinking?" I asked.

"How did all this happen to me?" he smiled.

It was a priceless moment.

WE DROVE NORTH ON NORTH MEMPHIS STREET AND past a Hill Country Blues sign, which designated Holly Springs a historic part of the famed Memphis Blues Trail. About a mile or so up the road, off to our left, stood five large, crumbling buildings. This was the former high school and college campus where Joe's life made an abrupt and pivotal turn. He shared stories of his dorm room, his MI experience, and his disappointment in the condition of the old buildings, which stood there, forgotten in time. There they were in front of us, decaying as the sun set to the west. Joe seemed to leave the campus with a heavy heart.

In less than two hours, we all had been taken back to the past. The mood in the car was somber as we headed north and out of town toward Memphis. I decided to turn on the radio and station after station was in Sunday evening broadcast mode: church programs complete with choir music, a gospel spirit, and an enormous amount of soul. As we rolled toward Tennessee, 92.7 WKRA-FM out of Holly Springs provided our soundtrack, complete with *hallelujahs* and *amens* and talk of Satan and sin. After the gospel song ended, an R&B remake of Bob Dylan's *Tonight I'll Be Staying Here With You* came through the speakers and lightened the mood considerably.

Our time in Mississippi was poignant and eventful.

That night we stayed in a fancy hotel on Beale Street in downtown Memphis, ate barbeque, and drank beer. We all slept well that night, with a tremendous sense of accomplishment: New Orleans, Columbus, Tupelo, Holly Springs, and Memphis in three-and-a-half days.

THE NEXT MORNING, OUR HOTEL ROOM WAS TRANSFORMED into our studio. Andre did a terrific job lighting the area; it looked like a *60 Minutes* set. For another 90 minutes we captured

Joe's story for the documentary. He spoke of his last time through downtown Memphis and the night he and Mrs. Allen were led to that rural country house and were forced to pay the magistrate, as he stood in his robe inside his living room. Joe recalled, once again, how he vowed he could have died that night because he was not going to take a beating.

We again discussed his temperament toward white people.

"I'm not sure why I don't hate whites. The only explanation I can give to it is to remember how I was raised. How my parents taught us not to hate. There's nothing to be gained by it and usually, it will not change anything. No one suffers more than you, the one who perpetuates the hate."

Later that day, we drove to Memphis International Airport. Andre and Joe had developed the friendship I knew they would and I felt closer to Joe than ever before. He had opened up to us and shared the most intimate and raw emotions he had carried with him nearly his entire life. Joe and I hugged Andre and he went off to his gate and back on to LaGuardia in New York City.

If there was one negative to the trip, it happened next. Joe and I went through airport security. Being a frequent flier, I knew the strict Transportation Security Administration rules but Joe forgot to take several items out of his pockets. This, of course, alerted the metal detector and prompted a secondary screening. I was cleared and stood nearby as Joe was put through a ridiculous amount of stress. The black, overweight TSA agent all but told Joe to strip as part of the "standard procedure." Joe was confused and became flustered and at one point—because his belt was now off—his pants fell down to the ground. At any other point this would have been humorous but here out in the open of an airport security checkpoint, it was anything but. I was furious. This treatment—of a WWII hero in my eyes—was absolutely ludicrous and unnecessary.

Joe looked bewildered and emotional.

I didn't want to risk arrest but made my displeasure known. The search continued another few minutes and I had had enough. I walked over to a nearby supervisor seated behind a raised desk.

"Hello. I know you all have protocol but my traveling companion is an 85-year-old WWII veteran who has been searched for nearly ten minutes. This is ridiculous. His pants even fell down at one point. Where is the common sense here?" I said in a slightly raised voice.

He looked at me like I'm sure he's looked at hundreds of ticked-off passengers and said nothing. I walked away and back to Joe. The TSA agent spent another few minutes running items through the X-ray machines and barking orders, and then Joe was allowed to get dressed.

"This is ridiculous!" I said to the agent at least half my age.

As we walked away, the supervisor called the agent over and began a conversation. They both looked at us as I glared back. I doubt they cared much.

If they only knew this man's story, I thought.

We then caught our flight back to Denver.

I'VE TRIED TO CONDUCT AS MUCH RESEARCH AS POSSIBLE germane to Joe's incredible story. As is the case for any writer or journalist, Internet searches proved invaluable and it was during a simple search of Joe's birthday—March 25, 1926—that revealed a disturbing reminder of the unjust world into which he was born.

Had you been in Mingo County, West Virginia, the morning Savilla went in to labor, the town would have been buzzing about the latest nigger set for execution. The headline in the *Wayne County News* that day: *Negro Hangs Next Month For Attack On Mingo Woman.*[4]

Everyone in the area got his or her news from the paper, which was established in 1874. Its motto: *The most effective force in building a good community is a good newspaper.*

The story was reported that Harry Sawyer, a Negro, confessed to robbing and assaulting a white woman, Mrs. Cullen Amburgy. The alleged crime happened around 9:00 p.m. on March 18 when the wife of a local dentist was beaten, choked, and robbed of $1,000.00 worth of jewelry. According to Sawyer's confession reported in the local newspaper, Amburgy was knocked unconscious and "he committed the crime for which he shall pay with his life."

The article did not mention the woman was sexually assaulted but it was understood. The crime, indeed, was heinous. However, according to the information available, the accused received anything but a fair trial. It is obvious his race was the reason.

A "special" grand jury was empaneled and deliberated less than a half hour before it returned an indictment. Just one witness, a police captain, was called. With the indictment in hand, Sawyer entered the courtroom and on the record, entered his confession. According to the newspaper account, the trial "was one of the speediest held in Mingo County in many a year. He was in the courtroom less than five minutes from the time he entered his plea of guilty until the death sentence was passed by the judge."

Judge Bailey ended the brief "trial" and told Sawyer, "I sentence you to hang by the neck until you are dead."

The defendant had no lawyer.

There were no appeals.

Hours after he was sentenced, the now-convicted railroad worker was on a train in police custody, in handcuffs, and on his way to the West Virginia State Penitentiary in Moundsville. Most cells during the time held three prisoners in a five-by-seven-foot confined space. Two prisoners slept in bunks while a third took the floor.

Harry Sawyer was hanged before sunrise on April 19, 1926. The public was invited to attend.

All four men executed by the state of West Virginia that year were black and Sawyer was the only convicted criminal who died for a crime other than murder.

He was 24-years-old.

CHAPTER TWENTY-TWO

WISDOM

I'm not concerned with your liking or disliking me...
All I ask is that you respect me as a human being.

— JACKIE ROBINSON

JOE AND I RECAPPED OUR TRIP TO THE SOUTH DURING ANOTHER interview session in his dining room in late October 2011. I was so proud of him and the success of our journey; little did he know, I was in full pursuit of getting the headstones produced for a ceremony the coming year.

"The whole process we went through over those four days was like my life moving in front of me, like I've not seen before. It brought back memories, like in the cotton fields. Names of people that I had long forgotten, people who were in the fields with me—I could visualize going down those rows picking cotton, two rows at a time. They were in overalls and T-shirts. It was hot. I can see those faces as if it were just yesterday. It was just awesome to be taken back into that time period."

I've often wondered why I felt such an instant connection with Joe. Sure, his story is remarkable and his service admirable—but there is something more and there has been from the moment he came into the KOA studio with me in March of 2011.

During one of our final sessions, I decided to ask him about our relationship.

"It's personal. We're friends. And if I had another son," he said and paused slightly.

"I hope it would be you."

My heart melted and soared at the same time.

"I feel the same way," I said and looked him in his eyes.

We sat across the table from one another and let the moment sink in. I loved this man as if he were my own blood. Then Eula broke the silence.

"We have to hang you on the family tree someplace, don't we? You know more about us than anyone else," she laughed.

IN LATE SPRING OF 2011, JOE FINISHED READING JAMES Bradley's *Flags of our Fathers* and talked about it during one of our sessions. The book sat on the tabletop to my right as he not only described what moved him but how it took him back to his time on the island in 1945.

"It had a tremendous impact on me. I wept on several occasions while reading what happened to Bradley's father on Iwo Jima. I thought about the pride that I had and have maintained of being in the service and all of the good things that have happened to me. And then I read about James' father and the tremendous atrocities that they went through," he said.

He again struggled for words.

"In reading the account, I thought that what happened to me was really nothing compared to what they went through on the frontlines. Today, if I'm in a veteran's group setting and we all have our red *Iwo Jima Survivor* caps on, it really makes me uncomfortable when people come up to say 'Thank you.' I really don't know what to say in return. Saying, 'You're welcome' sounds so shallow to me. I appreciate it but none of us thought we were heroes on Iwo."

JOSEPH LANIER IS A MAN OF FEW REGRETS. HE DOESN'T LONG to live in his wartime or segregated past; however, decades after WWII, he told me that at times, he's longed for a few mementos of his time in the Navy. He wishes he still had that pea coat and his dog tags.

"I am so different today than when I was young. I'm talking emotionally—the way I'm made up and the way I relate to people. It is important to me that people like me and I like them. It is important that I can take the adversarial things that occurred in my life and step back from it all and make a decision on how I should approach it or how I should deal with it. And at the same time, I recognize I'm not as good as I think I am in a lot of instances."

I looked Joe in the eye and felt a need to console him a bit, though that was likely the farthest thing from what he needed.

"You know what that is, Joe? It is wisdom," I said.

"Yeah, yeah. I guess if you live long enough. That's true."

J OE HAS SPENT DOZENS OF HOURS SINCE THE SPRING OF 2011 speaking with Denver-area school children about his life experience. There is nothing more fulfilling for me as the chairman of The Greatest Generations Foundation than to see generations connect, whether in the classroom, over a cup of coffee, or a program back to Normandy or Iwo Jima.

When Joe speaks, he draws instant respect and attention by comparing today's society and the one he knew both in Mississippi and the Navy.

"I tell them freedom is not free, that someone has to defend that. Sometimes, it's the ultimate sacrifice. I also tell them to look at the past and learn from it, because as has been said, if you don't learn from it, you're going to repeat it. Your generation is the next school board member, the next mayor, state senator—all the way to the President of the United States. I get fulfillment from being able to say this to these kids and to see them sit there and look at you; it's like some are in awe as if this is the first time they've heard it.

This is my contribution to this country that has given me the ability and the opportunities to move in a direction that for a long period of time, people of my ethnicity were unable to do."

What has fascinated me, since I became intimately involved with WWII veterans, is just how many of them either went to their graves or spent most of their lives in silence. They were so traumatized by their experiences or felt insignificant or simply wanted to forget that they said very little to anyone, even to their wives and children. Case in point, Papa never knew a thing about Joe's actions in service. There was never a dinner where the two of them talked about Iwo Jima. Joe barely said a word to Eula, that is until I began to pry into his life as a part of more than 100 hours of discussions and taped interviews.

"I don't know that he really ever spoke about it," Eula told me, Joe seated to her right.

"I knew he was in the Navy, somehow that came up, but I can't remember the first time we even talked about anything in the war. A lot of stuff I'm just learning now. When he talked about Roosevelt dying while he was on Iwo—I was in the fourth grade in Oklahoma. I never thought I would meet someone who at the time was out there, somewhere. My brother never talked about his time in uniform, either."

Joe is adamant he never purposely avoided talking about his service.

"I didn't avoid talking about it but I just viewed it as something I did. I mean, heck, I was *out* of the service before I was 20. My personality, for lack of a better word, is that I don't dwell a lot on the past. I'm a dreamer. I look ahead."

O N Thursday, December 2, 2011—a frigid Denver night—Joe was honored by Colorado U.S. Senator Michael Bennet at an event in the African-American neighborhood of Five

Points. The third floor of the Blair-Caldwell African-American Research Library was filled with neighborhood politicians, community leaders, fellow veterans, a few students, and Joe's family. The Senator didn't come upon Joe after a staff alert or Google search. Instead, one day earlier in the year—while on a visit to Washington with The Greatest Generations Foundation—Joe decided to drop in on the democrat.

"I met Mr. LaNier in July of this year, in the midst of the debacle that was the debt-limit debate. Not a fun time to be in Washington, for anyone. We talked for about 30 minutes. He came in at a time where, honestly, I was feeling low; the morass in D.C. was having an impact on me and after meeting him, I felt rejuvenated. You can only imagine what a breath of fresh air it was to have someone like Mr. LaNier come by. His story is incredible; inspiring even. And it's a reminder that despite all the foolishness we see from Washington and the difficulty of the times, there are still many reasons to believe that things can get better and that they will. This is what it's about," the senator told the crowd.

He spoke of Joe's background, his service, and the racial injustice during the 20th century.

"We take inspiration from Mr. LaNier's story. His is a story of triumph in the face of adversity, a testament to persistence in the face of overwhelming odds. That is the story of America. In tough times, we always find a way to move forward, to press on, and to form a more perfect union. Mr. LaNier has said that his service in World War II provided him with opportunities he would have never experienced otherwise. I think it's equally true that our generation would have never experienced the opportunities we have enjoyed if it wasn't for the service and sacrifice of Americans like Mr. LaNier. And now, it's our generation's duty to do the same."

The audience broke into applause.

Bennet presented Joe with framed comments from the Congressional Record. The name, Joe LaNier, and his war accomplishments were made a part of the official record of the United States Congress on Tuesday August 2, 2011.

Congressional Record Volume 157, Number 120. Senate Floor. Page S5243:

Mr. President, today, August 2, 2011, I wish to thank Joseph Conklin LaNier, II for his service to the United States of America as a member of the U.S. Navy during World War II, and for choosing to make Colorado his home. His has been a life of service for Colorado and for all Americans.

We can all learn from Mr. LaNier.... His story exemplifies the successful transition that many returning veterans have made from active duty to civilian life.

Mr. President and all other Members here today, please join me in honoring the life and continued work of Joseph Conklin LaNier, II. A man who, despite all the discrimination he faced, is proud to be an American. A man who, despite returning home after the war and being denied his right to vote while wearing his uniform, is proud of his distinguished service in the Navy. A man who recognizes that even in the face adversity, one can find a way forward and help our country to become a better place, a more perfect union. For his perseverance, hope, service and patriotism, I thank and commend Joseph LaNier, a great citizen of Colorado.

I brought my wife, Lori, and our boys, Ryan, Nathan, and Jake to this special honor just a block from the Rossonian Hotel, where Joe and Charles had listened to music and drank beer back in their mid-20s. As we walked up three flights of wooden stairs—the boys' snow boots clomping along with every step—I felt so proud of Joe. I also felt lucky, once again, to know his story and to be the one to outline to you his amazing life.

After the benediction, most of the people in the dozen rows of chairs cleared and folks went back out into the cold night air.

Several, though, hung around to talk with Joe and to shake the senator's hand. Here was Joe, 85-years-old, dressed as usual in a tie, sweater, and a smart-looking suit, getting accolades he never asked for yet richly deserved.

Bennet, the former Denver Public Schools superintendent, has appeared on my morning show on 850 KOA numerous times, both as an administrator and senator, but this was the first time we met in person. I asked him several questions about Joe and one in particular about race and how not so long ago, Joe served in the U.S. military—in a U.S. Navy uniform—yet was segregated.

"It shows how a democracy is not perfect and how we have made strides as we've realized our mistakes," Bennet said.

"It was finally Harry Truman, in 1948, who desegregated the U.S. military and only then, did things start to get where they should have been all along."

Bennet and I talked about the importance of honoring this generation of daring, courageous, humble Americans. We both discussed how, before too long, they will all be gone and he harkened back to his own family story as to the importance of World War II veterans.

"It's a part of my own story. It's a miracle in my own family that my grandparents were able to get out of Poland in the early 1940s. They somehow made it out and came to America. Joe is important to Colorado," he told me.

"There's no one really like Joe and people of his generation. They all represent a time where the western world, as we know it, very well could have gone the other way. We owe a great debt to men like him."

I thanked the senator for taking the time to honor my amazing friend and before he left, I introduced him to my children, who were all waiting patiently—munching on the cookies and lemonade provided at the back of the library. Bennet paused for a picture with my boys and eight-year-old Nathan, in particular, was star struck. He had told me on the drive to the event that he was excited to meet a *real* U.S. senator. When I told Bennet this information, he quipped, "You're not planning on running against me, are you?" to which Nathan responded: "No, I'd rather be a wide receiver," with a smile on his face.

The boys thanked Bennet and he was quickly off to another event. We waited patiently a few more minutes while Joe answered questions from strangers at the front of the room near the podium. He then noticed Ryan, eleven-years-old.

"Hey, heyyyy!" Joe exclaimed as he stooped over a bit to give a grandfather-like bear hug.

All three of my kids, almost in unison, cried out, "Hiiiii, Joe!"

It was priceless.

Joe, as usual, embraced Lori as if she were a family member. I hung back to soak it all in and watch him smile and love my family.

Finally, we made eye contact and I approached him with a smile and open arms.

We hugged, long and loving like so many times before in that incredible, special year.

"I'm so proud of you," I said. "You deserve this, Joe."

CHAPTER TWENTY-THREE

BACK TO IWO, WITH HONOR

I can imagine no more rewarding a career. And any man who may be asked in this century what he did to make his life worthwhile, I think can respond with a good deal of pride and satisfaction: "I served in the United States Navy."

—PRESIDENT JOHN F. KENNEDY
U.S. NAVAL ACADEMY
AUGUST 1, 1963

MY WIFE, LORI, AND I PICKED UP JOE RIGHT ON TIME, about 4:30 p.m. on Friday, March 9, 2012—it was the eve of our journey to Iwo Jima. Our youngest, Jake, was in the back seat ready for a potentially long ride in traffic out to Denver International Airport. As I got out of our SUV, I noticed Joe already coming out to his small porch, Eula and Joe III right behind him. We all smiled and I asked Joe if he was ready for our adventure.

"Oh, yes," he said as he laughed.

He gave Eula a sweet kiss goodbye and wheeled his own suitcase out to where I parked. With Joe out of earshot, I asked Eula if he was ready and how he was doing emotionally. She told me he was excited and ready, and then informed me of my assignment.

"I want you to be sure he does two things," she said.

"One, be sure he takes his medication. And two, don't let him eat too much sugar!"

I laughed and was instantly taken back to the lunch I had with Andre and Joe right before crossing into Mississippi five months earlier. After the meal, Joe looked at me and told me to be sure I didn't tell Mama about the dessert he was about to order.

Lori and I hugged Eula and Joe III goodbye and we walked back to our SUV. Joe was seated with his seat belt on when I opened the rear door. Little did he know, but on the floor in a black, three-ring binder was the story of his life. I decided on this journey back to Iwo Jima he could read the manuscript of this book to date. I picked up the binder and handed it to him.

"Joe, this is your life."

The manuscript wasn't by any stretch finished but it was getting there. Nearly 400 pages and almost a year's worth of work, travel, love, and compassion were now in his hands. He was overjoyed and we weren't 200 yards from his front door when he began to read.

It was an emotional moment for me and Lori knew it. As we drove, Joe chuckled every now and then as he read. Lori grabbed my hand and held it tight and smiled, which told me every amount of energy I had put into this man's story was worth it.

We hit major traffic as we made our way to our next stop, which was to pick up a Marine, Jim Blane—4th Marine Division, 20th Regiment on Iwo Jima—a man I consider a close friend. Like Joe, I met Jim through The Greatest Generations Foundation and grew to know and respect his amazing story. Jim joined the Marine Corps at 18—went 18 months without seeing or talking to his parents—and on Iwo, received a Purple Heart. On my first visit to Sulfur Island, I had the amazing opportunity to travel with Jim and a select-few WWII veterans to both Okinawa and Iwo, the journey that almost never happened.

After hellacious traffic, we finally made it to Jim at his assisted-living facility in the Denver suburb of Aurora and then got on our way to catch our evening flight to Los Angeles. With goodbye kisses and hugs to Lori and Jake complete, Joe, Jim, and I walked through door 604 on the west side of Denver International Airport where Tim Davis, TGGF president, greeted us.

Upon check-in, American Airlines personnel took incredible care and showed great respect to our aging veterans. Five of the twelve, headed back to the South Pacific, were Colorado residents;

the other seven would meet us in L.A. The airline escorted our group through to a special TSA screening line on Concourse A, and I, of course, had flashbacks of the last time I walked with Joe through that TSA security line in Memphis. This time, it was different.

There was a reverence and a sense of thanks from the people who knew these men deserved to be treated with extra-special care. They were treated to nearly an hour inside the Admiral's Club, where Tim and I toasted a cocktail to the program about to commence. Fifteen minutes later, another of our travel companions arrived and joined us at the bar.

CONGRESSMAN ED PERLMUTTER, A DEMOCRAT FROM Colorado's Seventh Congressional District, had been instrumental in getting the first TGGF group to Iwo Jima in 2010, and as if by a good amount of karma left over from that program, he was able to make this journey in early 2012. Ed fought like hell to get that group of Marines over to Iwo, after a plane diversion (our original plane destined for Iwo was instead diverted to Haiti for the devastating earthquake in January 2010) and a mechanical malfunction on another. I will never forget waiting at Kadena Air Force Base on Okinawa when a senior officer came into a lounge area to inform our group they would not be able to make it back and how sorry he was that our veterans had come this far, only to be turned away.

On that journey in February 2010, Jim Blane was one of the most impacted veterans. On his 13th night on Iwo Jima, *Banzai* attackers lurked in the fear-filled darkness, as cordite, gunpowder, and death permeated the air. He sprang from his foxhole to engage the enemy and opened fire into the area where live rounds emitted. Jim—as fear and anger pulsated through his body—had his helmet shot right off his head but miraculously, the teen from Illinois was unharmed. He bent down and picked up his steel helmet, only to find a hole the size of a 50-cent piece had been blown into it.

Jim had already landed on Roi Namur in the Marshall Islands and had been a part of military campaigns in Saipan and Tinian—but on the night of March 3, 1945, six Japanese soldiers came out of nearby caves on Iwo Jima and engaged Jim in a firefight. One Japanese bullet would find him and end his time on the island—it was a smack, then sizzle throughout his left foot; the bullet tore flesh and broke through skin, tendon, and bone in a millisecond. Any Marine with a shot-up, bloody, and broken foot would do more harm than good in his unit. Blane was transferred to a beach hospital before he was evacuated to Guam the following day.

Blane never knew there was a label connected with the nightmares that continued for decades or why, as a retired senior citizen now dedicated to helping other WWII veterans receive their VA benefits and proper commendations, certificates, ribbons, and medals, he was so depressed. He sought help through the VA in Colorado and was told he suffered from serious, debilitating post-traumatic stress disorder, or PTSD. Sure, he had heard of it and its predecessor, *war fatigue,* but he had brushed it off far too long to impact him six decades later.

On this trip back to Iwo, Jim—stocked with hours of support and guidance from his counselor back home—would tackle Iwo Jima one more time. But we had no way to get there.

That's when the Congressman stepped in. While we waited on Okinawa, Ed was in D.C. and phoned Japanese Ambassador Ichiro Fujisaki, sent emails, called the Marine Corps, and went into a dogged, hyper-drive pursuit to make sure these Coloradans weren't stranded at Kadena. The White House was even apprised of the situation. At one point, Ed was on the phone with the White House as his Frontier Airlines flight was about to taxi for takeoff back to Denver. The flight attendant yelled at him to either "get off the phone or get off the plane!" He told her it was a phone call to the White House but she didn't care. Ed flamed with anger but he understood. He vowed *there's no way I'm giving up and leaving these vets stranded.*

In the end, with what I feel was part divine intervention and incredible, tenacious behavior by a politician—indeed, simply a good man—we received word from nearly 8,000 miles away that a special C-130 cargo plane was being fueled to take us on a three-hour flight to what many Marines referred to as "the pork chop" because of Iwo's distinct shape.

Congressman Perlmutter's tenacity and fighting spirit would pay off when we invited him to travel with us again to Iwo Jima in March 2012.

He immediately accepted.

As Ed drank a glass of cabernet with us inside the Admiral's Club on March 9, 2011, I told him once again how much I appreciated his effort to get us to Iwo the first time. I was incredibly happy he was coming with us. His colleague, Congressman Bruce Braley from Iowa, would connect with us in Los Angeles. Bruce's father had fought on Iwo Jima, which made the journey incredibly personal.

Ed ended up being my seatmate on the Friday night flight to L.A. and I told him highlights of Joe's amazing life and how I desperately wanted his story to become known now, instead of posthumously.

"I want you to do something when you're done writing Joe's story. I want you to write your own story and how it relates to Joe. This has been a journey for you, too," Ed told me during our flight.

When I told him I was including a lot of firsthand accounts within the pages, he was pleased. It reminded me how Lisa, Joe's daughter, had told me many months back how my relationship with her father was special enough to put down on paper. As Ed and I talked, Joe was across the aisle and behind us a couple of rows, reading from the large three-ring binder, which contained the story of his life. I felt an enormous sense of pride and my fears of not doing his life justice were allayed.

OUR SMALL COMMUTER JET LANDED IN LOS ANGELES AFTER 9:00 p.m. and our group was again treated to VIP service. American had a staff of greeters and a special bus that transported everyone to a nearby hotel where we would sleep only a few hours before heading back for the beginning leg of our flight to Guam.

As we checked in to the hotel and passed out keys, Joe looked tired. With his key in hand, he began to walk toward the elevators and as I was talking with him, a tall man about my age came up from behind him and made reference that "Joe will be fine, he's got bodyguards everywhere." It was Larry Lewis, son of Joe's best friend Charles Lewis from back in Columbus. I was stunned and totally unaware Larry had planned to visit the man he refers to as "Uncle Joe." It was incredible to see Joe's face light up. They hugged and Joe introduced me as if I were his own son.

Larry was 42 and at 6' 7", looked as if he could play for the Los Angeles Lakers. I would come to find out later he played parts of two decades of international basketball in both Spain and Japan. He could not have been a nicer man. But it wasn't just his surprise visit that made a long day a lot better. He had brought a special guest who waited out in the car: it was his father, Charles Lewis. Joe was thrilled at the chance to see the person he'd known longer than anyone alive today.

We walked from the lobby through automatic double doors and Larry's silver Range Rover was in front in the valet circle. Joe walked around to the passenger side while Larry opened the door and simultaneously told his father who was just outside the car door. Alzheimer's disease is such a cruel, silent, and debilitating thing   seemingly tougher on those on the outside, those who love and are able to remember.

Charles looked older than 86 but the nearly 86-year-old I knew in Joe defied the odds. Larry again explained to his father that it was Joe, from Columbus, who was in town and it finally seemed to click. The best friends hugged and laughed a bit while Sonia, Larry's wife, got out of the car. She hugged "Uncle Joe" as her eight-year-old son stood by holding a Star Wars Lego ship and then introduced herself to me.

We all walked back inside the lobby and sat in a small waiting area. Charles and Joe sat on a two-person couch and Joe tried to hold a conversation but sadly, it was mostly one-sided. Joe tried to explain my role in going to Iwo Jima, and every now and then, there seemed to be a flicker of understanding. Just when I thought it was futile, Charles exclaimed, "Joe!"

It was a special moment.

As the two friends talked, I got to know Sonia and her family's story—how she grew up in Miami, was a speech therapist, had two children born in Spain, and how Larry had never been back to Columbus. They had just returned from living in Spain, where after 17 seasons of foreign basketball, Larry retired at 42-years-old, unheard of in professional basketball. As she talked, she held her little four-year-old girl, asleep in her lap. I glanced occasionally across the room to watch Larry soak in the conversation between his father and Joe.

With every minute that passed, the kids grew more tired and it was soon time to go. I knew the goodbye wouldn't be easy on my friend. Larry and Sonia—in a matter of less than 30 minutes—could not have been more gracious, friendly, and appreciative of my writing Joe's story. I told them how much Joe talked about Charles and how much he meant to the LaNiers. Joe and Charles slowly walked back to the double doors and said their goodbyes, and sadly just minutes earlier, Joe had to remind Charles that Larry was his son. I hugged Larry and Sonia, truly hoping I could see them again.

Despite the attempt to put a positive spin on it, the visit was indeed sad. I knew it was hard for Joe to see his friend in a way perhaps he never had. As Joe turned back around, I tried to console him a bit but with tears welling in his eyes, I thought it best to put my hand on his shoulders and let him get up to his room. How lucky I was, I thought, to have this time with Joe, especially considering Charles was almost exactly the same age. They had shared Mississippi swimming holes and talked of pretty girls; they worked together and dealt with the same segregated, racist society. But now, they were not the same.

"It's just so sad," Joe said as he shook his head.

With a long face, he turned around toward the bank of elevators and went up to bed.

WITH NO MORE THAN SIX HOURS OF SLEEP, OUR GROUP WAS up before sunrise, March 10, to catch a 5:30 a.m. bus, a half-mile to the American Airlines terminal. When we convened in the lobby, a group of at least 50 Patriot Guard riders were already in place to escort our two busses the short distance to check-in. I have held the guard riders in high esteem since they came on my radar at Ian Weikel's funeral in Colorado Springs back in 2006. The majority of them served in Vietnam or the first Gulf War and in my estimation, they possess what is right about our country.

As we walked outside, my friend Donnie Edwards—a San Diego native and former linebacker for the Kansas City Chiefs and San Diego Chargers—was there to send us off. I had met Donnie the previous June in St. Mere Eglise, France, as part of the anniversary of D-Day in Normandy and found he shared the same passion for our veterans. It was extremely gracious of Donnie to come and say goodbye to these WWII heroes, especially considering he was heartbroken he couldn't come with us past the ticket counter at LAX. He had just missed the deadline to go to Iwo Jima, since access is controlled by the Japanese government and opens to U.S. citizens just one day a year.

We all climbed on the shuttle and after a few minutes, we started to roll toward the American terminal when the roar, then purr, of dozens of Harley engines kicked up. I looked at Joe.

"Whoa! What's that for?" he said.

"That's for you, Joe!" Donnie and I said at about the same time.

A police and Patriot Guard escort led us to the terminal, where yellow balloons, American flags, and over-the-top friendly, American Airlines representatives and staff greeted our veterans. A wonderful ceremony at our gate sent the vets off in style and made the nearly six-hour flight to Honolulu more bearable. Nearly all of the veterans in our group were complementarily bumped to first class, including Joseph Conklin LaNier II. After all of the years of being told where to sit, where to enter, what to say, when to say it, and what to do, Joe was seated in row one, seat A. It was just awesome to see. Meanwhile, I went back to row 33.

At the gate ceremony, the crowd was told that 60 percent of all American Airlines pilots are veterans and 10 percent of all company employees worldwide have served in the military. Impressive. As we rolled back from the gate on our Boeing 757 headed first to Hawaii, the captain came over the intercom to welcome his VIP passengers and with that, applause broke out in every row of the aircraft. Captain also informed us that the Los Angeles City Fire Department would send us off with a water cannon tribute. Select airline reps and ramp workers in their yellow vests, six Marines in full dress-blues, and one Army soldier stood at attention as we rolled under the hundreds of gallons of water—arched from the yellow-green Truck 80—and headed toward the runway for takeoff.

As I contemplated the trip ahead, I looked out on the beautiful, L.A. morning and off at the hazy San Gabriel Mountains some 40 miles to the east. I had a headache, the kind you get without enough sleep. I missed my kids and my wife. And then I thought of Joe's life to this point. I thought about the lives of these 12 men from various parts of the country who didn't know one another but shared a common bond and a common theme. Collectively, they lied about their ages in order to enlist; they received Purple Hearts and went back for more; they limped from injuries suffered 67 years earlier; they would do it all again. And because this Greatest

Generation was also the silent generation, our aim was to change that over the course of the next week.

We took off at exactly 8:00 a.m. from runway 25-R.

I CHECKED ON JOE AND THE VETERANS ABOUT MIDWAY THROUGH the flight to Honolulu and discovered that one of our vets on the program had an incredible family link, and it just so happened, he was seated next to Joe. As fate would have it, Joe's seatmate was Ralph Whitlock, an 85-year-old former U.S. Navy sailor currently living in Parker, Colorado—less than ten miles from Joe. Ralph's grandfather fought for the Union in the Civil War. Amazing, I thought. Here we were en route to an eventual stop on Iwo Jima and the two men seated in row one, seats A and B, had family lineage that dated back to the Civil War era. Joe's grandfather a slave, Ralph's a Union soldier who served from 1861-1865.

SEEING THE NORTHWESTERN TIP OF OAHU WAS A WELCOMED sight for everyone in our group. We would have about three hours to stretch our legs and enjoy the hospitality in the Honolulu International Airport Governor's Lounge before our nearly eight-hour flight to Guam. The time in the lounge was an excellent bonding experience for people in our TGGF group to introduce themselves and for our students, from Ohio State University, to hear stories from the men they would shadow for the next week to places on our agenda: Guam, Iwo Jima, Saipan, and Tinian. After light snacks and drinks, I had the chance to address the small crowd and welcome everyone to Pacific Theatre program. Two months earlier, I had been elevated from board member and named Chairman of The Greatest Generations Foundation, a position I was proud to take and instantly accepted.

I urged the students to soak in their time with these men of incredible courage and sacrifice. They were a part of a fighting force that changed the course of world history, a message I preach to anyone who will listen. After the brief remarks we headed to the terminal and our United Airlines flight to Guam, where we spent the next two full days touring invasion beaches of Agat to the south and Asan to the north. The veterans also met with the governor of Guam, Eddie Calvo, who showed his deep appreciation for their service and what the United States military meant in the liberation of Guam in July 1944.

A DAY BEFORE OUR DEPARTURE TO IWO JIMA, JOE AND I talked at length at a small outdoor table at the Hilton Guam, overlooking the turquoise Tumon Bay. Maintenance workers were off 50 yards away, cleaning the pool that morning for sunbathers later in the day. Tiny frogs—half the size of a fingernail—hopped and skipped along the ground. It was a muggy morning, the kind you expect when you're in a tropical climate, and every now and then, a sprinkle of rain hit our table.

"In my mind, it's surreal because we came here but we didn't get off ship. We were passengers. We stopped in the harbor south of here in February 1945 and I had never heard of Guam. I just knew it because that's what they told us when we stopped," he said.

No more than 300 yards away from our table—overlooking the bay—a Japanese pillbox remained intact where it had been for more than 70 years; its machine gun slits easily visible despite an overgrowth of vines. Palm trees swayed in a gentle breeze and whitecaps broke along the reefs perhaps a quarter-mile offshore. Birds chirped as Joe recounted his first visit to the region.

"No announcement was made about Guam until we made it here. Again, it was all 'destination unknown.' I never felt I would ever have a chance to come back here and to then get to Iwo and that was part of my sadness. It has been stated that the Japanese aren't all that happy about tourists going back to the island in the first place. I knew that and my thought was that I probably would never get a chance to see this again. But here we are. In many ways, it represents an end to the story."

IN LOS ANGELES TWO DAYS EARLIER, WE CONNECTED WITH OUR historian for the Pacific program, retired Marine Captain Dale Dye, a true patriot and friend. I met Dale and his wife, Julia, in April 2008, in Melbourne, Australia, and during that TGGF program, we brought back U.S. WWII veterans for the spectacular ANZAC Day celebration and parade. It proved to be one of the most patriotic events I have ever experienced. Every April 25, tens of thousands pay tribute to those who served in the Australian and New Zealand Army Corps (ANZAC) and fought at Gallipoli during WWI.

You have, no doubt, seen Dye in numerous Oliver Stone films, including *Platoon, Born on the Fourth of July, JFK,* and *Natural Born Killers.* Perhaps his most famous role was that of Colonel Robert F. Sink—Commander, 101st Airborne, 506th Parachute Infantry—in the HBO miniseries *Band of Brothers.* Dye served as the military advisor to its companion piece, *The Pacific,* where he again assisted the actors and directors, Tom Hanks and Steven Spielberg. His contributions as military adviser to countless Hollywood projects cut the bullshit out of productions and instilled realism, accuracy, and authenticity from a boots-on-the-ground approach.

The Cape Girardeau, Missouri, native climbed his way up from enlisted private to captain during a career that included three tours in Vietnam, where he earned the Bronze Star and three Purple Hearts as a member of the 1st Battalion, 5th Marine Division. He retired in 1984 after 20 years of service. Dye has shown his dedication and true appreciation of members of the Greatest Generation as well as to those of us connected with TGGF, as we honor our aging veterans who take their final journeys as part of our programs. We are forever grateful for his contributions.

"YOU KNOW, LOOKING OUT THERE ON THAT WING I CAN'T help but think about that guy in the movie who looked out his window and saw that alien-thing tearing up the engine," Joe laughed as we sat on the tarmac at Guam's A.B. Won Pat International Airport, aboard a United 737, about to head to Iwo Jima. He referred, of course, to that iconic scene in John Landis' *Twilight Zone: The Movie*—a scene that terrified, yet intrigued me as boy in 1983.

After little sleep, the alarm went off at 2:30 a.m. in our hotel room that overlooked one of the beaches in the northern invasion zone of Tumon Bay. It saw 3rd Division Marines, thousands of them, storm ashore under Japanese resistance back in July 1944. My hotel roommate, TGGF President Tim Davis, was up early with me and fine-tuned the last minute details as I went down to the fifth floor to make sure Joe was up and ready to go. He greeted me with a smile and a 'Heeeyyyyy' as he let me in the room at 3:15 a.m. For the documentary, I recorded Joe getting ready—teeth-brushing, pill-taking, shoe-tying. I then sat him on his bed, where we talked about the day ahead. He was incredibly anxious, in a positive way.

I phrased my questions carefully, not wanting to have him repeat himself just a few hours later, but I did ask about the emotions running through his mind.

"I don't have an emotional release that I need to make in relationship to my time in the service because I came from such a restricted lifestyle until I was 17. What I will remember most is all of the things I saw that I did not know existed. I even enjoyed the times where I was in harm's way; it wasn't that I took it lightly, instead it was like, 'This is happening to me.' I had never, *ever* had any visualization of what my life was going to be after 17 because there was no apparent option to me except to do menial things," he said slowly and carefully.

"I think when I get there, I will be able to recreate all of it in my mind."

The night before we had all learned there would be two ambulances on Iwo Jima and six separate medical stations set up at various points on the island during our stay. The veterans also heard that should there be a serious injury or medical emergency, a special flight would be standing by to transport them to a military medical facility on Okinawa, hundreds of miles northwest. Our tickets informed us of our time of departure: United Airlines flight 1862 at 6:30 a.m. with a return on flight 1863 at 3:30 p.m. Joe and the 11 other veterans with the TGGF program—8 Marines and 3 Navy boys—would have the better part of six-and-a-half hours of reflection on Sulfur Island.

A T THE AIRPORT, OUR VETS MINGLED WITH OTHER VETER-ans and their escorts and family members. History buffs who paid thousands to travel to Iwo Jima sought out their stories, autographs, and pictures at gate 14. The veterans visited with other elderly men, strangers who had one thing in common; they all shared the same tiny bit of hell in the Pacific 67 years earlier. The TGGF group linked with other groups on this special day—the only day of the year the government of Japan will allow commercial flights to land on Iwo Jima.

President Lyndon Johnson and the United States returned Iwo Jima and the Bonin Islands back to Japan at 12:15 p.m. local time on June 26, 1968—less than eight months before I was born. At that time, the American flag was lowered and the flag of the Rising Sun—the red "meatball" as veterans call it—was raised, where it remains, atop Suribachi. As their soldiers had done so often—that is to say "disappear" into the tunnels and caves on Iwo—so, too, the name *Iwo Jima* officially disappeared in June 2007. The Japanese now refer to the small island as *Iwo To,* which also means Sulfur Island. Iwo Jima veterans I know still fume when they talk about giving the island back; the island they fought so hard to secure. None of them refer to it as Iwo To.

We were on the second of two flights headed to Iwo that Wednesday morning. The first flight had taken off about 30 minutes before us. United Airlines had a special pre-boarding for these incredible men and I documented Joe as he walked up to the friendly gate agent and handed her his ticket that read:

> *Depart: Guam   Arrive: Iwo Jima.*

Joe proudly wore his distinctive red cap stating, *Iwo Jima Survivor,* a light-brown khaki shirt, and a pair of emerald-green golf pants—again the kind only an 85-year-old man could get away with wearing. Seated in front of Joe, was the Navy Boatswains Mate Second Class, Jim Baize, who enlisted at 15-years-old—*15-years-old.* A deadly mortar round had blown him out of LCVP-13 as a part of the second wave on invasion day, February 19, 1945. He floated unconscious in the bloodstained foam and rough shoreline waters off Iwo before he was pulled to safety. The Indiana native received two Purple Hearts for injuries suffered during his service in the Pacific.

Behind Joe sat Marine Sergeant Al Eutsey; first wave on Green Beach, as a part of Combat Team 28, the Marines responsible for the eventual iconic raising of the American flag on D+4 atop Suribachi. On March 1, 1945, Al was severely wounded by shrapnel on Iwo and during evacuation out of extreme harm's way, he watched one of his stretcher carriers shot to death. The stretcher dropped to the sand and Al fell into a small ditch in agonizing pain. The remaining corpsman and stretcher carriers tried to get him out once again but Japanese bullets and explosions again detoured the plan; Al was dropped in his stretcher "at least twice" more. Fifty years later, at a reunion of the 28th combat team, Al saw one of his life-savers from that fateful day and asked him, jokingly, why he had been dropped so many times. Al told me when he asked the question, the man held up his hand and said, "See where I have no fingertip? That's what was blown off while I was trying to get you out!"

JOE WAS IN GREAT SPIRITS AS HE SAT IN ROW 30, SEAT A, ON March 14, 2012. I was next to him in the middle seat and prepared to use the next 90 minutes to capture his mood and feelings, and record this momentous return for the once-upon-a-time loner from rural Mississippi. He knew he would get back in just a matter of hours, after Mother Nature had pulled the rug from beneath him and other veterans almost exactly a year earlier.

We chatted a few minutes before takeoff and I took pictures so we could both show our families back home. Like in Los Angeles a few days earlier, we taxied down the tarmac under a stream of water shot in a ceremonial arch over our path, courtesy of a fire truck from the Guam Airport Fire Department. As droplets of water covered the window in front of him, Joe began to nod off, then jolt awake, as we hit bumps in the concrete.

At 6:47 a.m., Wednesday morning, March 14—2:47 p.m., Tuesday afternoon in Colorado—we rolled down the runway. As we did, Joe, the God-fearing Catholic, crossed himself seconds before we lifted off from Guam headed to Iwo Jima. While Joe looked out at the water and clouds, Eula was back at home in Colorado, wondering what her husband was about to encounter.

"Here we go, Joe," I said as the thrust of the engines practically drowned out my voice.

"Alright," he smiled.

As the jet lifted off the ground, Joe clenched his left fist and thrust it several times in front of him, symbolic that this time, there was no stopping him. He would soon walk again on the black volcanic ash of Iwo Jima.

"Finally," he said and paused as he looked out his window.

It was my moment to reflect on Joe's previous attempt to get to Iwo Jima a year earlier.

ON THE ONE HOUR, 45-MINUTE FLIGHT ACROSS THE PACIFIC Ocean from Guam to Iwo Jima, Joe and I ate cheese omelets for breakfast, which he washed down with tomato juice on ice. Our in-flight entertainment was a documentary on traveling back to Iwo titled, *Goin' Back,* which included violent, vivid, death-filled images of the war these men could never forget. I jotted down on my notepad: *I wonder what the other 11 vets with whom I didn't get a chance to talk before takeoff are thinking right now as they travel back.* The video described the one million pounds of bombs dropped on Iwo and how, thanks to hard-working Seabees, 50,000 U.S. troops ended up in various camps at the base of Suribachi. The video informed our flight that Iwo's tallest point was six times shorter than Colorado's lowest. We leveled off at 38,000 feet and I gazed past the sleeping Joe to look out at the puffy clouds and blue water below.

"I never thought there would ever be the possibility of seeing Iwo Jima with my own eyes again," Joe said just moments before he dozed off.

OUR FLIGHT BEGAN TO DESCEND INTO IWO JIMA AIRSPACE and a few minutes later, from behind me, Al exclaimed, "There it is!" But it was a false alarm. It was land but only a tiny speck that looked like a Chinese man's hat. A short time after, it came into view: Mt. Suribachi was out our left windows. The captain took the 737 off the southeast coast and we looked down on Green, Red, Yellow, and Blue Beaches, where deadly bloodbaths took place on D-Day. As we continued northeast, infamous Iwo landmarks could be seen from above: the Quarry, the Amphitheatre, Hill 382. These sites witnessed tremendous loss of life and acts of heroism.

Each veteran on the flight had a window seat; each one of them peered out their window, mind racing. Some of their foreheads rested on the clear plastic of the window as they took it in from a vantage point they'd never seen in person.

In the northern section now below us, General Tadamichi Kuribayashi spent the final days of his life; it was a place where he knew he would die.

The flight continued around the island—now headed southwest—and Joe looked down on the black, volcanic-ash beaches he first touched February 24, 1945. Our jet offered a perfect view of where he lived, in that foxhole, for two long months and then above it, on the plateau, for another four. Again, I documented his reactions with my video camera.

The captain flew around the island twice to ensure everyone on both sides of the aircraft could see the now-lush locale below. It didn't look like hell but it had once been the deadliest area, per square foot, in all of WWII. We circled and landed on the sole reason for wanting Iwo Jima in the first place: an airstrip, one of the former Motoyama airfields.

I instantly thought how ironic, that while Joe lived on the beach under war conditions and the threat of Japanese *Banzai* soldiers and mortar fire, our plane landed no more than a 20-minute walk, if that, away from where he dug the first foxhole in his life.

"Welcome to Iwo Jima," the flight attendant announced.

Joe looked out his window and we rolled to a stop. He shook his head back and forth in disbelief as he snapped a few photos with his weathered digital camera.

"Well, I'm back on Iwo Jima, a place I thought I'd never see again," he told me.

Joe was ready to go.

With sunglasses secured to his shirt and camera around his neck, he was ready to touch the ground with his own feet. I scurried off the plane with a news crew out of Denver and our TGGF photographer, John Riedy—absolutely one of the best in the business. Years earlier I had urged John to become a part of our veteran programs and he jumped at the chance; since our initial conversation, we have traveled the world together supporting these amazing men in their own journeys back to the battlefields. John donates his time and has captured easily more than 20,000 images on multiple TGGF programs. He is also a great friend and cares for the men he captures via stunning digital images.

As we set up our cameras on the tarmac, the vets nervously waited to deplane. I had to capture the moment Joe stepped back on Iwo Jima, and when he appeared at the jet doorway on top of a portable set of stairs, my heart pounded. He made his way down and I watched with pride as my friend touched down. Joe was immediately greeted with a handshake and smile from three-star Lieutenant General Kenneth Glueck, Commanding General, 3rd Marine Expeditionary Force and Commander, U.S. Marine Forces Japan.

Joseph C. LaNier II was back on Iwo Jima.

"W HERE'S THIS HOT WEATHER YOU GUYS HAVE BEEN telling me about?" Joe laughed as a chilly wind blew across the concrete runway.

It was not tropical or warm, and high clouds drifted above. I shook his hand and welcomed him back and then we walked a quarter-mile to the large hangar normally operated solely by the Japanese.

"Sir, I have you down as a distinguished visitor," a Marine sergeant explained from a table as Joe signed a check-in registration sheet inside the hangar. Joe and I received DV stickers, *Distinguished Visitor,* and headed through a hallway back outside to await our ride to another part of the small island.

I remained incredibly grateful for every moment with my friend, every second we were there that day. Marines and sailors from U.S. bases in Tokyo and on Okinawa were our transportation escorts, and we climbed into a small passenger van along with several others and drove out of the airfield and down past large satellite dishes and several small buildings operated by the Japan Maritime Self-Defense Force (JMSDF). The killing fields of Iwo

Jima were all around us but there was no way of knowing 67 years later. Unlike when the fighting was at its height, small shrubs and vines had grown up all over the island.

Due to the firepower unleashed in the months prior to invasion, Iwo Jima had been stripped and scorched of all its vegetation, which subsequently took years to reappear. By official accounts, so much unexploded ordnance remains that travel, other than in specified areas, is not only discouraged but prohibited. According to the "Iwo Jima Courtesy Brief" that U.S. visitors receive upon landing:

> We arc guests of the Japanese government and represent the United States. Act accordingly. It is prohibited to remove any artifacts, natural, historical or otherwise from the island. It is prohibited to raise, fly or otherwise show flags of any nationality or meaning on Iwo Jima. Please note that Iwo Jima still contains the remains of many missing Japanese and U.S. service members. It is essentially a cemetery and memorial site. The Japanese government conducts annual expeditions in an ongoing effort to recover, identify, and pay proper respect to their dead. If human remains are located, do not touch, move, or otherwise disturb the area. Report the location of suspected remains to the nearest Marine. One such area in the vicinity of the Sherman tank is currently being excavated and is *off limits to U.S. personnel.*

And finally:

> Caves, underground bunkers, and historical structures are off limits unless specifically designated. Centipedes, spiders, bees, wasps, scorpions, and rats are numerous and venomous/dangerous. Beware of unexploded ordnance. Do not touch *anything* that cannot be identified. Avoid the water's edge and no swimming! There are dangerous currents and aggressive sharks!

We continued on asphalt the next several hundred yards, making a few left and right turns before heading down a dirt road full of ruts and small ravines from the runoff of the 60 inches of average annual rainfall. The van headed southwest, on a road I was familiar with from my first visit to Iwo Jima during the previous TGGF program in March 2010. That was the trip that nearly never happened and had allowed our veterans just a three-hour window to experience past trauma and heartache.

Five minutes out from the airstrip—in the direction of Suribachi—we came to a halt, amid the dust kicked up from several of the other vans transporting other veterans and dignitaries to a ceremony later in the morning. As we climbed out, Joe and I stuck together. We knew immediately where we had to go.

"Let's go down to the beach, Joe."

"Alright," he said.

Joe returns to Iwo Jima, March 2012.
(John Riedy Photography)

We stood a half-mile above Blue Beach, where Jim Blane and the 4th Marine Division stormed ashore and faced not only the thick, volcanic-ash sand, but steep hills and plateaus that at best served to slow them down. Both large and small caliber Japanese weapons cut them down, seemingly from *within* the island. Progress that first day, like along most of the rest of the shoreline down to the base of

Suribachi, was measured in feet and yards. Though this was on the opposite side of the island he knew, Joe anxiously wanted to get to the shore, feel that sand again, and see those intricate lines of white foam on the wet, black volcanic coastline.

W E BEGAN OUR WALK DOWN ALONG A WELL-CUT TRAIL, which bottomed out at a Japanese pillbox that still stands with an eerie overlook of the beach and wide fields below. At its front, a rusted shell of a high-caliber machine gun pointed toward the sand, protected by a thick concrete blockhouse. This particular pillbox contained two rooms and judging by the twisted and rusted rebar and exposed concrete that protruded from its semi-hidden locale, it was likely hit by a Marine-fired mortar from the beach, grenades, or a round fired from one of the hundreds of ships offshore.

I was worried for Joe as we continued down the slope. One fall and he would find himself on a medical flight headed to Okinawa. As best I could, I escorted him down and with every step we soaked in the environment. Again, all around us: killing fields. I would later remark that Iwo Jima would have such a different feel if there were markers in each spot where someone had lost their life for their country.

Joe and I continued down the plateaus and tables that were so tough to conquer in those first few days on this side of Iwo Jima. As we drew closer to the beach, the ash mixture below our feet grew thicker. Off in the fields on either side of the path, tiny reeds of growth swayed in the ocean breeze—Iwo's version of tiny, individual stalks of wheat shooting toward the sun. Small sparrows darted in and out of vegetation, their song drowned by the increasing sound of the crashing surf. When we finally made it to where the surface below our feet was nothing but coarse volcanic sand, I turned the camera on Joe to capture his thoughts as he stood on the exact material where he first stepped foot, nearly 25,000 days earlier.

CHAPTER TWENTY-FOUR

PEACE

History is a cyclic poem written by time upon the memories of man.

—PERCY BYSSHE SHELLEY

SEVEN HUNDRED SIXTY MILES SOUTHEAST OF TOKYO, MT. Suribachi stood as our backdrop under a cloudless, brilliant blue sky as Joe began to recall his six months on Iwo Jima. He talked freely about Japanese attackers, the death, the black volcanic sand, and his time on this desolate speck in the middle of nowhere.

"Standing here on the sands of volcanic ash brings back fresh memories of 67 years ago. I remember the sound of the ocean beating on the sands. When I got off my ship, it was a matter of following orders. Living in a foxhole was small and cramped but it was all you had. You had to accept what you had," he told me, almost as if he'd rehearsed it in his mind.

As the turquoise waters churned behind him, Joe talked about the significance of his return.

"To the best of my knowledge, I am the first African-American to come back to Iwo Jima after the war. There's a sense of pride to me that I am representing all of the Navy's 23rd Special Seabees who served here with me. Being here, my mind goes back to Columbus, Mississippi—so far away. I'm sad that my father is not here to see that his son has come back to the place where his son made a contribution to our democracy."

During my first visit to Iwo Jima, I failed to bring canisters to collect its infamous sand. This time, my backpack was loaded with three plastic containers and plastic bags, and Joe filled mine for me;

I wanted him to collect the sand that I would treasure the rest of my life. I brought some back for close friends and my kids. We spent several more minutes standing with the gusty wind in our faces and ears, and reflected before our long trek back up for the remembrance ceremony. On the way back up the path, several people from the other groups greeted Joe as he slowly trudged forward. His red *Iwo Jima Survivor* cap acted like a beacon for strangers eager to hear his story.

It had already been a long morning when Joe started back up the slopes that witnessed thousands of deaths not seven decades earlier. On his way up, a Marine sergeant—42-years-old from Cincinnati—assisted Joe as I carried our gear. Joe began to tell them his abbreviated story and how he was segregated on the island.

"Oh, really? No kidding," the sergeant said, almost flabbergasted. He didn't know the history of blacks in the military.

If he only knew.

Joe thanked him for the help and made it the rest of the way to the top on his own.

T HE MEMORIAL WAS ABOUT 30 MINUTES FROM BEGINNING and Joe and I stood just off the dirt road that led to Suribachi. The place was busy with people putting the final touches on the program, from the color guard practicing a hundred yards away to the bands as they fine-tuned their instruments. About this time, three Navy females—all teenagers—approached Joe and asked if they could take their picture with him and hear his story. They were from the USS Germantown (LSD-42), based in Sasebo, Japan. She and her crew assisted with rescue-and-recovery efforts following the devastating quake and tsunami, almost exactly a year earlier. The young women smiled with Joe as I took their pictures with multiple cameras and as we left, Joe gave them some unsolicited advice.

"Learn from history because if you don't, you'll repeat it. If you learn from your history, you'll make a positive contribution to our society moving forward."

He smiled, said goodbye, and we made our way across the dirt road to our seventh-row seats on the left-hand side of the main podium. The U.S. delegation sat on the left side, with the Japanese delegation directly across on the right. Every man from Japan was dressed in a dark suit and dark tie; women wore black dresses. Those of us on the U.S. side were in a hodgepodge of attire; some wore suits but most of us in comfortable outdoor gear. Nearly 300 people assembled for the somber, one-hour ceremony.

The pre-ceremonial activities included patriotic music from both countries. The Japanese Ground Self-Defense Force Central Band was perched on the right above on a small, grassy plateau, while the III Marine Expeditionary Force Band from Camp Foster, Okinawa, alternated music directly across from their Japanese counterparts. With the playing of each country's national anthem— *Kimigayo* and *The Star-Spangled Banner*—the "Reunion of Honor" ceremony got underway.

"MAY TODAY'S CEREMONY NOT ONLY HONOR THE dead and express undying gratitude for those who fought here but deepen our resolve to further peace in our world. Grant us Your grace as we remember," the Marine chaplain concluded in his invocation.

Because of the earthquake, this was the first commemoration ceremony on Iwo since 2010. I sat there with Joe as speeches were delivered and I couldn't help but think what this area had witnessed during the time he was here the first time, in 1945. Lieutenant General Glueck, the man who greeted Joe when he took his first step back onto Iwo Jima, addressed the somber crowd with authority.

"We gather here today as men and women representing two great nations—two nations, who, after this battle, came together to build an alliance, an alliance which some consider to be the most successful in the history of mankind, achieving over 60 years of peace and stability in this critical region of the world," he said.

"May God bless the men who fought, suffered, and died on this island called Iwo Jima."

A U.S. Embassy official also delivered strong remarks as the wind off the ocean whipped the crowd.

"Today, we pause to remember so we do not repeat the past. If the people who fought here could see us today, they would not believe the alliance between our two countries. These survivors of Iwo Jima are the standard bearers of peace and democracy."

As each Japanese leader came to speak at the podium, they bowed to their American counterparts, a sign of respect. The second speaker's introduction caught my attention immediately. Yoshitaka Shindo, member of the Japanese House of Representatives—on this day a representative of bereaved families—walked up in a dark suit, white shirt, and dark tie; a blue-and-white remembrance ribbon was pinned near the left lower side of his suit jacket. As he stepped in for his prepared remarks, it sunk in to me exactly who he was. Shindo was the grandson of General Kuribayashi, who was defending Iwo Jima as best he could—in vain—exactly 67 years earlier.

"Japanese soldiers suffered the heat of underground bunkers, where the temperature rose to over 122 degrees, and fought desperately without food or drinking water. I think the soldiers who fought in this infernal hell stood up to this hardship for the sake of their parents and loved ones at home, and in order to delay the danger to them as long as possible," Shindo said in his native tongue.

"We, the bereaved families, would like to express our sincere sorrow for the loss of those who fought for their country and family, and we must pass down their history to the future generations so their sacrifice will not be forgotten. Less than half the remains of the Japanese troops were retrieved, with more than 12,000 of them still left on this island, which seems to be a place where time has stopped its movement."

According to the commemoration program, the United States lost 6,821 men and suffered 26,038 casualties on Iwo Jima over the official 36 days of fighting. The number of Japanese dead was listed as 21,570. It is widely believed just 216 Japanese soldiers were captured during *Operation Detachment*. The vast majority of Japanese who weren't killed by U.S. forces committed suicide.

TAPS was played to conclude the ceremony.

A S THE CROWD BROKE UP, I NOTICED THE OPPORTUNITY for Joe to meet Shindo and what happened next still boggles my mind. He had just wrapped up a brief conversation with Congressmen Braley and Perlmutter when I approached his interpreter, a man holding a clipboard.

"Would you mind introducing him to a WWII veteran who was here? He's Joseph LaNier."

In Japanese, the interpreter introduced the two men.

"Ah," Shindo said.

"Twenty-third Seabee," I added.

Joe stepped closer as Shindo shook his hand.

"So nice to meet you," Joe said.

"This is Mr. Shindo. His grandfather was the general here on Iwo Jima during the battle," explained the interpreter.

Shindo looked Joe up and down.

"You so fine, look so fine. So very fine," he said to Joe in extremely broken English. He made reference to how healthy and vibrant Joe looked at 85-years-old.

"You're kind to say that. It is so nice to meet you, it is my pleasure."

"Please take care," Shindo said with the nod of his head.

"I'm from Denver, Colorado. If you're ever there, come to see us."

The interpreter then took over as Joe smiled. Shindo smiled and again nodded his head as he heard Joe's words translated to Japanese.

"Den-vuh. So, so cold city! Please take care. Thank you very much," Shindo smiled.

The two shook hands again and parted ways. The entire connection lasted only 50 seconds but I remain thrilled that Joe had the opportunity to meet the son of Takako Shindo, whose father was General Kuribayashi.

AFTER THE CEREMONY, WE BOARDED ANOTHER MINIBUS and drove down the dusty dirt road, headed southwest toward Suribachi. What had been an often-deadly trek up chunks of volcanic rock to the top in WWII was now a drive on a paved road. It was pockmarked full of ruts and cracks, every one the result of significant earthquakes that constantly rumble through the area. When we arrived close to the summit we got out and walked the final 100 yards to the top, directly to the site of the iconic second flag raised on Iwo Jima less than a full day before Joe arrived.

He walked up to where the land flattened at the summit and in front of him stood a small memorial park. Joe's head was on a swivel. He had never seen the five-mile-long, two-and-a-half-mile-wide island from this vantage point, despite his six months on the sand and plateau below. His first stop was briefly in front of the Japanese memorial—two granite pillars on top of square granite slabs—in-between them, a large, unattached granite square. Japanese writing adorned each side of the pillars. Joe seemed in awe and soaked it in.

The top offered a beautiful panoramic of the blue Pacific Ocean, while 500 feet down the mountain, black beaches stretched at least two miles.

"I'm now at the top of Mt. Suribachi. When we were here securing the island, I never had a desire to come to the top. After 67 years, this is very important for me to come to the top of this mountain."

Joe and Steffan on Mt. Suribachi, March 2011. The 23rd Seabees landed on the beach below February 24, 1945.
(Steffan Tubbs)

We walked another 30 yards to the northwest, which allowed Joe to look down on the beach where he landed February 24, 1945. He pointed off into the distance and he visualized the foxholes, the carpentry shop, and the chow lines of his past.

"We built foxholes right down there, just before that widest spot on the beach. We started building those foxholes and built them to the north part of the island and we stayed there for two months," he said.

"That plateau right there, that's where I saw the Japanese soldier shot to death, right in front of me. The first time I saw the enemy shot dead was at the bottom of that plateau. Standing up here today, I get a perfect visualization of everything that I saw at ground level."

It was hard to believe we were there together.

"That's your side of the island, Joe."

"That's right. That's right."

Before we left, Joe sat in front of the right-hand side of the 5th Marine Division memorial. Behind him read the words:

23 February 1945
Old Glory was raised on
This site by members
Of the 2nd Bn. 28th Regt.
Fifth Marine Division

On the left-hand side of the small memorial:

"Among the Americans who served
on Iwo Jima, uncommon valor
was a common virtue." Nimitz
Dedicated to those who fought here by
the island command AGF.
Erected by the 31st USNCB.

A bronze replica of the American flag is placed over a bronze brass plate depicting the Rosenthal photograph.

Our time passed quickly on top of Suribachi. In a sense it was both his hello and goodbye to the island, squeezed into just a few minutes.

As our transport down the hill loaded, Joe and I paused and took in one more scenic look at our surroundings. Off in the distance, we could see the northern tip of the island, where in the late stages of the battle for Iwo Jima, U.S. forces had used loudspeakers in hopes of convincing General Kuribayashi and his Japanese forces to surrender. They never did.

Both Joe and I felt it important to pause, look around, and soak in exactly where we were. It was our moment to respect the dead and pay tribute to a key United States victory. It was my time to appreciate Joe's segregated service on the island. We needed this time; after all, the odds were against us ever coming back— especially together.

As the day wound down, I asked Joe how his day had gone.

He smiled a toothy grin.

"Great. Great. One of the best days of my life."

OUR DAY ON IWO ENDED WHERE IT BEGAN, AT THE LARGE hangar off the tarmac. Each person getting back on the United flight had their bags searched and were then electronically screened with a wand to be sure they weren't trying to smuggle some metal souvenir. Each person in line was covered with Iwo Jima dust, and nearly everyone brought back with them various amounts of that black, volcanic-ash sand as a somber memento. I must have brought back five pounds of the stuff.

As the temperature began to drop a bit and the sun crept toward the western horizon, we started our walk out to the United 737. Joe was upbeat but clearly tired and when he reached the temporary jet stairs, he paused a bit in his mind. His feet then took him off the surface of Iwo Jima and climbed each step until he reached the airplane door at the top. Joe took a final deep inhale of the heavy air, exhaled, and walked in toward his seat.

He didn't look back.

ONCE ABOARD, WE SETTLED INTO OUR SEATS. IT HAD BEEN a very long, but fulfilling and memorable day.

"I was not emotional about it but it was a refreshing vision to see where I lived. It was worth the trip to see it from Suribachi. I would come back and when I did, the first place I would go is where I dug my first foxhole," Joe smiled.

He slept most of the 90-minute flight back to Guam.

He had made it back to Iwo Jima.

He was at peace.

CHAPTER TWENTY-FIVE

NO REGRETS

There's a time for departure even when there's no certain place to go.

— TENNESSEE WILLIAMS

"I REALLY CONSIDER MYSELF A FORTUNATE MAN. GIVEN the area of the country I was brought up in, I have been able to provide for my family. I consider that fortunate. I have been very fortunate to have been born in the United States of America," Joe reflected.

The fact he is 43 years my elder is both a blessing and a curse. I am, without question, a better man today because of our chance meeting in March 2011. Yet, as he indicated to me on the outskirts of his family's cemetery in rural Columbus, I wish we had met sooner. He had already led an amazing life by the time I saw him for the first time in the Clear Channel lobby.

ON AUGUST 15, 1981, JOE AND TWO OTHERS WENT FOR a golf outing at the Pinery Country Club's *Lake Valley Course* in Parker, Colorado. Joe stepped into the tee box on the par-three fifth hole after grabbing a four-iron out of his bag just seconds before. From 162 yards away, the eight-handicapper took a practice swing, then addressed the ball perched on a white tee. He hit it well and watched it fly through the air, then bounce onto the green. It rolled in and gave Joe his first and only hole-in-one. He was part of a threesome that day and they served as witnesses.

"I couldn't believe it! Still can't," he told me.

The following year, Titleist Golf Division sent a letter informing him of the five "distinctive awards" he could choose from to commemorate the rare feat; he received a trophy from Foot Joy and became a member of the Crown Royal "Hole-in-one Society." Not bad, I thought, for the guy who wasn't allowed to play back on his hometown course.

A**S A PART OF HIS PHARMACY AND HOSPITAL CAREER, HE** exchanged letters with all types of elected officials including governors and senators; the one-time loner from Mississippi visited the governor's mansion in Colorado for a cocktail party. During the Carter Administration, he received a tour of the White House but never met the President. He frequently wrote letters to the editor and penned articles in every conceivable pharmacy-related publication. Joe was a member of the American Pharmaceutical Association, the Colorado Pharmacal Association, the American Society of Hospital Pharmacists, and the Colorado Society of Hospital Pharmacists. In most—if not all—cases, he was the only black man among the groups. That began to change over the years but Joe, indeed, blazed a trail.

I**N NOVEMBER 2000, JOE AND EULA WERE ON VACATION BACK** in New Orleans when he noticed his ankles swell. *Must be the change in climate.* He didn't feel normal and when they returned to Colorado he visited his doctor to explain his condition; it was a routine visit overall, until it was time to wrap up the appointment. Just before he was about to be sent home, the doctor had a premonition and suggested a cardiologist take a look. After an extensive exam, they discovered Joe had lived his entire life with an enlarged heart. He was put on medication to help shrink it.

Golf was still enjoyable and not a problem; walking the course and pulling a cart was just fine. But one Sunday before Thanksgiving, Joe felt a sharp pain shoot down his left arm. It went away quickly but it had registered in his mind. The following day he called his doctor and was told, "You just described a heart attack."

Doctors performed a five-hour, double-bypass operation on November 17. Recovery was normal, if not a bit slow for the active senior citizen. He lost weight, exercised more, and was told to watch his sugar intake. It changed him in the sense that he had a new appreciation for the fragility of life.

I N 1988, HE DECIDED TO GO TO MODELING SCHOOL IN DENVER— at the wise age of 68. *Someone* had to play those roles on the big and small screens. The move paid off with an appearance in a U.S. West telephone print advertisement and a small cameo role in an episode of the television series *Father Dowling Mysteries* starring Tom Bosley. Joe has kept his original Screen Actor's Guild or *SAG* card in his personal "memory book"—the wallet-sized card valid from December 1988 to April 1989.

The kid from Mississippi, the boy who thought the earth was flat, the teen who witnessed a racially motivated beating, the young man who joined the Navy and went on to become a pharmacist was, for a time, an actor and a model. *Only in America,* I thought.

Joe III went on to model as well and for a brief time, worked as a TV sports anchor and radio broadcaster, just like his father had done on the side. Lisa went on to become a concert pianist and loving mother to the only LaNier grandchild, Andrew.

D URING OUR JOURNEY TO COLUMBUS IN OCTOBER 2011, videographer Andre Greller and I visited as many parts of the small city as we could—all to get a feel of Joe's hometown.

Imagine our surprise when we read the marker in front of the birth-place of Pulitzer Prize-winning playwright Tennessee Williams. There, at the corner of Main and Third Streets in downtown Colum-bus, the plaque read: *Thomas Lanier "Tennessee" Williams was born here March 26, 1911.* Thomas *Lanier* "Tennessee" Williams. Joe has never been able to trace his family tree to the man who penned such classics as *The Glass Menagerie, A Streetcar Named Desire* and *Cat on a Hot Tin Roof,* but the possibility still boggles my mind.

Later that afternoon, we stopped at another historical marker across town. This one honored the late, legendary baseball broad-caster Red Barber. Andre and I stood in the middle of a landscaped island with two-lane streets on either side—once again in amaze-ment. The plaque here read: *Walter Lanier "Red" Barber was born near here February 17, 1908.* Walter *Lanier* "Red" Barber. Common name in the area? Yes. Bizarre, though, considering the presence of the Laniers and their connection with slavery and segregation. As with Williams, Joe has never connected the branch of the family tree with the Barbers.

What proved to be even more bizarre as I thought more about the potential significance: it was Red Barber who broadcast Jackie Robinson's first game with the Brooklyn Dodgers as baseball's color barrier was broken, April 15, 1947. As the late baseball broad-caster Mel Allen would say: "How about *that.*"

IN APRIL 2012, JOE, MY WIFE, AND I WERE INVITED TO ATTEND the annual TAPS Honor Guard Gala in Washington, D.C. Our friend Mike Buchen, CEO of Colorado-based Skydex Technolo-gies, urged us to make the trip and meet some well-connected guests who would be interested in Joe's story. Mike is an incredible supporter of our troops and has become a great friend. His small company—Skydex—has developed blast mitigation technology via the use of specially designed plastics, shaped in such a way as to absorb the tremendous energy from IEDs (improvised explosive devices), like the one that killed Ian Weikel in 2006. TAPS (Tragedy Assistance Program for Survivors) is a national charity that provides counseling, camps, and support for the children of servicemen and women who have either been killed in action or have committed suicide. TAPS has helped thousands of people, primarily children and widows, deal with their grief since its inception in 1994.

Joe looked handsome and dignified at the black-tie affair, which included some of the biggest names in Washington. Over the course of the evening, he shared in conversations with Joint Chiefs Chairman General Martin Dempsey, Marine Corps Commandant James Amos, and General Eric Shinseki, U.S. Secretary of Veterans Affairs. In a private conversation, Joe presented Shinseki with a small glass jar filled with Iwo Jima sand. The small token, so representative of Joe's life, stunned the four-star general.

"I cannot thank you enough for this, Joe. I will treasure it in my office," Shinseki said as he left the program.

Joe and Steffan meet Gen. Eric Shinseki, United States Secretary of Veterans Affairs, at the TAPS Gala, Washington, D.C., April 2012.
(Steffan Tubbs)

The following day we connected with both Congressmen Braley and Perlmutter and took a behind-the-scenes tour of the U.S. Capitol. Outside the House Chamber, where President Roosevelt delivered his *Day of Infamy* speech, Joe met members of Congress and was treated like a hero.

J OE HAS MADE ME THINK OF MY OWN DECISIONS IN LIFE, AND has proved time and again, he is much the wiser. Unfortunately—and inevitably—I had to eventually broach the topic of his own mortality, a sad fact that he has indeed more life behind him than ahead. The topic has made me think of my own mortality, as well.

"I think I will be remembered as a person who tried hard to be the kind of person I thought I needed to be. I hope they remember that I really cared about people and had no ability to hate. I also think I will be remembered as a good husband and father who provided for his family with every bit of gusto. I also want to be remembered for the respect that I have for my father. I live today by most of what he taught me and how he lived his life to show me how to relate to my fellow man," he said.

Life. Joe was able to live the life he never dreamed possible.

Liberty. Joe lived the life of *his* choosing.

Resilience. Joe succeeded despite the racism that had surrounded him.

On those three different fronts, he had come out on top.

As Joe spoke, I listened with as much emotion as ever, though I tucked it away.

"I view death as inevitable. I don't worry about it, but that does not mean I don't think about it. I know what life is like as I live; I have no idea what is going to happen after death. Based on my faith, I believe that as you go on into the afterlife, if you have lived the life on this earth by the Judeo-Christian ethic, you're going to be okay," Joe calmly mused.

"My philosophy of life is not to hate and I had no reason to feel patriotic growing up because we weren't even considered a part of the country in that sense. I didn't feel like this was my country because I wasn't treated as a person; all that came later. It was like I was here for the benefit of the power structure. Looking back..." he said and then paused without finishing his sentence.

"Looking back, I think I accomplished more than I had ever thought that I could accomplish in my life."

Life. Liberty. Resilience.

He then concluded.

"I think you have to be able to let go of adversity when it comes to you. You can't worry about it. You have to really feel that this too shall pass and that something better will happen."

Joe looked me in the eyes and smiled.

EPILOGUE

THE SHOVELS EASILY MADE THEIR WAY INTO THE DAMP soil, shaded by the high and arching canopies of trees that helped to hide the old graveyard. It was hot and humid for mid-June, and the air was filled with the sounds of myriad insects making their late-morning noise. The place was exactly the same as I had remembered it eight months earlier.

JOE, MY WIFE, AND I FLEW INTO BIRMINGHAM, ALABAMA, the day before, then drove west to Columbus that afternoon. Carlotta LaNier was also on our small United Airlines flight and rode with us for the two-and-a-half-hour drive into Mississippi. We all talked about her days in Little Rock and that infamous September when she became a part of Civil Rights history.

In many ways the graveside ceremony set for Friday, June 8, 2012, on the old Lanier plantation, was a culmination of a multi-layered set of factors: the ending for this book, the bringing-together of LaNier family members from different parts of the country and indeed their family tree, the proper markings for lives lost, and the often-over-used term *closure*. To me, the ceremony meant Joe would make good on the promise he made to his dead relatives at their graves the previous autumn. He would place simple, dignified, beautiful granite grave markers where his mother Savilla, brother Ira, and father Joseph had been buried.

LORI AND I GOT UP EARLY THAT FRIDAY AND MET JOE IN THE hotel lobby. We didn't have to say a word to each other about the significance of what would soon take place. It was understood.

We all drove just down the highway and into the gravel lot of Columbus Marble Works, where we were set to meet Key Blair and see the markers for the first time. After we parked, we walked into the front showroom and saw various samples of their cemetery work. It was at least 20 degrees hotter inside than out. As we made our way to the office door, a black man I had seen near a flatbed truck outside came in.

"Hi, we're here to see Key Blair," I said.

"Sure, let me go get him."

Within a couple of minutes, Key came into the showroom and warmly greeted us in a thick Mississippi accent. I immediately thanked him for all he had done to make this moment possible. It was his pleasure.

Key also informed us that for more than three decades, his Columbus location had provided the headstones for Colorado's Fort Logan National Cemetery, south of Denver. The Georgia-culled marble was crafted and stamped on these premises before being shipped west. What a coincidence, I thought. He then told us that two of his best men would be installing the markers, and one of them was in the showroom with us.

"He's ready to go. The markers, they're loaded on the truck right now," Key said.

We introduced ourselves and smiled.

"I'm Jimmy Peoples," he said.

I paused.

I must have heard him incorrectly. Then it registered.

Peoples.

The Peoples' boy.

My mouth opened in disbelief, and I quickly looked at Lori, equally in awe.

"Peoples?" I asked.

Jimmy smiled, not knowing why I repeated his last name.

Joe was also stunned at the irony.

"Yes," Jimmy said, likely wondering why we were making it a big deal.

"It's just that there's a boy in Joe's life with the last name of Peoples who had a significant impact on him. Have you lived here all your life?" I asked.

"Yes," he said, but he really didn't know much about his family history.

Jimmy was friendly, likely in his forties, tall, and weathered. He was dressed in a T-shirt, jeans, and thick construction boots. We made our way outside and as Lori and Joe went back to the car, I walked over and introduced myself to Jimmy's job partner, Byron Berry. There on the flatbed of the dusty truck, I saw the grave markers for the first time. They were perfect. I was proud.

T HE GATE THAT PROTECTED THE *LAZY ACRES* DIRT ROAD alongside the graveyard was padlocked when we pulled up. It was the same road Joe, Andre, and I went down that led to the garage sale the previous October. The morning of the ceremony, Joe contacted the property owners, the Youngbloods, via cell phone, and they instructed us to go back down Youngblood Road another 200 yards and then drive into the open field, where we could get close to the tree line. Just beyond that—within the grove of trees and vines, spiderwebs, and toppled headstones—we would hold the ceremony.

Several of the LaNier family had joined our small procession as we drove a quarter-mile through the field and to a stop. Car engines turned off, and we all filed out and began to gather. Introductions were made and hugs were shared before I told everyone I would be back within a few minutes. I wanted to go into the trees alone, to be sure I could still locate the gravesites we were so lucky to find eight months earlier.

I WALKED TOWARD THE DENSE VEGETATION AND RECOGNIZED the area where we had entered the first time. The voices behind me grew distant as I continued in through low branches, tall weeds, and over two strands of rusted barbed wire. There—past two larger trees covered in twisting vines—I saw the cross Andre had fashioned near Ira's uprooted headstone. The cross made of sticks and tied with vine was still in perfect shape. It had stood tall through a partial fall, full winter, and most of spring without falling.

It had kept watch over the three graves.

I was relieved beyond words to not only see the cross but to know we had found the right location. I was emotional. For the first time in the months of planning, it hit me that my dream for Joe was about to come true. I made my way again out of the trees and uneven ground and back to the small crowd near the parked cars.

I informed Joe and Lori; Joe's daughter, Lisa, and her husband; along with Carlotta and her husband, Ira LaNier Jr., that we could now head into the trees to place the markers. Other family members, who had driven hours to be there, also began to slowly make their way into the wooded, overgrown area. Joe had invited Father Robert Dore of Annunciation Catholic Church in Columbus to preside, and the two of them walked in together.

ONCE EVERYONE HAD DODGED THE BARBED WIRE, navigated the sloped terrain, and brushed off the biting ticks, they gathered near the gravesites and the solemn ceremony began. Father Dore held a blue, hardbound book, *Order of Christian Funerals,* in his left hand. With Joe standing to his right, he began with a prayer.

"My brothers and sisters, we believe that all the ties of friendship and affection which knit us as one throughout our lives do not unravel with death, confident that God always remembers the good we have done and forgives us our sins. We pray today, asking God to gather Joseph, Savilla, and Ira to Himself."

The words hung among the trees for a moment.

"Lord Jesus Christ, by Your own three days in the tomb You hallowed the graves of all who believe in You and so made the grave a sign of hope that promises resurrection, even as it claims our mortal bodies. Grant that our brothers and sister may sleep here in peace until You awaken them to glory, for You are the resurrection and the life. Then they will see You face-to-face, and in Your light will see light and know the splendor of God. For You live and reign forever and ever. Amen."

No one said a word.

"Oh God, by whose mercy the faithful departed find rest, bless these gravestones which will be laid to mark the graves of these people. May they rest here in peace until the Lord awakens them to eternal life, and may they have everlasting life and rejoice with You and Your saints forever and ever. And we ask You this, through Christ, our Lord. Amen. And may Almighty God bless you in the name of the Father, and of the Son, and of the Holy Spirit. Amen."

When Father Dore finished, Joe read from a folded paper program Eula had put together. She remained in Colorado but provided the memento that included a color picture of Papa in a suit; a black-and-white photo of Ira in a suit, boutonniere, and hat; and Mama, reproduced from her only known photo.

Joe read from the prayer—*Eternal Rest Grant Unto Them, O Lord*—printed on the inside of the single, folded sheet of paper.

"Lord Jesus, lovingly welcome into Your presence my deceased family, relatives, and friends who have completed their journey on this earth, and have gone to their rest in the hope of rejoicing with You forever in Heaven. Source of all life and love, in Your infinite mercy, look favorably upon their goodness, and forgive any sins they may have committed, so they may enjoy for all eternity the great rewards You have promised to those who believe in You. Amen."

Joe then spoke in his own words.

"I would just like to say to my mother and father and brother that I promised in October when we came that before I died, I would make sure they had a headstone at their grave. Eight months later, we have headstones to place."

He paused.

"It gives them an identity. We remember you."

Several people softly said, *Amen.*

Joe thanked Father Dore, who then walked out of the small clearing of trees and back to his car parked in the field. The rest of us remained.

Ira Jr.—or Sonny as he was known within the family—had parting words about his late father. Carlotta stood to his right.

"He died at the young, tender age of 27, and he left behind a loving wife and three young children. I don't have any memories of him but I do have accounts—stories that my mother shared with me throughout my life—about how my father loved me. To know that my father was a nurturing man gives me some comfort. It made me want to be like him, even though I had no idea what being like him was."

As Carlotta wiped away tears, Sonny concluded.

"As my Uncle Joe has said, I know they would be proud of this day. And I hope my dad would be pleased with how his wife managed to raise his children during some very, very hard times in Mississippi."

AFTER RESPECTFULLY WATCHING THE GRAVESIDE CERE- mony, Jimmy Peoples and Byron Berry from Columbus Marble Works walked back, through the bed of dead leaves and low-hanging branches, to the field. They stopped at the side of their flatbed truck where three granite headstones were nestled between pieces of wood. The markers were simple: a cross centered on the top, with names and dates of birth and death below. With care, each man carried one back into the woods. They meticulously used shovels to clear debris and then dug several inches of fresh earth. These spaces would be the final resting place of grave markers that should have been placed decades earlier. Most of the dozen people standing nearby barely said a word.

MAMA'S GRAVE MARKER WAS PLACED FIRST—ON A BED OF dry, powdery concrete mix. Once set, Jimmy and Byron used a level to make sure it was correctly positioned. The process was repeated for Papa's marker and finally for Ira's. Joe stood silently and watched from a few feet away. Patches of sunshine filtered through the tops of the trees; birdsongs filled the air. Before leaving, Jimmy wiped the tops of the markers clear of any debris. Most everyone in the LaNier family took pictures and said silent prayers. They then filed out of the woods.

Soon, it was just Joe and me in the clearing, looking at this overgrown section of land that time forgot. It was overwhelming. On this day, we didn't forget. His loved ones were remembered.

Before I left Denver, I packed one jar of Iwo Jima sand specifically for this moment. Joe didn't know, but I thought it would only be appropriate for him to sprinkle some of the black volcanic sand from another part of the world onto his parents' graves. Mama had died four years and four months before Joe landed on Iwo, and Papa never talked about it with his son. Now was the chance for the symbolic connection.

JOE OPENED THE FLIP-TOP LID OF THE SMALL JAR OF SAND AND held it in his left hand. He bent over the new grave markers and with his right hand sprinkled the coarse sand he had scooped up on Iwo Jima less than four months earlier. He then stood in silence over the graves and held his hat, his head bent down in prayer. Birds continued to sing. It was time to give his parents a final message.

Joe recalled seeing Papa in the audience during graduation back at Xavier; he warmly remembered Mama and her love. Both of them, he reiterated, died too soon.

"This is my thank you," he said as he looked at the Mississippi soil below.

"Thank you for being my parents."

The 86-year-old then stood at attention and raised his right hand to his head.

Tears welled.

Joe saluted the grave markers.

He turned around—his shoes crunching the leaves, twigs, and dead branches—and walked out of the wooded area and into the sunlit Mississippi field.

He didn't look back.

New gravemarkers for Savilla and Joseph LaNier in rural Columbus, Mississippi. Placed at a graveyard ceremony June 8, 2012.
(Steffan Tubbs)

Notes

1   Robert J. Schneller Jr., Breaking the Color Barrier (New York, NY: NYU Press, 2007), p. 162.

2   Edward Mayes, Lucius Q.C. Lamar: His Life, Times, And Speeches. 1825-1893 (Nashville, TN: Publishing House of the Methodist Episcopal Church, South, 1896), p. 633.

3   Olga Reed Pruitt, It Happened Here (Holly Springs, MS: South Reporter Printing Company, 1950), p. 47.

4   *Negro Hangs Next Month For Attack on Mingo County Woman* (Wayne County News: Wayne, WV March 25, 1926).